# STANFORD MOSAIC

### Reminiscences
### of the first seventy years
### at Stanford University

EDITH R. MIRRIELEES, '07, Editor

PATRICIA F. ZELVER, '46, Associate Editor

*Illustrations by Gilda Meyers, '60*

**366445**
Stanford University

Stanford, California, 1962

# EDITORIAL BOARD

# PREFACE

THE REQUEST to write a preface for this volume of letters is irresistible—and for two particular reasons: The request came from Miss Edith R. Mirrielees, and the letters record impressions of undergraduate experience at Stanford. I have always been anxious to find favor with a teacher as respected as Miss Mirrielees, and my interest in undergraduates is chronic, so I respond to the request.

I was an undergraduate in the 1920's—the "Roaring Twenties" as a TV program now depicts them—but in sobersided Toronto I did not hear them roar. As the late '20's passed into history, I was teaching in the Canadian West; I didn't hear them roar there, either. I heard about raccoon coats and hip-flasks and goldfish-swallowing contests, but these goings-on did not strike me as endemic; rather they appeared episodic, as a passing minority derangement which would give way to another.

There was prosperity—or so it seemed—and bull sessions in my senior year (1926–27) revealed no anxiety about getting a job; indeed, the job-seeker had choices! A few classmates were looking forward to a summer in Europe, but they were so few as to be considered very fortunate. The Atlantic Ocean was still very wide, although Lindbergh's flight during the summer after graduation narrowed it somewhat. The emergence of Stalin drew some attention, but such student interest as there was in international affairs was directed mainly to the League of Nations. The Locarno Pact and other agreements nourished hopes of peace and the outlawing of war; they did not then seem, at least to the wishful, to be fortresses on paper pads.

Then came the stock market crash and the great depression. Japan moved into Manchuria; Mussolini sent his legions into Ethiopia; Hitler rearmed Germany and prepared to unleash a whirlwind. The League of Nations crumbled and free societies struggled with the economics of domestic recovery and national preparedness. These extremities bore in on students of the 1930's. Properity was then doubtful; jobs were scarce; there were rumblings of major war.

War came. Tens of thousands of those who had been students in the '20's and '30's, who had argued the merits and demerits of *laissez faire* and of socialism, of splendid isolation and of intervention, were caught up in the war, and thousands did not return.

It is remarkable that undergraduates of successive generations persist so similarly toward curricular goals while changing external circumstance so differently directs or engages their extracurricular attention. The Roaring Twenties, the Depressed Thirties, the Warring Forties! Through all of these, students attained degrees in engineering and medicine, law and theology, humanities and science; but campus fashion and fancy changed in response to moods and pressures that were at work far beyond academic halls of learning and residence.

The Fifties, with their unprecedented acceleration of technological change, spawned by science, brought an assortment of new extracurricular pressures and preoccupations. Terrestrial problems had seemed complex enough, but now even these had been transcended by orbiting satellites. That world of the Twenties had become small, indeed, and as if to prove it and profit from it, undergraduates traveled earlier, farther, faster, and in greater numbers than their parents had. They became more world-conscious and knowledgeable—a change that is being reflected in their discussions. Still they proceeded toward their academic degrees in traditional areas of study—not, of course, without ready and ample suggestions for curricular improvement or without articulating ideas for the betterment of education in general and their alma mater in particular. In this they were but making their own footprints on a well-worn path which neither they nor their predecessors trod in vain!

I imagine that the letters of this volume will reflect several of the problems and pressures which have affected undergraduates over the years. I imagine, too, that those who have written the letters will recall with nostalgia, seasoned with the reflection of maturity, the memories of undergraduate days that will forever be their own.

If my imagination is in error in these particulars, I shall make occasion to have words with Miss Mirrielees for having enticed me into writing a preface to a volume of letters which I have not yet read.

J. E. WALLACE STERLING

iv

# INTRODUCTION

THIS BOOK OF LETTERS by alumni who once were undergraduates at Stanford has been brought together in honor of Stanford's having completed its seventieth year. It is not a presentation of the University's "great" (though some great are represented in it), nor of any special phase of University work or influence. As far as its editors could obtain material to make it so, it is a cross section of undergraduate life.

In letters dealing with the first twenty-five years, some eliminations have been made. As regards these, the editors both apologize and explain: Without them, there would have been even more justification than there now is for the comment of one of the editorial board, made after reading the early sections, "Why hunt for a title for the compilation? Why not just call it 'We Love Dr. Jordan'?"— a suggestion any graduate of any year preceding President Jordan's retirement would second.

Gathering and preparing the material for the book has been a pleasant undertaking in many ways but especially in three: Letters, whether contributed for publication or explaining why contribution was impossible, have been almost uniformly appreciative of the writer's undergraduate experience and, in a surprising number of instances, expressive of the lasting influence of that experience in shaping his later life. . . . Early classes are represented with a fullness that, after the passing of nearly seventy years, was not to have been expected. . . . And the repeated failure of the editors to draw reminiscences from any Hall of Fame athlete is more than compensated for by the contribution of the one writer in the United States who knows Stanford's athletic history throughout and in a detail both as to men and to events that no half dozen Hall of Fame members could rival.

EDITH R. MIRRIELEES
PATRICIA F. ZELVER

# CONTENTS

## FOUR

## FIVE

## SIX

## SEVEN

# STANFORD MOSAIC

# ONE

I F STANFORD UNIVERSITY's beginning had coincided with the arrival of its first president (June, 1891) or with the opening of its doors to students in October of the same year, the reminiscences from alumni which make up this chapter would call for no addition. In fact, however, preparation for the University began more than a decade earlier—though without conscious intention in its founders' minds.

In the early 1870's Leland Stanford bought a farm of 650 acres in the Santa Clara Valley. Farm by farm he continued his buying in the same sparsely settled region until his holdings covered more than 8,000 acres.

His first purchase and the two or three following seemed to have been made with no intent except to provide a summer home within easy driving distance of San Francisco—easy, that is, in the terms of the ex-Governor's way of driving and the quality of his horses. For his later land buying he had two other reasons, neither of them related to the land's final use. The lesser of the two was his need for space to exercise and train the trotters and racers which for years he had been buying and selling and which were now his most profitable hobby. The greater one, the overwhelmingly greater, had to do with his son, Leland Stanford, Junior, born after eighteen years of childless marriage.

From the time of the child's conception (itself almost a miracle in both parents' eyes) father and mother alike had shaped their lives with his welfare constantly in mind. Once he was past his infancy, country living was obviously desirable for him. Obviously, too, the heir to the Stanford fortune could live on no mean scale. Yearly, mother and son made longer stays at the farm, Stanford joining them when he could. And yearly the property in the Santa Clara Valley grew not only in size and value but in its varieties of cultivation. It had been named the Palo Alto Farm, but "farm" was soon a misnomer; it was an estate, kept and cultivated for beauty as well as use.

3

Along with the growth of the estate, Stanford's fortune from other sources grew steadily larger. There was occasional discussion with friends of putting part of that fortune to some public use—a museum? an art gallery? — but always the discussion ended inconclusively. There was time enough; Leland, Junior, was still a child. Decision must wait until he was old enough to say the final word.

At fifteen, he was taken for a prolonged trip abroad. In Florence, after weeks of failing health and illusory improvements, he died. He was two months short of his sixteenth birthday.

His death left his parents stripped of hope and purpose. Stanford, worn out by watching and final shock, dropped down on a couch close to the room in which the body had been placed and gave way to his despair, "I have nothing now to live for." Only half conscious, he heard what seemed to him his son's voice answering him, "Do not say you have nothing to live for. Live for humanity." As the voice ceased, he passed into complete unconsciousness. When he woke hours later it was to find himself repeating, as though the words had been dictated to him, "The children of California shall be my children."

Under the impulse of his dream Stanford decided, Mrs. Stanford agreeing, that the memorial they erected to their son should be a university. The first decision being made, others followed on it quickly: The university should be in California. It should stand on the home farm. It would be open to both sexes. The instruction in it would be practical—instruction by which a graduate could earn a living. And it should bear the dead boy's name, the Leland Stanford, Junior, University.

The word *practical* broadened its meaning as Stanford discovered through talks with Eastern educators how practical the seeming impracticals could be. The name was gradually shortened in general use, once by the dropping of "Junior"; again by omission of "Leland." The rest—West Coast location, country surroundings, men and women on equal footing—these determinations, formulated though they were in the horse-and-buggy era, gave to the University a shape and tone that, even into the era of jet travel, has held its own.

With main purposes clear, however, the University was as yet no more than a rich man's dream. Changing the dream into reality filled and over-filled the time between the founders' return to the United States and the final opening date—a date that, after being set, had twice to be moved forward to allow for unforeseen delays.

Part of the delay was because of the slowness with which the necessary buildings were completed. A still larger part sprang from the difficulty in finding a president—one who both satisfied the donors and was himself willing to face the risk of leaving whatever was his present post for the headship of an institution not yet in being. The discovery of David Starr Jordan, successful president of the University of Indiana, ended the Stanfords' search. Both husband and wife were quick judges of character. "Within ten minutes," as Dr. Jordan remembered it, he had been offered the presidency. This was in March. In May he and his family reached California. At this point the reminiscences which follow take over the Stanford story.

*It has several times been suggested to us that there was a limit to the beneficence of education—but we have thought differently. We do not believe there can be superfluous education.*

LELAND STANFORD
Address at laying of the cornerstone

# "The University and I Were Young Together"

## EDITH MONICA JORDAN, A.B. '97

*Edith Jordan (Mrs. Nathaniel Gardner) taught until her marriage, in the Los Angeles Polytechnic High School. Marriage reattached her to a university, this time to the University of California at Berkeley. She has spent most of her life in Berkeley—though, as she says, with always a "bit of red" showing. There and elsewhere she has lectured extensively, chiefly on foreign affairs.*

*Her present contribution was first given as a speech at an Old Timers' Dinner in 1957*

ON JUNE 26, 1891, a rather limp-looking group arrived at the railroad station in Menlo Park. The party consisted of the David Starr Jordan and the Orrin Leslie Elliott families. Crossing the continent was not so easy in those days, and we were all very tired.

Senator Stanford met us with friends who wanted to see what the new president was like. After cordial greetings we were all driven to Escondite Cottage, the only place which could be occupied on the campus proper.

There are four things which particularly stand out in my mind about these very early days: Escondite Cottage as a home and the center of an interesting story; the personal kindness of Senator and Mrs. Stanford, who were in California during the whole summer; the all-around unfinished look of the campus buildings; and the dust, the tar weed, and the "stickers." The University office was very soon opened in a brick building nearby, and the first entrance examinations were held on the porch at Escondite. Later as the members of the new faculty began to arrive and prospective students came to look around, an office was opened in a building just completed on

6

the Quadrangle. There were desks furnished for the officers but there were no telephones. In fact, telephones in the University buildings had not been included in the original plans. It was 1906 or 1907 before a real telephone service was installed.

There was, however, a telephone at Escondite, and often I walked back and forth with important messages. Sometimes I took a luncheon to my father, who ate with the others seated on the edge of the Quadrangle. As for food, "Mr. La Pierre, of Mayfield, came to us through the hayfield."

As the summer progressed the houses on the "Row" were taking shape, and the Quadrangle and Encina did not look so unfinished.

Early in August two young women, Lucy Fletcher and Eleanor Pearson, came to the campus, eager to start a school for girls. There was an old house some distance from the University with a ghost and some furniture. The young women acquired more furnishings, a good cook, and a horse and buggy. Many of the newcomers found it a good place to board. A young man who wanted some tutoring and a job came to look after the horse. His name was Herbert Hoover. When they opened as a school in September I was among the pupils, often walking to Escondite for week ends.

On October 1, 1891, came the formal opening of the University. The story to June, 1895, has been often told by the "Pioneers."

My class, 1897, remembers the "six pretty long years" or *lean* years. In June, 1893, the Jordan family was vacationing and my father was half way up Mt. Shasta when the news reached him of the death of Senator Stanford. The Lean Years began. The Stanford will went into the probate court. There was no money with which to run the University. The Jordan family had to give up the anticipated new house, the plans for which were unsigned on Senator Stanford's desk. The house the early students knew was built by my father, not by the University. All of the faculty had to take cuts in their salaries . . . sometimes they were fortunate if they got anything at all.

When things began to look brighter, came the suit brought by the United States Government against the Stanford estate relating to money borrowed to build the Central Pacific Railroad. It was said that Mrs. Stanford could not win until it snowed in California. March 2, 1896, was a cold, drizzly day with snow on the neighboring hills. The word came that the Supreme Court of the United States had decided against the Federal suit. There was rejoicing among the student body, and at a rally under the oaks in front of the Jordan house the parrot learned the Stanford yell. The next day everybody went to the mountains to play in the snow.

University finances were still under a strain. There were still advisers who wanted Mrs. Stanford to close the University. What kept the University going were: Mrs. Stanford's devotion and loyalty to the memory of her husband and son; father's enthusiasms, his will to see the university of his dreams develop; the absolute confidence between the two in spite of many difficulties; the willingness of members of the faculty to hold on and go ahead in spite of personal loss and lack of necessary equipment.

A small personal incident may be interesting here. I was going with my father to a "Big Game" when they were still played in San Francisco. Father looked at my navy blue hat with a gold trim. He refused to let me go with him until I acquired a red hat. I have since worn red where it shows, although I have lived for more than half of my life at the University of California.

Commencement exercises in 1897 were held in the old gymnasium. There was little ceremony and no caps and gowns. My thrill was when my father handed me my diploma. My excitement was saying good-bye to my friends who were also graduating or those who were going away for the summer. As I walked slowly home, I thought that Stanford and I had gone quite a distance together and that we were both growing up. As I looked back, I saw how much Stanford had meant to me. As I looked ahead, I saw I was really somewhat prepared for the cold, cold world. As I looked farther forward, I saw what a wonderful future there was for Stanford when the lean years were over. The classes after 1900 would enjoy a larger and a better University built upon the ideals of Mrs. Stanford and the carrying out of the enthusiastic plans of my father and his young faculty. But still the University and I were young together, and a very good time we had.

# "My Name Is Jenness"

## JAMES FREEMAN JENNESS, A.B. '92

*The Reverend James Freeman Jenness was a member of Stanford's first graduating class. He took a degree, also, from Boston University, then served for thirty-nine years as a minister in the Methodist Church. Fifteen of those years were spent in Latin America, where he held pastorates in Argentina, Chile, and the Canal Zone.*

*Following his retirement he and Mrs. Jenness returned to the vicinity of the University. Their home has been in Palo Alto since 1932.*

I ENTERED STANFORD as a senior the day the University first opened its doors for the admission of students. That is what I had made up my mind to do as long ago as early July when I visited the campus with a group of young people, most of whom were students of a neighboring college.

We were greatly impressed by what we saw that day—grounds, buildings, nature, and the brain and hand of man conspiring to create the marvelous institution which Stanford University has come to be. As we were about to separate, one of the fellows said, "Jenness, I want to make a motion. You be chairman and put my motion to this bunch." Then, after a few moments of silence, he said, "Mr. President, I move we all stay at home through August and September, then on October first come here and register as Stanford students."

This may have been intended as a joke, but "the bunch" appeared to take it seriously, as most of them voted "aye," and on the first day of October were in the long line at the Registrar's Office on the Stanford campus. There were seven who were admitted as seniors, and a considerable number who ranked in the lower classes.

There was another member of the first graduating class at Stanford for whose coming I was more definitely responsible. He was my brother, older than I by nearly two and a half years, but he had stayed out of school for two years, giving me the chance to catch up with him and be his classmate at Boston University. I wrote him about my visit to the Stanford campus and my decision to transfer to the new university, suggesting that he do the same.

At first, he appeared not to be at all interested. However, after a couple of weeks' use of the fastest mail service then available, I received a telegram saying he would come, and when the opening day at Stanford arrived, we were rooming together at Encina Hall.

That brought the membership of the Class of 1892 up to twenty-nine—twenty-seven men and two women. On the first Commencement Day President David Starr Jordan said, "Every university has its first graduate. That doesn't mean very much, but it does mean that he receives the first diploma. I am giving that first diploma to C. K. Jenness."

To my thinking, my brother's getting the first diploma ever handed out at Stanford was much more important than Dr. Jordan made it sound. It was even more important than the exciting baseball game played on Commencement afternoon, faculty against graduates, with Dr. Jordan filling first base for the faculty and I first base for the opposite team. Evidently, I was not the only one who thought the first diploma of historical importance, for it has found a permanent place in the Stanford collection.

Senator Stanford must have been a happy man when Dr. Jordan accepted the presidency of Leland Stanford Junior University. He had cause to be, for Dr. Jordan and his wife were both eminently fitted for the positions they were to hold. This was soon shown by their successful contacts with trustees, faculty members, and students. Both had the ability to remember names and faces of the almost countless numbers of students whom they knew throughout the years of Dr. Jordan's administration. I shall mention two evidences of this ability which I met with long after I had ceased to be a student.

Ten years after my graduation, having been absent from Stanford during that time, I came to Palo Alto as minister of the First Methodist Church. A few days after my arrival I went over to the campus.

As I was standing with a group of students, I became aware of a stentorian voice behind me saying, "Hello, first baseman." It was Dr. Jordan, not only recognizing me but remembering that long ago faculty-graduate game in which we had played in the same positions.

The years rolled by, most of them being spent far from California. In 1932 I became a retired minister. The next year my wife and I returned to Palo Alto to spend our remaining years. The first time I saw Mrs. Jordan I said, "Mrs. Jordan, my name is Jenness; I was a member of the Class of 1892." Quick as a flash came the answer, "Oh, yes, I remember. There were two of you, C. K. and J. F. Which one are you?"

*The work the world will not let die was never paid for—not in fame, not in money, not in power. . . . No man was hired to find out that the world was round, or that valleys were worn by water, or that the stars were suns. No man was ever paid to burn at the stake, or to die, that other men might be free to live.*

DAVID STARR JORDAN
*The Higher Sacrifice*

# Memories of '93

## Arthur Henry Barnhisel, A.B. '93

*Arthur Barnhisel entered Stanford his junior year, as a member of Stanford's second graduating class. Following his graduation he took graduate work at Cornell University, and theological studies at San Anselmo Seminary.*

*He was a Presbyterian minister for ten years in Los Gatos, California, and in Tacoma, Washington, and was a delegate from the Northwest to the World Council of Presbyterian Churches which met in Liverpool, England, in 1904.*

*In 1907 he resigned from the Presbyterian Church and engaged in business. He was chairman of the national committee to prepare a code of ethics for real estate business, president of the Northwest Real Estate Association, member of the Tacoma Library Board, and a member of the board of trustees of a non-profit corporation fostering social welfare programs for senior citizens.*

YOU HAVE ASKED for contributions of personal memories to be included in a book recalling early days at Stanford. This request is quite urgent as those days are rapidly becoming prehistoric. But how can anybody write something regarding anything of those beginnings that hasn't already been written by somebody? It would necessarily be very incidental and equally unimportant. The great people, places, and events have had complete coverage. The records can be found in any alumni or other respectable library.

It has seemed logical and well, therefore, in beginning this chapter, to follow a certain illustrious example by merely stating that in the beginning there was a vast wilderness with chaos brooding over primitive darkness. Out of this came a dream and a purpose and the voice of a man and a woman crying out of their heart's agony, "Let there be more light in our small corner of this world." Leland Stanford and Mrs. Stanford built Stanford University and dedicated their

12

great estate with stone buildings and chosen men to be leaders and teachers to help under God in bringing more light and human freedom to all men.

But no university can be a living thing with merely a vast area of acres nor complete with college buildings—not even with the most select and skilled leaders and scholarly teachers. To complete a university there must be the last supreme essential—a body of students.

The next step, therefore, in bringing order to this dedicated purpose was the bringing together of the 500 men and 200 women who came from nearly every state of the union and every corner of the earth to form the raw material of the first student body constituting Stanford University.

In the first days of Stanford's opening there was a good-natured chaos as 500 men and 200 women students tried to find their way around. A few came with full credentials for entrance as juniors or sophomores. Most of these candidates for the first three classes—'92, '93, and '94—were reasonably prepared with qualifications for matriculation. The real chaos was evident as the body of thrilled and determined would-be freshmen became the raw material for this first full four-year Pioneer Class. There seemed to be thousands of such milling about and around the campus.

Stanford had been nationally publicized. Men and women came who had given up all thought of college until the challenge of the Cardinal sent out the call to all comers. Many of these had partial credit for entrance that called for examinations in part. These pioneer classmen assumed that everybody on the Farm had to pass in something to make the grade.

Even the professors on the pioneer team of experts were young. President Jordan limited his first line faculty to professors not over forty years of age. Word was passed around that one of the freshmen with a worried look met a friendly boyish-looking newcomer, became chummy and confidential, slapped him on the back, and whispered, "Buddy, do you think you'll make the grade?" The newcomer answered, "I certainly hope so." A few days later this freshman found himself in an English class with this precocious "buddy" as one of Dr. Jordan's discoveries—a brilliant young professor, age 26, who proved to be Professor Edward Griggs of the English Department. Dr. Griggs later became one of America's outstanding lecturers.

Even President Jordan was informal as he moved among the students. A certain naïve freshman took a dare, approached Dr. Jordan, and greeted him with a "Good morning, David." This bold freshie won his challenge as the president came back with "Why so formal, Joe? My friends call me Dave."

Of the few fundamentals that were a "must" for Stanford, English came first. Our head professor, Anderson, one of President Jordan's picked stalwarts for the famous first faculty, presided in the rather informal give-and-take discussions. This master in literature was a rugged individual—a man's man. The feminine class majority adored him. His gruff exterior, including voice, was shadowed by a stubbish black mustache which never dulled the edge of a tongue with a sly and sometimes wicked humor. One of his favorite masterpieces was an occasional surprise examination. Students would be in place on bell-call. The headmaster would not appear, but the questions chalked on the large front blackboard would grip attention.

We had been studying Dante's *Inferno*. The test required accurate, but random, quotations. The lines that had burned themselves into my memory somehow gave a brimstone urge to use as a caption:

> "Oh Hell! What Do Mine Eyes
> In Grief Behold!"

The test was completed and left for reaction—which turned out to be oblivion. The professor never mentioned it to my knowledge.

Fifteen years later, however, a Stanford man who had attended Anderson's courses wondered if I could be the one who had taken liberties with Dante's *Inferno*. It seems that this bit of attempted humor was passed on from year to year with a chuckle of enjoyment in telling others of the daredevil who had fired that random shot. So that lost arrow was found years later buried in the tough, but tender, heart of that grand old oak.

Regardless of Professor Anderson's superficial gruffness, he was greatly beloved and a fascinating inspiration to the eager students in his classes. After retirement from Stanford, his last years were spent in Italy writing his own life's *magnum opus*, a translation of Dante's great work, a new high of his own and one of the world's best.

Friendly informality with the thrill of a new world being conquered was the eager attitude of all comers. It was not too difficult for serious-minded young scholars to meet the entrance tests. Time to work out credits was generously allowed. After all, these challenges of a new experiment in education where "The winds of freedom blow" had been widely advertised. President David Starr Jordan had been lecturing throughout the western states, seeking ambitious university prospects; Stanford simply had to have customers. The state university at Berkeley, with its 1,000 students and its heavy financial problems, resented this new educational upstart as being surplus in the western field. However, customers came. The ranks were filled. Entrance requirements would never again be so generous. The weeding out process began later as order succeeded chaos. The first four pioneer classes (with their own organizations) gradually became self-disciplined. Stanford University became a living, moving body with no "Ivy Wall Traditions," but throbbing with ambition and warm in the spirit of friendship and high ideals. The dream of the founders, Senator Leland Stanford and Jane, his wife, was now in the beginning of its fulfillment. With the brilliant genius of Dr. David Starr Jordan, Stanford's first president, the miracle progress of the decades to follow steadied into stride.

*The professional schools of a university may be in a great city, but a college should be in a town so small that college interests overshadow all the rest.*

DAVID STARR JORDAN

# Camping in Encina

DONALD HUME FRY, A.B. '95

*Donald Fry followed a career in electrical engineering until his retirement. After retirement he took up painting and pottery, now his absorbing interests. His paintings have been exhibited in many places in the Palo Alto area where he and his wife live.*

WHEN I FIRST CAME to the Stanford campus in the fall of 1891, it was to take entrance exams. At that time Palo Alto's station was not imposing! It was simply a long wooden bench with a protective roof. Only a few of the many Southern Pacific trains stopped there. There was no bus or rig of any kind which would have taken me to Encina Hall, so I accepted some kindly advice and got off at Menlo Park. From there I walked to Encina, lugging my Gladstone bag. It was *heavy.*

When I reached the hall, I got a shock. Encina was not ready for occupancy. There was no bedding as yet and the kitchen was unfinished. Also, the electric generator, which was to furnish Encina and the whole campus with light, was still in its boxcar. The only good news: there was one student already living in Encina. If one could make it, why not two?

So I set out to find this one and only Encina resident. His name was William Greer—a large, rawboned man with a big, red beard. He had come from Boston and M.I.T. He had a solution to the problem which affected many others as well as him—he had brought with him when he came west a camper's bed roll. This on top of the regular mattress made a very comfortable bed. As for "eats," he walked to Mayfield whenever he was sufficiently hungry. Q. E. D.

I could not emulate Greer and his bed roll; I accepted, however, a suggestion and a trunk rope, roped two of Encina's mattresses together, then crawled in between them to sleep. It was not a comfortable bed but it worked and had this advantage: I did not oversleep.

I was up and dressed by six o'clock and just in time for a hearty meal our cook had concocted for the night crew of workmen striving to put the finishing touches on Encina. I was the only student to share this—the first meal cooked in Encina.

Roble (the girls' hall) was a little behind schedule, and for several days after our kitchen was in working order the coeds walked over in a bunch, two by two, had their meal, then returned to Roble while we residents had "second table."

In those early days a hungry crowd would congregate in front of Encina's dining-room door before every meal. The doors opened out; consequently, the front of the line had to back up. There was pushing and struggling before anyone could get in. In one such jam my heel came down on the toe of the man behind me. I was mortified, for the lad was lame and walked with two canes. However, he assured me I had not hurt him, "not in the least." But imagine my feelings when on the very next occasion I repeated and stepped on that same lame lad. Again, he assured me I had not hurt him and invited me to come to his room at "lights out," which I did. I found him already in bed, reading by candlelight, his two legs standing beside him! This lad, George Gardner, in spite of his handicap of two wooden legs, yet with his canes and his bicycle got around with the best of us.

Electric lights were comparatively new when Stanford started. The plan was for the University to generate its own D.C. current. However, when classes were begun the generator was still in its boxcar, and we had to use candles. In fact, even after the generator was operating, it was shut down at 9:30: "lights out." The plant operator dimmed the lights at 9:15 for a few seconds as a warning, and we looked up our candles and matches and had them ready for 9:30.

When Stanford opened we had no track. A few of us would jog over to the Stanford trotting farm to train, but that was unsatisfactory. In the first place, we had to pass too close to Roble, and some of the occupants objected to our indecency. Also, by the time we got home again and reached the dining room, there was apt to be only beans left and they rather cold. We were glad when we had a track of our own, our first one a quarter mile behind Encina.

Greer—the first Encina occupant—did not go in for track but was addicted to cross-country running and frequently, after "lights out," took a run of a mile or two. Also, he made a habit of starting off on Saturday, his bed roll on his back, returning late Sunday. Whether or not he had those overnight trips in mind when he got that bed roll, it certainly served him well as the first man to sleep in Encina.

*At the time of the opening, the electric connections had not been made. Mrs. Stanford forbade the use of kerosene, since lamps might explode and the dormitories be set on fire. So life went on by candlelight, for a brief time in Encina, for some weeks in Roble.*

ORRIN L. ELLIOTT, Registrar

# That Second Thanksgiving

## HERBERT HOOVER, A.B. '95

*Herbert Hoover is so widely known not only in the United
States but throughout the whole Western world that to pre-
cede his reminiscence with a paragraph of biography is superfluous. As concerns his relation to Stanford, he is a graduate of Stanford's first four-year class, he has been a member
of the Board of Trustees for fifty years, and for more than
fifty years has been the University's constant and generous
supporter. His two sons attended Stanford, Herbert Hoover,
Jr., graduating in the Class of '25 and Allan Hoover in the
Class of '29.*

*The excerpt below comes from his memoirs and is pub-
lished here with his permission and that of his publishers,
the Macmillan Company.*

WE ENDOWED our University with a football team. Probably because I had been able to save the money for uniforms and
equipment of the baseball team, I was made the manager. We arranged a game with the University of California to be played on the
University's second Thanksgiving Day. The game was to take place
at the Haight Street baseball grounds in San Francisco. We had seats
for a total of 15,000 fans. We bought new uniforms for our teams
from a dealer on the sales expectations. We printed seat-numbered
tickets for only 10,000 as we did not expect more visitors than that
number. When the game came on, two things happened to disturb
the managers.

First, the attendance piled up to nearly 20,000. We had no such
supply of tickets. So we set up an alley of our college boys from the
box offices to the gates and sold tickets for cash—the purchasers being
carefully watched so that no outsiders crowded in without having
first paid their respects to the box offices. At that time few bills were
in use in California. We dealt in silver and gold. The cash piled up

19

behind our entrance-selling boys to the extent it spilled on the floors; we had to rent a wash-boiler and a dishpan from nearby householders for the price of a free ticket.

And while these difficulties were being solved, the captains of the two teams turned up, demanding to know where was the football. We had overlooked that detail and had to delay the game for a half hour while we sent downtown for two pigskins.

I did not see the game, but to our astonishment we won. After the game the California manager and I retired to a hotel with our money, now transferred to grain bags, and sat up most of the night counting it. I had never seen $30,000 before. The bank the next morning found that we had $18 more. We were well financed for the next season.

*Where could a genius devoted to the search for truth . . . find on earth's round a place more advantageous to come and work in? "Die Luft der Freiheit weht!" All the traditions are individualistic. Red tape and organization are at their minimum . . . Eastern institutions look all dark and huddled and confused in comparison with this purity and serenity.*

WILLIAM JAMES, visiting professor, 1905–06

# Running for Office

## CARL HAYDEN, ex-'00

*Carl Hayden has served his native state, Arizona, in the United States Congress for fifty consecutive years—from 1912 to 1927 in the House, since 1927 in the Senate. Earlier than 1912 he was already in politics, having been elected as treasurer, then as sheriff of Maricopa County. The paragraph which follows is excerpted from "Washington Conversation," February 18, 1962, and is Senator Hayden's answer to the question of whether he had ever lost an election.*

*It is reproduced here by permission of Senator Hayden and of Columbia Broadcasting System because it presents a phase of undergraduate life not elsewhere touched on, and also because a book of Stanford reminiscences containing nothing from Carl Hayden would be a book seriously lacking.*

I WAS CANDIDATE for president of the student body at Stanford University. Herbert Hoover's brother, Theodore Hoover, was one candidate. I was another, and a gentleman by the name of Diggles. Diggles had a very good organization. I had the most votes on the first time, and then we had to run it off, like a Texas primary, and everybody thought I had run so well in the first ballot that there was no question. I went around all over the campus telling them that Diggles had a good organization, was getting the votes, and please come over and vote for me. But I remember that there were at least four students from Arizona who promised to go but didn't, and I lost by four votes.

# TWO

T HE CLASS OF '95 was Stanford's first full four-year class, holding thus a distinction no other class could claim. Members of the Class of '96, as their own Commencement Day approached, may have pondered on what means were left for a merely second four-year class to escape oblivion. At any rate, whether by pondering or by inspiration, a means was found. Removing a paving block in the Inner Quad from the exact center of the space which fronted the yet unbuilt Memorial Church, they inserted in its place a bronze plate bearing the class numeral and with the class roll entombed beneath it.

Permission had to be obtained for removing the fraction of pavement, and for a while its coming was in doubt, every inch of the University and most of all that close to the prospective church being precious in Mrs. Stanford's eyes. The President, however, may have influenced her, for he was wholeheartedly in favor of the plan. A year later, meeting with the Class of '97, he quoted to them their predecessors' action, both as an example for other classes and also as a symbol:

> The date when the first circuit of the Quadrangle is laid shall be as far in the future as the Crusades are in the past. Who can say what crusades lie before the class that completes this circle—in the far-off year of 5097? I like to think that in like fashion our university influences shall extend through the life of our country. Each of you shall be a Stanford memorial plate.

His capacity to endow a local action with worldwide significance was one of the many in which his listeners delighted. For twenty-odd years, as the reminiscences of those years show, he was himself the prime Stanford symbol. Hardly a graduate left the campus without bearing his mark. Only an occasional one failed to carry away the recollection of some special man-to-man aid or praise or counsel from

23

him. Sometimes the aid or praise was ill bestowed, but this was a risk—or so the President saw it—that had to be taken. "I get into more trouble than most people," he admitted, "but then I have more chances."

Not that undergraduate admiration exhausted itself on the President. Within their separate circles, some professors were surrounded with it. Marx, Anderson, Jenkins, Branner—in the eyes of any one of their followers, to have missed being in their classes and learning to know them was, in effect, to have missed going to Stanford at all.

And even with these and other special admirations set apart, relations between faculty and students were cordial throughout the opening years. Each freshman on entering chose a major subject and so acquired a major professor. As a result, he began his four years with knowledge of at least one of his teachers. Usually he added liberally to the number. And a friendship once having been formed, nothing was likely to disturb it. Grades for classwork, term grades, final examinations—these academic hurdles were installed for a class or not installed for it at the option of the individual instructor. Most instructors established some of them; some did away with all. A report sent to the registrar's office might carry grades or bare pluses and minuses at its maker's pleasure. "Every Professor Sovereign in his own Department" is one of the scribbled directions to himself still to be found in Dr. Jordan's notebook for the year 1891, and sovereign each one was. It is not invention but sober fact that the professor of philology, beloved and reverenced scholar, once halted his students on their way out from the last class of the term. "A moment, if you please! Seven of you are here, and I haf but six name cards. If you will do me the kindness to find whose name lacks—" For the intent scholar who needed no urging, the early Stanford was Utopia. So was it, too, for the inveterate loafer.

The campus formed the boundary of most students' interests. What went on beyond it, even what affected the University, lay lightly on their minds if at all. The years following Senator Stanford's death, for example—the "six pretty long years" in Dr. Jordan's moderate phrase—were for faculty and administration years of gnawing anxiety. Not so for undergraduates. Each favorable court decision in the suit brought by the United States against the Stanford estate was marked by student celebration. Betweenwhiles, earning a living as nearly half were doing in whole or in part; beating Berkeley in the Big Game; carrying on their class or clique rivalries—these occupied their minds much in the order in which they are set down here. As for the suit? The President had told them in the beginning that Mrs. Stanford would win. Well, then, she would win. Why worry?

War with Spain in 1898 impinged a little on the usual campus absorption; eighty men volunteered for service, enough football men among the eighty to cause Stanford to lose its "Big Game" against the University of California for the first time in its history. The war, though, was come and gone before interest could reach a lasting height—only two of the eighty killed and most of the others safe back at the University.

The building of Memorial Church and its dedication were thrilling events for boys and girls, many of whom had never before seen so fine a structure or so elaborate an opening. Its being nondenominational puzzled freshmen, but presently they took pride in its having a standing held by no other neighboring church—again, a campus pride in being different.

With the beginning of the Twentieth century, however, University sorrows and tragedies accompanied it which could not be overlooked; the three chief of these alumni reminiscences deal with these fully. In the main, though, once the immediate tragedy was past, the color of life for the undergraduate continued to be red, and life itself expressed only in superlatives. The finest climate on earth, the greatest president in the United States, the University bigger with every year—why worry?

Not everyone saw it so, especially not everyone on the east coast. The Stanfords' decision to spend in California the fortune that had been amassed there was regarded by many educators as sheer folly. And publicists from the first had been either violently for the new enterprise or violently against it. On the "against" side, witness the comment appearing in *Town Topics* for June 1899, its author Colonel William D'Alton Mann:

> . . . *Mrs. Stanford's donation is just so much money wasted. . . . The irreclaimable desert that separates California from the populous regions of the United States will confine the opportunities of the "university"—it is and must remain for another century an academy—to those living in the immediate neighborhood . . . Indeed, it is difficult to conceive a more foolish misuse of a splendid opportunity than to dump twenty or thirty million dollars into a third-rate western university. It isn't philanthropy at all, it is hysterics.*

There were enough Job's Comforters east of the Hudson so that it can be taken for granted Colonel Mann's diatribe went west. If so, its reception there must have disappointed the senders. By 1899, Stanford had celebrated eight Commencements. A fair part of its student body had crossed the "irreclaimable desert"—crossed it by rail and found it set with towns and irrigated ranches. The majority, however, were "the children of California," and there precisely, as president and youthful Old Guard alike saw it, lay Stanford's opportunity. The University had taken raw material, boys and girls whose families had never contained a college-educated member, and by instruction and example and the contagion of enthusiasm had turned them into explorers in the sciences, strugglers in the arts, holders and expounders of an altered attitude toward life. In a sense not calamitous but benign, it had set brother against brother—the man whose chief interest was of the mind against the one whose interest was in acquisition or in the gratification of the senses. . . . There would be failures in plenty, but the work was there to be done. Eastern jeers did nothing to reduce its importance.

# Mrs. Stanford's "Boys and Girls"

## MARY HAZEL PEDLAR, A.B. '06

*Mary Hazel Pedlar (Mrs. Frederick Faulkner) makes no mention, in her account of visits to Mrs. Stanford, of her own undergraduate interests. Her most continuous extracurricular activity and the one which was most to affect her post-college life was with the* Stanford Daily, *then the* Daily Palo Alto. *Following her graduation she entered into newspaper work in San Francisco and continued in it until, some years before her husband's death, he found it necessary to move to Sacramento.*

*She now lives in San Jose with her sister, Clair Pedlar Tuttle, '07.*

IN STANFORD'S FIRST YEARS the student body was so small that it was possible for Mrs. Stanford to know many of the undergraduates and for most of them to have firsthand impressions of her. I was myself only a junior at the time of her death, but, along with others, I had had two visits at her home. They are among my valued recollections, and they make up the substance of this reminiscence.

The first was in 1904. The fall semester (no quarters then!) was well under way when news reached the campus that Mrs. Stanford, who had been traveling abroad, was again at home. Spontaneously, a group of students decided to go over after nine o'clock closing of the library and extend a welcome to her. Up and down the Row, through the dormitories, and around the Quad the word ran: Everybody was invited to go along.

Nine o'clock came. Students trooped out of the library to join others waiting in the arcade of the Outer Quad. Under a full harvest moon, an eager crowd, its numbers steadily increasing, started on foot across the fields to the Stanford home. At first, there was laughing and singing. The last quarter-mile, though, was walked in silence to make sure of the planned serenade's being a surprise.

As we reached the lawn and the first notes of our singing broke the stillness, a lantern-hung veranda and garden burst into light, with chairs and tables dotting the lawn. Somehow, the grapevine had carried news of our coming, and our hostess was ready for us. The serenading continued nonetheless, each number received with appreciative applause. After the singing, while bowls of punch and platters of cookies were passed, Mrs. Stanford spoke to us, first collectively, then individually—the University's mother greeting her "boys and girls."

The second experience was initiated by Mrs. Stanford herself. About to embark on another of her trips (her last) to Honolulu, she expressed a wish to see the women students before her leaving. Women students, how they carried the responsibility of being Stanford students and what they accomplished, had a special interest for her, since she had been largely responsible for their admission to the University and had stood steadily for their having an equal place there, even though limited to lesser numbers than the men. Now she greeted us in her home, showing us through the rooms on the lower floor, pointing out and commenting on objects she, or she and Senator Stanford, had gathered during their travels, then leading us into the dining room for tea. Half a dozen upperclass women (how I wished I could have been one of them!) helped her with the serving.

Such recollections seem perhaps unimportant in these magnificent days when the University has its hundred-million PACE Program; when, once all-inclusive, it now fosters Stanfords in Germany, France, Italy, and Japan! But to this alumna of more than fifty years ago, the present glories constantly recall the spirit of the Founders and especially of the one I knew, whose steadfastness and idealism gave us the Stanford that was and so laid sound foundations for the one that is and the one that is to be.

# The Earth Shook

## PAUL CARROLL EDWARDS, A.B. '06

*Paul Edwards has followed newspaper work since well
before his freshman days. His adventures as an undergraduate reporter are a part of his reminiscences. Since those days
he has held a succession of editorial posts on Western newspapers, and has been editor-in-chief of Scripps-Howard papers in California and in Texas.*

*In 1943 he was elected to the Stanford Board of Trustees.
He became emeritus in 1953, but Board action provided for
his continuing an active member—as, of 1962, he still does.*

*As coeditor of* The Memoirs of Ray Lyman Wilbur, *he has
completed the massive task of bringing together and preparing for publication the notes, documents, and speeches of
Stanford's third president. The work, begun in 1957, was
published in 1960.*

*He is married to the former Georgina Lyman, Class of
'07, and is the father of Paul Edwards, Jr., '37, and Carroll
Emma Edwards (Mrs. Paul Vernon), '42.*

I WAS A CAMPUS KID in the years 1896–97, visiting my sister, the wife
of Professor Rufus L. Green, one of the faculty men Dr. Jordan
brought with him from Indiana University. The Inner Quad, Encina
and Roble Halls (the old Roble, that is, afterward called Sequoia),
the men's and women's gyms (not the present ones), the central
building of the Museum, and the powerhouse (now one of the engineering buildings) were about the extent of the University plant.
Three strings of boxlike faculty residences stood starkly in an oat field,
the present Alvarado, Salvatierra, and Lasuen Rows. The football
field was a ploughed rectangle of adobe (about where the temporary
buildings now stand behind the School of Education) with a modest
tier of bleachers on one side. Games were played on the bare ground,
and they were dusty and dirty. That was in the era of the "big push"

brand of football—the "flying wedge," etc. For other boyhood diversions there were bicycle trips to Mrs. King's Inn on King's Mountain (walk up most of the way and coast back down with a small pine tree hitched on behind for a brake), trout fishing in San Francisquito Creek (it ran all the year round then, and steelhead came up from the Bay in the fall), and the annual camping trip in the redwoods of Big Basin, on which Professor Green took his family every summer vacation.

It was five years later that I returned as a freshman to enter with the Class of 1906. Stanford had been going ahead with big strides meanwhile. The Outer Quad was almost finished, Memorial Church was complete, and plans were maturing for the new library (on the site now designated for the new Graduate School of Business) and the men's gymnasium (about where the Laurence Frost Memorial Amphitheater is now).

I had worked all summer in Indianapolis, my home, to earn railroad fare and expense money for the trip to Stanford. But the last morning before arriving, I breakfasted at a Harvey eating house. When I started to pay my bill, I remembered I had left my wallet under the pillow in my Pullman berth. I rushed into the car to retrieve it, but the berth had been made up and the porter was stoically uncommunicative. While the search was proceeding, the train moved out. The wallet was not recovered, and I arrived at Stanford totally penniless. However, I wore a "beany" cap and a pair of peg-topped trousers which I thought were very collegiate. My sister took me into her family, which relieved the financial strain. A few days later John Ezra McDowell, assistant registrar, found me a job as campus correspondent for the *Palo Alto Times*.

Having been a campus kid, I thought I knew more about the place than any of my classmates. But I kept those thoughts discreetly to myself. My high school record did not afford enough entrance credits of the right kind. I was obliged to take four exams, including English composition, required of all entering freshmen. The most that can be said is that I slid in by a hairline margin. In those days all subjects were elective. I helped myself to a veritable smorgasbord of intellectual offerings, satisfying, I fear, a rather aimless appetite and ending with more spots on the napkin than solid credits on the registrar's records. I appeared in Professor George Price's senior embryology course in my sophomore year, causing him to look at me askance. But when I convinced him I really was interested, he assented with his customary kindly philosophy. Embryology admittedly was a bit off-beat for an English major.

Extracurricular activities consumed much of my time. I was campus correspondent for newspapers throughout my college career. Writing led me to the staff of *The Sequoia*, literary magazine, and ultimately to its editorship. And literary pursuits led to dramatic activities because the English Club in those days justified its existence by staging revivals of early English plays under the expert coaching of Professor Lee Emerson Bassett, bless his memory. All productions were presented in the Assembly Hall (now the Graduate School of Business). Topping the stage was a stained glass dome, very ornate, but interfering considerably with theatrical lighting and scene handling. We sought permission to build a "gridiron" over the stage from which to suspend and operate drop curtains. But "NO" in a loud and firm voice was the answer from Charles B. Lathrop, business manager of the University and Mrs. Stanford's devoted brother. That stained glass dome could not be covered, he decreed. It took two long years to break down this official opposition.

Staging plays in those primitive conditions was a lot of fun—and work. I'm sure I put in more hours in the Assembly Hall than in classrooms. Unlike today, no credits were given for dramatic activities, more's the pity so far as I was concerned. Compared to the professional-like productions now put on by the Department of Speech and Drama, our amateur efforts were crude and sometimes embarrassing. In one Junior Class opera, I remember we had a sort of Romeo and Juliet scene in which the heroine was to lean out the window of a tower and sing to her Romeo below. She leaned too far out and Juliet and tower came tumbling down on center stage.

The rowdiest dramatic event was an alfresco Junior vaudeville performance staged usually on the football field. In my junior year I played a feminine role (there were no coed participants ever), and it led well-nigh to a campus scandal. My part was to burlesque a

Palo Alto milliner. The name was camouflaged, of course. I wore a Mother Hubbard and a sunbonnet. Next day, word reached me that the most famous Palo Alto milliner, who took the gibe to herself, was coming to the campus to horsewhip me. Well—she didn't come! But I steered clear of Palo Alto for several weeks.

The annual Sophomore-Freshman Rush was the lowest form of interclass activity. The object was to see which class could "hogtie" the other. It was a brutal and bloody affair. In my sophomore year, as I remember, the two sides, after scouting each other through the Arboretum, clashed on Palm Drive, about midway between the Quad and the El Camino gates. Fresh macadam had been spread on the roadway. When the gladiators wrestled on that inhospitable surface of sharp-edged broken stones, the carnage was dreadful. So dreadful, indeed, that the University authorities banned the rush thereafter forevermore.

Another less sanguine class event was the Junior Plug Ugly. Junior men affected gray plug hats as their official headgear. The tradition started, it is said, when a San Francisco hatter with a large surplus stock of the hats hit upon the clever scheme of selling them to students. The Junior Class immediately proclaimed them a monopoly. They decorated the plugs with their class numerals and any other frescoes that took their fancy. It wasn't long before the seniors served notice they would smash the plugs on a certain date. It was a lively encounter and so colorful that it became a campus tradition. For juniors, a recognized status symbol was to be still in possession of the most beaten-up plug on the Quad. Juniors looked quite "far out" in their plugs compared with seniors who wore impressive sombreros.

A serious note was introduced into University life in 1903 when a typhoid fever epidemic struck down a number of students, faculty, and faculty children. It was then that the students became closely acquainted with Dr. Ray Lyman Wilbur. He was the University physician. The skill and precision of his ministrations throughout the epidemic gave comfort and confidence to everyone. He was the one who discovered the source of the infection in the milk supply from a dairy on Alpine Road, and he personally guarded the place with a shotgun to prevent issuance of any more milk until the danger was over.

Mrs. Stanford's death and the earthquake were the tragic events of my college days. The campus was shocked and saddened when news came that the surviving founder of the University had passed suddenly in Honolulu on the last day of February, 1905, in her seventy-seventh year. First reports were that she had died of poisoning, but they were discounted quickly by findings of the physicians who attended her. The cause was rupture of the coronary artery. As correspondent for a San Francisco newspaper, I was sent on a number of wild goose chases to find supposed caches of poison on the Stanford estate and to interview her servants. One of these forays was at night to the home of Miss Bertha Berner, her secretary, who lived in Menlo along San Francisquito Creek. When I rang the bell, a second-story window was flung up and an impressive masculine voice said, "I have a shotgun, and if you don't go away immediately, I'll let you have it!" I sensed it was the charge and not the gun that was being proffered me, so I retired quickly in good order and reported to my newspaper that Miss Berner was not available for an interview. The newspapers and press wires made a shameful sensation of the so-called poisoning story for several days.

The University immediately went into mourning. Classes were suspended and social activities canceled. Mrs. Stanford's funeral services were held impressively in the magnificent Memorial Church which she had erected so recently to the memory of her husband. Faculty, alumni, students, and many prominent citizens filled the Church, and many more stood outside during the services. Clergymen from practically all denominations attended, marking the nonsectarian significance of the church which Mrs. Stanford had decreed. The casket was borne by students. Tears were in the eyes of many as the cortege passed under Memorial Arch and down Palm Drive to the Mausoleum where Mrs. Stanford was reunited in death with her husband and their beloved son. For many months thereafter it was almost impossible to realize that the University was without its devoted, wise, patient, and loyal patron who had carried on so courageously after the Senator's death.

Everybody got up early on the morning of April 18, 1906, because Mother Nature set off the alarm clock at 5:13 a.m. She didn't just ring a bell, but gave every sleeper such a good shaking it was impossible to stay in bed. The day already had dawned, but a new dawning came with the realization that a very severe earthquake had visited the campus and surrounding areas. I was spending the night at my sister's home. Plaster rained down from the ceiling, the furniture went into a dance, and I joined the dance trying to get into my clothes. There was an ominous rumble like distant thunder and the sound of voices in various notes of fear and dismay. A fraternity house down the street where a beer bust occurred the night before was shaken off its foundations and spraddled out like a hen sitting on eggs. One of the brothers, jostled awake and still a bit exhilarated, looked out the window and survey the scene. His stentorian bass voice drowned out the rest: "Now look what rum does!"

A cloud of dust was rising above the Quad. It became almost immediately obvious that the University plant had been severely damaged. A quick look revealed that the spire of Memorial Church was gone, the mosaic façade had collapsed, the tall chimney of the powerhouse had fallen, and the just-completed men's gymnasium and the half-finished new library were in ruins. Word came that tragedy had struck Encina Hall. My brother-in-law, Professor Green, and I hurried there with others. We found one of the heavy chimneys had plunged through the roof, carrying four rooms with it to the basement. Students were in the wreckage, broken water pipes were raining streams into the shambles. Professor Green took charge of the rescue work. All but one student were quickly extricated. The one unfortunate was Junius Hanna, whose life was crushed out by the falling timbers and masonry. Of the two fatalities on the campus, the other was Otto Gerdes, night fireman at the powerhouse, who paused long enough to throw off the master electric switch, possibly preventing fires, and then ran out only to be caught by the falling smokestack. One other casualty was narrowly averted when a poetic senior, living on the top floor of Encina, leaned out a window and grasped the eaves-trough, hoping to pull himself up to the roof, a maneuver he couldn't bring off. There he dangled, shouting, until a fellow student reached out and dragged him back into the room.

All houses were evacuated and the University was closed for the remainder of the term. My class of 1906 was robbed of its Commencement. Gallant fraternity men stood guard through the night over their Greek letter sisters, who slept on the verandas of their houses. There had been rumors that inmates of Agnews Insane Asylum at San Jose had escaped and were roaming the countryside.

In mid-morning I remembered suddenly that I was a campus correspondent and my paper, the *Bulletin*, in San Francisco, would want the story of the disaster at Stanford. John Cushing, correspondent for the morning *Call*, had the same idea. So we made hasty notes of the damage to the University, hired a team and surrey from Jasper Paulsen, Palo Alto liveryman, and headed for the city. No trains were running; telephone and telegraph wires were down. When we reached Colma we were warned by refugees who were streaming out of the city that our rig would be commandeered by General Frederick Funston's troops, who had taken charge and declared martial law. We didn't fancy losing our mobile equipment, so we put it in a livery stable in Colma and started walking toward the inferno. All the way up we had seen the black pall rising to the north.

By ten o'clock we came to Potrero Hill and looked down on the city. It was a sight I shall never forget. Seemingly, all San Francisco, from the bay to the ocean, was in flames. But we soon discerned that the light of the fire raging in the downtown and Mission areas was reflected in the windows of houses on the western hills, making them appear to be burning also. A huge mushroom cloud of smoke was boiling up from the burning section, similar to the sight we have become familiar with since Hiroshima. We made our way down to Van Ness Avenue, intent upon getting to our newspapers. There we were halted by an armed sentry who said we could go no farther toward the central district.

"We're newspapermen," we told him with assurance. "We've got a big story about the earthquake damage to Stanford University. We must deliver it to our papers."

"What papers do you work for?" the soldier asked, unimpressed by the importance of our news against the background of a whole city being consumed. We told him, "Well, boys," he said, "you might just as well sit down and rest. Your newspapers burned up hours ago."

We roamed around the edges of the fire through the night, watching a suddenly dispossessed population wandering awe-stricken away from the fire, bearing only what they could carry in their arms or drag in perambulators, toy wagons, or trunks. Cushing caught a ferry to seek his family across the bay. I reached the Valencia Street Southern Pacific depot by daylight. But no trains were running to take me back to Palo Alto. A relief station had been opened nearby, and I went to work there, handing out potatoes and bread to refugees. It was two weeks before I returned to the campus. By then it was almost a deserted place. The students were gone, the buildings closed. I realized, with a catch at my throat, that my Stanford student days were over.

But what a glorious four years it had been! And what a momentous period in the University's history! The first "stone age," as Dr. Jordan dubbed the years of intensive construction, had been achieved. Life on the campus, academically and socially, had formed a pleasant pattern. It was a close-knit community. Faculty and students enjoyed a delightful camaraderie.

Dr. Jordan frequently strolled along the Quadrangle arcades, tipping his hat gravely to coeds or stopping to talk with students. He was accustomed to drop in uninvited, but always welcome, to dormitories and fraternity and sorority houses for a chat in the evenings, or sometimes for lunch or dinner. Occasionally, he would bring along guests to whom he was showing the University in all its facets, particularly the life of the students. One Sunday morning he was escorting a tally-ho load of distinguished Chinese gentlemen over the campus. He stopped at the Kappa Alpha Theta house (his daughter was a member) and ushered the mandarin-clad dignitaries to the front door. The young ladies, catching one glimpse of the celestial invasion, and being mostly in Sabbath morning dishabille, fled to the seclusion of their bedrooms upstairs. One who had dressed early for church opened the door and ushered the party in. Dr. Jordan, followed by his curious guests, entered and explored the lower floor. Then a general alarm spread through the upper floors. "They're coming up!" some one shouted. And up they came, indeed. Fortunately, the bedrooms were interconnected. When the invaders passed down the hall from one empty room, the astonished Thetas scampered back into that room from the one about to be shown. The game of hide-and-seek went on until Dr. Jordan, apparently oblivious to the consternation, led his gorgeous-robed party back to the tally-ho and proceeded on his hospitable tour. "Tally-ho" became a warning signal in the Theta house thereafter.

The annual Junior Prom was, I thought, the nicest social event because it utilized the very heart of the University, the Inner Quad, for its locale. It was given at night. The Quad was converted into a fairyland by Japanese lanterns. Booths were arranged by the women's living groups between the classroom buildings. Stanford swains promenaded their ladies around the arcade from booth to booth where they were received with refreshments and hospitality. It was a delightful affair; I'm sorry it was discontinued. The Senior Ball, held each year in Encina Commons, was another outstanding social occasion.

The whole tempo of college life was serene. To be sure, there were occasional mild explosions, as, for instance, a "peerade" or the mysterious issuance and distribution of an anonymous "Bawlout" sheet full of scandalous innuendoes about students and faculty. But, generally, the atmosphere gave true meaning to the favorite descriptive term "The Farm." As university communities go, it was indeed idyllic. . . .

I see I am growing sentimental. And long-winded as well. I'd better close these recollections before I reach the point of no return. But who can recall old Stanford days without letting his affections show?

# In a Scholar's Study

OLA ELIZABETH WINSLOW, A.B. '06, A.M. '14

*After graduation from Stanford Miss Winslow taught in a private school in San Francisco, then at the College of the Pacific. In 1914 she accepted a position in the English department in Goucher College, Baltimore, where she remained until 1944. In that year she was invited to Wellesley College as a visiting professor for one year, a visit which was extended until her retirement in 1950. Since retirement she has been on the staff of Radcliffe Seminars, an adult education project. Among her published works are* American Broadside Verse; Meetinghouse Hill, 1630–1788; John Bunyan; Master Roger Williams; *and* Jonathan Edwards, 1703–1758, *which won the Pulitzer Prize for biography in 1941.*

*She now lives in Sheepscott, Maine, in a two-hundred-year-old cottage, with a garden that her western friends say is worthy of a one-time Californian.*

A S THE YEARS GO ON I find it is the classroom that remains in sharp focus, while the details of what we call "college life" grow dim or else recede altogether. Not that the subject matter of these fifty-minute periods is remembered for itself; not at all. Rather it is the man at the desk, the way he entered the room, his tones of voice, his gestures, his fleeting expressions as he talked; these are clear memories, even at long distance. There is also something else, not easily caught in words. Classrooms have an individual significance, entirely apart from all remembered pictures.

Among my Stanford teachers whose classrooms have such a significance I wish to pay tribute to the one presided over by Professor Ewald Flügel, to whom I owe what was probably my first conscious wonderings about the scholar's devotion (a dedication it was for him) to inquiry into times far past. Emendations to the *Beowulf* text was the subject of the course, and he went at it as though our present peace of mind, even our life happiness, depended on finding out the precise word and syllable the one-time scribe had written. Why does it matter so much to him, I wondered, as he interrupted himself time after time to write German bibliography on the blackboard or balance one textual emendation against another.

Later on, as a supplement to another of his courses, I spent my Saturday morning in his study, and under his direction alphabetized words for a portion of a Middle English dictionary he was making. The words were written in pencil on little squares of paper torn from used student bluebooks, jagged of edge and troublesome to handle. At that time I knew nothing of Middle English or linguistic studies, but this room in which I worked, books to the ceiling on all sides, tables loaded with papers, work in progress on every side, became Saturday by Saturday an eloquent commentary on the scholar's life and the beginnings of an answer at least to the what of this particular scholar's dedication. I had been a reader all my younger life and had fancied myself at home in a library, but this was a new world in print and I was an outsider.

It was later, much later, before I knew for myself something of the excitement—in fact, the drama—of literary research, and had hints of the satisfaction it brings to the initiate. In this recall of Stanford days, I like to think that perhaps something in my own experience with books is owing to Professor Flügel and the intangible significance of his long-ago classroom in the life of one of his students.

*The study of literature is an effort to think honestly about literature— to think till it hurts, for pain is the test of all honest thinking. Out of such pain rises a strenuous joy; the purest, no doubt, the least disappointing that this earth is able to afford.*

ALBERT LEON GUÉRARD, Professor of General Literature

# My Days on the Stanford Farm

## PHILIP DAVID SWING, A.B. '05, LL.B. '07

*Philip Swing practiced law in San Bernardino and El Centro, California, and in 1919 became Judge of the Superior Court of Imperial County. In 1920 he was elected to the United States Congress, where he served six terms. While there he cosponsored, along with Senator Hiram Johnson, the Swing-Johnson bill which, becoming law, authorized the construction of Hoover Dam. He was also responsible for other important water legislation. From 1945 to 1958 he was a member of the State of California Water Resources Board and successive Water Commissions, which formulated the State of California Water Plan. He now practices law in San Diego.*

*He is the father of two daughters, one of whom, Phyllis Swing Hind, was in the Class of '44 at Stanford.*

I ENTERED STANFORD in September, 1901. I was to room with my brother, Will Swing, '03, in Encina Hall. He was being "sent to college" by our rich uncle. I was "going to college" on my own. Will had been valedictorian of his high school class at San Bernardino and as such made a hit with my uncle at the graduation ceremonies. After he congratulated Will, he offered to send him to college.

Two years later I, too, was valedictorian of my class, and again my uncle congratulated me; but, his offer to help me was conditioned on my waiting two years until he had finished sending Will through. I decided, though, that the time to go to college was when I was in the mood. So, after working all summer at the Santa Fe shops in my town (I worked there each subsequent vacation), I took the money I had earned and left for Stanford.

At the Palo Alto Railroad Station I took a horse-driven vehicle owned by "Uncle John" and headed down the mile road through the unbroken arboretum, seeing for the first time the magnificent Stanford Arch and Memorial Church in the background. Reaching the open palm-lined circle, we continued to Encina Hall, which was to be my home for the next four years. After matriculation I went to the student employment agency and got a job waiting on table at the student dining room, which then was between Encina and the Quadrangle. Between the Quadrangle and the post office there still remained the "Camp," the row of low whitewashed frame houses formerly occupied by the construction crew when Stanford was being built. These were then occupied by the elite of us financially poor students.

I arrived at the "Farm" a poor boy from the country, possessed of no financial resources but with a determination to get a college education. Stanford accepted me and gave me my opportunity. I found that here, in a University founded by a multimillionaire, was a really democratic institution where sons of poor and rich met on a common level and "Frats" and "Barbs" mingled without class distinction and accepted each other as social equals.

From my professors I received not alone the information contained in the daily lectures, but more importantly, the knowledge of how to study, how to think, how to look at and co-ordinate facts and evaluate happenings and events.

From David Starr Jordan I got the most. I think he left his imprint indelibly on the mind and character of every student who came in personal contact with him. I took his course in the Origin and Evolution of Man. Into it he put not merely biology, anthropology, zoology, and paleontology, but also his entire philosophy of how man should live and conduct himself with relation to other men in organized society. In welcoming our freshman class, he gave us a preview of what life on the Farm was to be. He said, "We have no rules here. We merely expect you to act like ladies and gentlemen. But, if you do not, we will pick you up by the nape of the neck, carry you to the edge of campus, and drop you off." He accompanied the remark with an impressive gesture as though he were picking up an insect between his thumb and forefinger and dropping it out the window. I was duly impressed.

On another occasion, I remember his telling his attitude toward politics. He said, "I always vote the straight Republican ticket. When I go to the polls and receive my party ballot, I examine it, and if it is not right, I scratch it and make it straight." I was again impressed and in later years, while I, too, was a Republican, I exercised the Jordan privilege of jumping across the party line to vote for whomever I thought was the best man.

A later president, Dr. Ray Lyman Wilbur, was, in my day, a practicing physician with his office in Palo Alto. But he gave part time to caring for the students, with a small office on the Inner Quadrangle where he kept specified hours. I remember my first contact with him; I had spent a miserable night with alternating chills and fever. My joints ached. My head throbbed as though someone were pounding on it. I feared the worst. The next morning I rose early and was at Dr. Wilbur's office long before the designated hour. When he finally arrived, I recited in detail all my symptoms and told him how I felt. He looked down my throat and had me say "Ahh," then counted out a dozen white pills. "You have a cold," he said. "Take these as directed; begin with two when you go to bed tonight." "What a doctor!" I told my roommate. "He can give disease a twelve hours' start and be confident he will overtake it." Dr. Wilbur's reputation did not rest only upon his ability to treat the bodies of Stanford students but also on training their minds. He later demonstrated that he was one of the truly great presidents of the University.

Dean Abbott of the Law School, in addressing our freshman class, said, "There seems to be an unusually large number of students who think they want to become lawyers. Let me say to you, unless you are willing to work all the days of your life like a horse, get out of here now while there is yet time." At the end of more than 50 years of practice, I know that never were truer words spoken.

Much as I gained from my professors, I must give credit to association with my fellow students for a large part of my mental growth and character development. My closest friends were those students living with me in Encina Hall. The one with whom I had most personal contact and to whom I feel I owe the most was my roommate, Tommy Coen. We lived together the last two years after my brother, Will, graduated.

Tommy formed an eating club in Mayfield on a share-the-cost basis. This group who ate together there was an interesting one: Tommy Coen, who later became Chief Counsel and then President of an indemnity and insurance company, a subsidiary of Cudahy Company of Chicago; Ben Day, who became Chief Counsel of Southern Pacific Railway with headquarters in New York; Oscar Gibbons, district attorney of his home county; Morris Oppenheim, long-time municipal judge of San Francisco; Louis Roseberry, State Senator and later trust officer for the Security First National Bank of Los Angeles, author and recognized authority on trust law; Arthur McQueen Dibble, an outstanding lawyer in Portland, Oregon; Alex Sheriffs, superintendent of schools, Santa Clara County; and Frank Hathaway, a government administrator for Indian oil rights in Oklahoma. In the three-times-a-day mile walk between Encina and Mayfield, we discussed everything, both trivial and profound.

I had neither time nor money to spend on social activities. Like Arthur Dibble, who was accustomed to declare, "I court but one mistress, and that is the law," I, too, was "courting the law." However, Encina was allowed one dance annually. In my senior year the boys insisted that I go. When I told them, "I can't dance," they replied that they would teach me. When I told them I knew no girl I could ask, they said they would fix that, too. So during the recreation hour, 6:30 to 7:30, they took turns teaching me to dance. Ten days before the dance, a boy who was waiting table at the Roble dining room took me over to Roble and sent for Miss Hazel Severy, '07. When she appeared he said, "Miss Severy, this is the guy who is going to take you to the Encina dance." That was it. The date was made. I was a miserable dancer, but Miss Severy graciously discharged her social obligation by inviting me to the next Roble dance.

Every student in the University loved Mrs. Stanford, then well along in years. She personally had come to the rescue of Stanford when its finances were tied up in litigation. Worn with the responsibility of guiding the University's affairs through the troubled early days, she left in 1903 for prolonged foreign travel. In 1904 she returned to her home on the "Farm." A large group of us students, led by our band and cheer leaders, marched to her home and serenaded her. She finally appeared on the porch and, after warmly greeting us, invited us into her home. I was greatly impressed with the warmth of her personality and dignity of bearing. In the spring of 1905 she went to Honolulu where her death occurred unexpectedly.

In the Euphronia Literary Society I had gained valuable practice in debating. As a senior I made the 1905 debating team, receiving a gold pin suitably engraved, and at the end of the year I was appointed class orator. I took as the motif for my remarks the story of how David Livingston, lost in the wilds of Africa, stirred Henry Stanley to brave the dangers and make the long trip to bring him back. In like manner, I said, our invisible hands reached out from the Farm across the vast Pacific to bring back to Stanford our beloved benefactor to her final resting place.

The silence when I concluded disturbed me. I said to Tommy as we left, "I failed." "No," he replied, "they were too deeply moved to applaud. Their silence was a tribute to Mrs. Stanford and also to you."

Looking back, I realize that Stanford opened the door to me for a new future—for a fuller and a more useful life, both for myself and others. It sent me out into the world with faith in myself, with a compass to guide my course, and equipped with the necessary tools to gain my goals. Whatever I have accomplished in later years I owe in large part to the knowledge, experience, and training received at Stanford.

*. . . Jordan—not all-wise or completely tolerant, but a sort of educational Moses, part poet, part legislator, patient and moderate—except, of course, in his enthusiasm for fish.*

HANS ZINSSER, Stanford professor, 1910–13

# Via Stanford to San Quentin

## Leo Stanley, A.B. '08, M.D. '12

*Dr. Leo Stanley has steadily pursued his medical career since leaving Stanford. He served as chief surgeon of San Quentin Prison until his retirement in 1951, except for four years spent in the United States Navy during World War II. He is now a relief surgeon on Pacific liners.*

THE VIEW OF STANFORD from Palm Drive with the steeple of Memorial Church behind it was my first never-to-be-forgotten impression of Stanford. I was seventeen, a country lad, dressed in ill-fitting store clothes and a celluloid collar. With another lad from the cow country of San Miguel, I had come on this hot September day to apply for registration at Stanford and take the test in English 1B, that stumbling block that all must get over to get in.

As we walked toward the Quad, I realized that neither of us had ever seen such splendor—the sandstone buildings, the Circle bordered with red geraniums, the wonderfully laid out grounds. All we had been accustomed to in our grain-producing village in the Upper Salinas Valley were small wooden buildings, the largest of which was the livery stable.

At the end of my first year, 1904, my money ran out. Working in the summer harvest did not provide means for another year at Stanford. Nevertheless, I returned to Palo Alto, hoping that in some way I might continue in school.

There was a job piling lumber with Dudfield, but this did not pay enough. I had to watch my old classmates coming back, happy and hopeful, knowing this was not for me.

One whole year I worked on the Southern Pacific as "peanut butcher." As I look back on this experience, however, it was, in the long run, better than a year at college—learning about people, studying their characteristics and peculiarities, finding how to get along with them.

The next fall I had a little money, and I knew that if I hashed I might maintain myself. All the trials and tribulations of working one's way through college were mine: riding a bicycle three times a day to Palo Alto to wait on table, getting fired for not washing the dishes properly, and many other vexations. But it was wonderful to be in the University and have such friends as beloved David Starr Jordan, Vernon Kellogg, Robert Swain, and scores of others who gave lavishly of their kindly help and interest.

Then came the earthquake. We hashers were domiciled in the attic of the Stanford Inn, located on the site of the present Cubberley Building. At 5:13 the San Andreas Fault slipped. I was thrown out of my double deck bunk. Looking out, I saw the great stone library fall in clouds of dust and mortar, leaving the steel birdcage, its frame, entirely devoid of cover. I hurried out to see more. A hasty survey showed the Arch irreparably damaged, the church in ruins, the statue of Agassiz plunged neck-deep in the concrete in front of the Zoology Building (Dr. Jordan said this was Agassiz in the concrete instead of the abstract), many of the other buildings in ruins. The impressions gained that day can never be erased.

Out of Stanford at last and on to Cooper Medical College. Working the "Sunday picnic trains" to Santa Cruz as newsboy, together with a modest loan, finally got me an M.D.

At Cooper one of our instructors was Ray Lyman Wilbur from whom we learned much. After graduation I got a job as doctor at San Quentin. One of my classmates, Jim Cutting, went to the state hospital at Agnew. At a Stanford gathering several years later, Dr. Wilbur dryly remarked that in medical school he did have two pretty good students. But one of them went to State's Prison, and the other to the Insane Asylum.

# Prelude to Astronauts

## EARL JONATHAN HADLEY, A.B. '08

*Since his graduation Earl Hadley has worked as a reporter and editorial writer for* Collier's Weekly *and for the* New York Evening Sun, *and was assistant managing editor of the* New York Globe. *He has also engaged in economic research and in general writing. At present he is the Governor of the Society of Colonial Wars in the State of New York.*

THINKING BACK to my sophomore year, the year of the earthquake, I am moved to point out a possible resemblance in the psychology at Stanford on the eighteenth of April, 1906, and that which could conceivably reappear under atomic assault. It is true that there were no radios to take up the slack in 1906, but with power systems out of commission, there might be a similar shutout.

Be that as it may, in the course of the morning following the big shake at 5:13 a.m., word traveled around the campus that Chicago was down, New York had been pitched into the ocean, and we were all that was left, a miraculous fragment of another Lost Continent of Atlantis.

At that time, about one-third of the student body came from outside the state of California and one of the first things the outsiders had done was to rush to the campus telegraph office to let their families know that the senders were still intact—which, as I have indicated, was before we had heard that families weren't there any more. As the day wore on my brother (Clyde M. Hadley, '06) and I, from Puget Sound, grew firm in a devoutly regional conviction that, whatever might have happened to the rest of the country, Nature simply wouldn't do that to the Pacific Coast. That was for sure!

It was with growing confidence, therefore, that he and I in the evening, although the whole northern sky was crimson from the flames of San Francisco, went around to the telegraph office again to see whether our wire had gotten through. The telegrapher laughed patiently. He told us that he had put 300 telegrams in an automobile for San Jose, to be dispatched there; at San Jose, 3,000 mesages had been loaded on the car and sent around the Bay to Oakland; at Oakland, 15,000 telegrams had been put aboard a train for Salt Lake City, to be mailed out from there. This, while it did nothing for our families, was nonetheless reassuring, indicating as it did that the country, as far east as Utah, anyhow, was still in business.

Because of the general overturn on the campus and our going up to the city on a relief expedition, it was a lapse of days before my brother and I reached Olympia, Washington. Even so, we arrived before our telegram (which never did). We got our money's worth, though; as a result of our blackout, when we went about the streets we created a flutter similar to that created by a modern cosmonaut coming down out of the super-sky. Yet the difference between then and now is that while cosmonauts are already getting to be a little routine, we were the first of our kind.

NEAR-ALUMNUS ODE

*Was a bank robbed?*
*The Irwins did it.*
*Was a train-butcher, plying his necessary trade*
*    between Menlo and Mayfield,*
*Looted of his peanuts?*
*Watch the Irwins!*
*Oh Gosh! It was lucky we were out of California*
*When the earthquake came along*
*And shook down the Arch,*
*Or the Committee on Student Affairs*
*Would, of a verity, have traced it to the Irwins.*

WALLACE IRWIN, ex-'00

# THREE

IN THE FIRST DECADE of the Twentieth century at Stanford, the three outstanding happenings were, in a sense, public happenings. The typhoid epidemic, Mrs. Stanford's death, the earthquake—everyone at the University, everyone in the surrounding countryside knew of them in detail, shared in greater or less degree in their effects. The events themselves and their results, then, are amply shown in the reminiscences of those who were students at the time.

The second decade moved otherwise. Its most noteworthy actions were those taken by the Board of Trustees—actions usually unknown or unimpressive to students until their results appeared. Set down chronologically, the four history-making actions of the Trustees were these:

In 1912 Herbert Hoover, '95, was elected to the Board to take the place of Whitelaw Reid, whose term had expired.

In 1913 the Board elevated President Jordan to the newly created post of Chancellor of the University.

Also in 1913, under the urging of both Trustees and faculty, Vice-President Branner reluctantly consented to fill the presidential chair for the two years remaining before his retirement.

In 1915 Ray Lyman Wilbur, '96, accepted Stanford's presidency. He assumed the post in January 1916, and continued in it for twenty-seven years, the longest term of any Stanford president.

The changes resulting from Herbert Hoover's election as a Trustee come first in time as also in importance. It had been the policy of the Trustees to hold each year a substantial part of what was received from the Stanford estate as a reserve against emergencies. The part so held was then invested with the utmost caution—a phrase which, interpreted, means at low interest. Under the persuasion of the new member, both policies were relaxed. The amount held for emergencies was cut down. Caution in investment, though it was caution still, was based on widened information. As a consequence, funds assigned for academic uses were increased—though still far from adequately.

Reversal of yet a third Board policy, though it was slower in showing results, was in actuality the most important of the three—perhaps, all its consequences considered, the most important any Stanford Board has ever made.

It had been the Trustees' custom to carry on their financial work in secret. The secrecy was so complete that neither Dr. Jordan nor Dr. Branner knew what was to be spent for what until the spending was done, and even then, as Dr. Branner pointed out, "by accident or courtesy." The advantages to the Board were that reporters could be brushed aside, protests—either public or academic—prevented or rendered useless. The disadvantages, however, were large and growing—the breeding of rumors, derogatory always; the certainty in many minds that things hidden meant things that would not bear the light; worst of all, the encouragement of a comfortable widespread belief that the Stanford fortune, once sufficient, was sufficient still and contributions from other sources both unnecessary and unwanted. In view of these drawbacks, the Board now decided to publish a yearly financial statement, so that "what was spent for what" could be known to anybody who took the trouble to read.

"It is marvelous," Dr. Jordan wrote to his successor, "how Hoover is handling the Board. . . . Mr. Hopkins said that Hoover gave them more ideas in ten days than they had had before in ten years." If one of those ideas was for breaking down the wall of secrecy and so developing public good will, a look at today's University, built up by gifts from many sources, justifies the extravagant sounding "marvelous."

Dr. Branner, knowing his term to be short, attempted no novelties. Two sentences from his inaugural speech express both his method of working and his philosophy:

*Being a practical man, the problems of life appear to me simply the problems of each day as the days bring them along. . . . I believe in the reasonableness of most things as they are.*

His informed watch over "things as they are" allowed him, even within his two years, to tighten procedures in the president's office, to enforce authorized lines of communication between faculty members and president or Trustees—improvements, both of them, tending to make life more livable for administrations to come. "I did not want this job," he explained in one of his letters, "but the Trustees persuaded me that all the other live men were dead and buried, or some such fol-de-rol; so here I am, repenting at my leisure and trying to add up six columns of figures and make the total come out bigger than anybody else can."

Whatever his success with figures, his individual success in office was unquestionable. As his term approached its end, Trustees and faculty alike urged him to prolong it. To this, though, his refusal was absolute. Six months more he would stay for the Board's convenience; beyond that, no more. The Stanford campus remained his home, however, so long as he lived.

*Education will assume ever greater priority because there will be increasing need for men and women not only trained in science and technology but also for persons with knowledge of foreign languages and cultures. . . .*

J. E. WALLACE STERLING

# The Innocent Decade

BRUCE BLIVEN, A.B. '11

*Bruce Bliven has spent most of his working life as a jour-
nalist in New York City, where he was managing editor of
the* New York Globe, *editor of the* New Republic, *and American correspondent for the* Manchester Guardian. *He has
published several hundred magazine articles, written two
books and edited two others, taught in three universities,
and lectured widely throughout the country. He is at present
back on the Stanford campus doing research for a new book.
He is married to Rose Emery, '14; they have one son, Bruce
Bliven, Jr., who is also a professional writer, a fact that has
hopelessly confused the cataloguers of the Library of Congress.*

THE ELDERLY always color the memory pictures of their youth
brighter than life. As we pause to rest awhile on the steps leading up to the guillotine, our recollections become more vivid as they
recede in time. Making due allowance for this propensity, it seems
to me that the decade that ended with the guns along the Marne in
1914 was an exceptionally happy time and Stanford University, where
I spent the very middle of that decade, an exceptionally happy place.

We were all so young, as we climbed into the ten-cent open carriages and drove in the August heat out Palm Drive to see for the first
time the red roofs of the Quad against the Santa Cruz Range and to
smell the tarweed! We surely must have been several years younger
than today's students of the same chronological age. Though the
Twentieth century had been ushered in formally not once but twice,
at the beginning of 1900 and 1901, we were really living in the Nine-
teenth. It is the fashion now to laugh at that era, but the laughter
becomes a little hollow when we look at today's smog-drenched,
bomb-haunted world.

It was not merely the excited seventeen- and eighteen-year-olds, assembling for the autumn semester, who were naïve and optimistic; the whole Western world shared this state. When the decade began, Gregor Mendel's wonderful work with sweet peas, forgotten since 1866, had been resurrected only four years earlier; but Darwin's doctrine had already taken firm hold, and colored the thoughts of even those loyal churchmen who with their conscious minds rejected it. Evolution was a philosophy centered upon mankind and intended for our benefit; it meant that everything would constantly get better and better for us, who were the center of the universe. Under the beneficient influence of natural law, the Twentieth would go on from one plateau of peace and prosperity to another. To be sure, poverty and disease still existed in some parts of the world, but they would be done with any minute now. And it was hard to remember that they existed at all, if you were in your late teens and basking in the golden sunshine of the Golden State.

When the Innocent Decade ended, the teachings of Freud were just beginning to impinge on the American public consciousness; the first popular magazine article about him appeared only in 1913, two decades after his work had begun. All the dark (but on the whole health-making) knowledge of man's barbaric unconscious that he taught us still lay, so far as most people were concerned, in the untroubled future.

Norman Angell did not write his reassuring book "proving" another great war was impossible until just before the decade ran out; but his philosophy was already so generally accepted that when the book appeared it locked into the pattern of our thinking with no commotion. To be sure, there was a Kaiser in Germany who rattled the saber occasionally—he had done so once at Agadir in 1911—but Europe was far away from the tawny hills of the Santa Clara Valley, where the live oaks stood out like green-tinted kernels of popcorn scattered on a rumpled tan cloth.

And anyhow, we were too busy to be bothered, as we got ready for the slow roll of the college year. The men of each of the four classes had to purchase their rigidly prescribed distinctive headgear: gray caps for the freshmen and red pork-pie soft felt hats for the sophomores, while the juniors wore gray felt plug hats, painted over

with the record of each man's college activities, and the seniors had
forest-ranger sombreros, decorated with class numerals carved into
a leather band. (Nobody would have ventured out of doors with a
naked head.) The upperclassmen wore tan corduroy trousers, con-
scientiously dragged through dirt and spattered with ink to remove
that obnoxious look of freshness. The girls had to supply themselves
with Peter Thompson dresses (or their equivalent, a middy blouse
and an ankle-length skirt).

In addition to all the other events of a busy year, the men looked
forward to two annual pitched battles. In one of these the freshmen
and sophomores, rolling in a sea of mud, tried to tie each other up
with long strips of cotton cloth; in the other the juniors wearing their
new "plug-ugly" hats sought to battle their way against senior resistance up the "Law Steps," leading from Lasuen Street toward the
northeast corner of the Inner Quad. Any junior whose hat was not
crushed in the melee was disgraced. (Some of them, scandalously,
may have secreted themselves later and ruined their own headgear.)

What were we like, in those far-off days? We were, for one thing,
pure children of Victoria's era, though the apple-cheeked little Queen
had been dead for three years when our decade began. Authoritarian
religion was starting to crumble and with it the authoritarian discipline of the home, but they were still important. The father dominated the family—at least in theory—partly because he was the only
breadwinner. Divorce was remarkedly rare. Our backgrounds were
overwhelmingly lower-middle class; in many cases we represented
the first generation to go to college, and so were pulling our families
up the social scale a little. Always allowing for occasional exceptions, our childhoods had been reasonably happy under firm but tem-
perate parental discipline.

We were well-behaved. Whatever may be the facts about juvenile
delinquency today, there was very little of it in our ranks, a fact that
is of course not particularly to our credit. We were the children of
our time, and if we had been born sixty years later, we should certainly in all respects have been children of today. To be sure, we
were hostile to the older generation; every crop of young people is.
But our hostility was to their ideas; it created no impulse to destroy

for the wanton sake of destruction. In my home town of 2,300 people in the Mississippi Valley, I cannot recall a single case of damage to property by young people during my whole childhood except an occasional uptilted outhouse on Hallowe'en, readily repaired in an hour.

Our morals were good, especially those of the girls. Of the five hundred undergraduate women only three or four in a whole college generation were subject to gossip as being "loose." This was not so true of the men; something of the frontier tradition of wine and women still prevailed, though undoubtedly there was a large minority—perhaps even a majority—who were in fact as chaste as the college women, whatever they may have said to the contrary.

There were periods during which it became fashionable to drink too much (the drink was almost always beer or whiskey, though California is a vineyard state). But here, also, the noisy excesses of a few made them seem more formidable in numbers than was in fact the case. On a much lower level: no nice girl would have dreamt of smoking in public, and not one in a hundred did so privately; a maiden in my class, discovered in her room with an inexplicable lighted cigarette, had to talk very fast to avoid being suspended.

The automobile had not yet wrought its enormous moral and social revolution, snatching a whole generation of young people out of the front-porch swing and into the remote recesses of Lovers' Lane. When I came to college there was, I believe, exactly one car owned by a student and he was forbidden to reach his living quarters by any route other than the continuation of Palo Alto's Embarcadero, now called Galvez Street. A little earlier there had been only one faculty automobile, owned by Dr. Ray Lyman Wilbur, the University medical officer; legend says that to keep out of sight of Mrs. Stanford, who disapproved of the horseless carriage, he had to reach his home by a circuitous route through College Terrace and along Mayfield Road.

Mrs. Stanford had lived into our decade; she died in 1905. But the horde of youngsters advancing on a college campus quickly tramples down memories; when I arrived in 1907, she seemed as remote as her husband who had been gone for fourteen years, or as

Queen Victoria, with whom I tended to confuse her. As for the University itself, so far as I knew it had been there forever; it is hard for me to believe even now that the whole institution was two years younger than I was.

We were parochial. Of the many world events during that decade, few reverberated more than faintly along the sandstone corridors beneath the red-tiled roofs. The Russo-Japanese War which began with the decade was noted chiefly because President Teddy Roosevelt, according to general belief, had ended it by his proposal for a peace conference at Portsmouth, New Hampshire. True, the San Francisco earthquake and fire made a deep impression, because men were killed and buildings destroyed on the campus. The voyage of the United States Fleet around the world a year later also bit in; we could and did go up to San Francisco to see the ships enter the unbridged Golden Gate. But other things seemed remote: Peary's discovery of the North Pole, Bleriot's first airplane flight across the English Channel, the dynamiting of the *Los Angeles Times*. Even great world events—the Italian-Turkish War, the Mexican Revolution against Diaz, the birth of the Chinese Republic—were hardly more than the hum of angry bees far off across a drowsy landscape.

At the very end of the Innocent Decade the Panama Canal was opened, and we knew about that, since it was to be celebrated (a year late) with expositions in San Francisco and San Diego. But almost unnoticed went the beginnings of great changes—the dissolution of Standard Oil, the first Federal income tax, Henry Ford's minimum daily wage of $5.

It is startling to think of today's commonplaces that were rudimentary or nonexistent when the decade ended. Radio for home entertainment was still five years away, and television a third of a century. Electric refrigeration, air conditioning, automatic washing of dishes and clothing were all in the future. Frozen foods were only a vagrant dream of Clarence Birdseye. Lord Rutherford's great experiments which opened the door to atomic fission were still six years away, and the discovery of insulin, seven. The sulfa drugs were twenty years off, the antibiotics twenty-seven, the anticoagulants still longer. Though Simon Binet had begun his revolutionary work on the intelligence quotient, it was not introduced to America (by Dr. Lewis Terman of Stanford) until two years after the decade ended.

The automobile continued to be a rarity, and a cross-country journey a great adventure, accompanied by ropes, shovels, tire patches, and extra cans of gasoline. Motion pictures were popular, though the price had gone up from five cents to ten or even a dizzy quarter. They were of course silent; at the end of the decade, sound movies were still thirteen years away, and effective color farther still.

Price comparisons must be discounted, since the average value of money was three times what it is today, but even so, some items seem modest. Tuition at Stanford was free to residents of California except for a "syllabus fee" of a couple of dollars; students from out of state had to pay $30 a year. Room and board at the Cardinal Club in College Terrace was $16 a month; outraged roars ensued when the money-mad manager put the rate up to $18. At "the Greek's" on University Avenue you could get a pretty good three-course meal with beverage for twenty-five cents (reckless plungers ordered stewed oysters a la carte for the same sum).

How did we compare with today's students? No one will ever know; there are too many intangibles to let us do more than guess. It is the fashion of elderly alumni to announce that they never could have hurtled today's entrance requirements, but this is probably not so. The scatter of intelligence along the scale is about the same in one generation as in another.

In those relaxed and sunny days there was certainly less urgency in the air. Commencement orators then as now told us that the fate of the world rested in our hands, but they didn't mean it—not as those who talk to graduates in nuclear physics mean it today. As is always true, some of us studied hard and some did not; success in later life came to most—but not all—of the best students and to some of the poorer ones.

Parenthetically, nearly all of us could read and write and spell. In the first grade, my classmates and I had been forced to memorize the alphabet, and had learned how to sound out syllables and words, going on to read easily and well. In my whole course from elementary school to college, I can recall hardly a student who needed a remedial-reading course, required I believe for forty per cent of the freshman classes in many big state universities today.

If most of us assumed in the Innocent Decade that the world would never see another major war, this was not true at all. There walked the campus in those days a man-mountain, a human volcano pouring forth a rich lava of scientific truth and moral perception. Students could and did fall into step with him as he walked between his home and his office, and never failed to hear something worth remembering. David Starr Jordan was deeply troubled about the possibility of more war. He pointed out the deleterious eugenic effect of killing off the bravest and best of any generation, leaving the second-raters to become future fathers. Geneticists nowadays are not so sure about the long-term physical results of war, but no one can doubt the great humanitarian spirit of this man.

I often thought of him, and his wish that mankind should live up to its best potentials, when in my later years I went as a journalist to Hitler's Germany, Mussolini's Italy, and Stalin's Russia. The Stanford motto, *Die Luft der Freiheit weht,* seemed more than ever significant in these lands where the wind of freedom did not blow at all, and you could not be sure that it ever would again.

We all take too much for granted, and this is especially true of the young; none of us realized how blessed we were to be in this place and in contact with such leaders, in the Innocent Decade. You may laugh, if you like, at our funny clothes, our quaint ceremonials, and our verdant, verdant ingenuousness. As for me, I shall only smile a little.

# In the Day of a Man Named Jordan

## ROBERT LEWIS DUFFUS, A.B. '10, A.M. '11

*Robert Duffus began his writing career by brief periods
as editorial writer on the staffs of the* San Francisco Bulletin,
*the* San Francisco Call, *and the* New York Globe. *Since 1937
he has been a member of the editorial staff of the* New York
Times. *He is the author of many books and magazine articles, among them, and of special interest to Stanford people,*
The Innocents of Cedro, *the story of two undergraduate
years spent as a member of Thorstein Veblen's household.
He is married and the father of two daughters.*

THE FIRST TIME I saw David Starr Jordan he was not behaving
like a college president. He was dressed in a baseball suit with
a cap over one eye and standing near where one of those new buildings that I can't quite now think of stands. Perhaps it was the site
of the Hoover Library.

At any rate Dr. Jordan was playing baseball as part of a faculty
team which was trying to subdue, as I believe, a gang of seniors.
This was at the end of August, 1906, shortly after the Declaration of
Independence but before the invention of the jet airplane. I believe
I have seen a photograph of Dr. Jordan standing at the plate and
tapping his foot gently with his bat. What he did, I believe, was to
hit the ball to a point somewhere between third base and the County
Road. He did not run. I suppose his doctor had told him not to. But
he could certainly hit. We students—if I may include those of us
who were not even freshmen, as yet, because we had not registered—
invented a yell which went as follows:

> *Cigars, cigars, cigarettes, beer,*
> *Faculty, faculty, we're right here.*

In those days I neither smoked nor drank. In a way I was wasting
my time.

61

I don't know who won the game. I don't know that anybody cared. It was a mellow sort of day. The Sierra Morena looked all right with its redwood spikes and its soft brown bald spots, and the hills rolled up toward it.

The other memory that clings to my mind again includes Dr. Jordan. This must have been on the Sunday following the baseball game. Dr. Jordan held a little meeting on the lawn in front of Roble Hall, which was then full of the most beautiful girls in the world. These girls emerged to join the rugged males who had come to listen to Dr. Jordan, and we all sat on the brown grass and soaked in sunshine. I remember what Dr. Jordan talked about. It was the Shinto religion. And he made it sound poetic and dreamy. Some of Palo Alto's clergymen thought Dr. Jordan should have made us go to church. They didn't think Dr. Jordan was orthodox. I suppose he wasn't. But on that morning he displayed warm, unsentimental, and masculine love of the world and of mankind.

The day stayed with me. It is a treasure I put with several other days and I will not sell at any price. Two world wars, the atom bomb, and the dismal fear that comes across the world have not tarnished that long-past Sunday morning. I retreat into it sometimes. It is pleasant there.

*I was called, unseen, unheard, unread, to Stanford University. . . . My prospective parents-in-law . . . frowned upon Stanford. Its president, David Starr Jordan, had an ominous reputation. He called himself a member of the Church Universal, that is to say that his mind was a theological blank. He had come out brazenly in favor of evolution. Much later, they were to discover the better side of Dr. Jordan.*

ALBERT LEON GUÉRARD, Professor of General Literature

# Accent on Adventure

## FRANK TAYLOR, EX-'18

*Frank Taylor, a professional writer, has written more than 600 articles, about half of them for the* Saturday Evening Post *and* Reader's Digest. *He has also written several books, among them* High Horizons, *which is the history of United Air Lines, and* Black Bonanza, *the story of Union Oil Company and the petroleum industry. He acknowledges that he has been accused of operating a factory known as the Taylor Writing Works, with specialists to put in the commas, apostrophes, jimdashes, and so on, but that this is not true. "I still sweat them out the hard way, being a writer who writes by perspiration rather than inspiration."*

*He is married to Katherine Elizabeth Ames, A.B. '19, and is the father of two sons, Robert and Paul, both of whom attended Stanford.*

EACH STANFORD GENERATION is sure its day was the Golden Age of Stanford. Ours really was. We came to The Farm in the last great period of world peace and left it (without graduating) at the start of the greatest age of war, both hot and cold. We came in horse and buggy days, saw the first auto on the campus (I actually owned one, an old Model T Ford, bought to expedite the selling and delivering of Wear-Ever aluminum pots and pans). We were the pioneers in flying machines, crystal set radios. We still had the red Toonerville trolley that rocked through the arboretum from Palo Alto to Stanford. My date (who's still dating me) had the inevitable choice after the movie of walking home and spending two dimes for ice cream at Sticky Wilson's, or riding home and squandering the dimes for carfare. We always walked. Ah, youth!

My most inspiring recollection is of Dr. Jordan, great and shaggy, ambling down the Quad, tipping his hat to all students, with even frosh doffing beanies in return. And the evenings when he would stroll unannounced into Encina Hall and start talking about any topic under the sun and including the sun with the first two or three students he encountered. In no time the word spread through the Hall, and he was surrounded by an audience sitting on the floor. He was the last completely educated man, I would guess, who knew all about everything.

Another fond memory is of Stanford's first journalism class. We had one mentor, Professor Everett Smith, whose idea of teaching journalism was to plant his feet on the desk and regale us with first-hand experiences of old *New York Sun* days. Looking back, I can think of no better way to fire young hopefuls with the derring-do of reportorial enterprise as practiced in pre-Guild days. We never learned what we couldn't do in Professor Smith's class. So it never occurred to me when I left the Farm that I couldn't be a war correspondent. In my ignorance I became one less than a year out of Stanford and I have been working down the ladder ever since.

I've asked my date what she remembers most vividly, since we have a joint bank account of memories of days on the Farm. She recalls Roble Bridge, a narrow foot structure over San Francisquito Creek, which we reached somehow after clambering over stiles, or via the shaded eucalyptus lane. She remembers Roble Bridge because the legend was you married the first coed with whom you crossed. So that's what we did and she hasn't had a chance to forget it during these past four decades.

She remembers also, she says, the rousing day when I kicked open the door between the Roble kitchen and the Roble dining room, as we hashers always did, with a tray stacked high with plates of food for the hungry girls. Somebody had spilled something slippery on the floor under the door and I came down in the noisiest crash in Roble's history, with the plates and the food all over me. A dame would remember something like that!

She also says she remembers the dates in the old "Dippy" office, where she sat on a stool waiting for me to put the paper to bed and then write some stories for the San Francisco papers (at 15c per inch) after which we dashed to Paly to get the copy aboard the train in time to make the morning news.

I like to recall the spirited meetings in a private dining room of the old Stanford Inn, which they tore down to make room for the Library, food for the mind being more important, I suppose, than food for the stomach. There we launched the *Stanford Illustrated Review*. The founders of that then belligerent journal—Al Griffin, the Randau brothers, Goodie Knight, Herb Marschutz, to mention a few —were thinkers with chips on their shoulders. No subject was too big for us to tackle. How I've wished in the years that followed that I could be as sure of things as we were around the festive board (dinner, 50c) in the old Stanford Inn.

The toughest decision I had to make at Stanford was the one at the end of my junior year to leave the Farm. I had been elected editor of the Daily for my senior year and there was a salary as well as honor involved. I felt that I had it made—for my final year, at least. But we thinkers had been thinking about the war in Europe and how we ought to be helping make the world safe for democracy, a quaint idea we had in those days. The easy, fast way to get overseas was to organize an American Field Service ambulance unit. It was the call of adventure versus the life of Riley. The spirit of venture drummed into us by Everett Smith, Dr. Jordan, Dr. Wilbur, and other faculty members won hands down. My understanding Econ prof, Dr. Murray Wildman, even loaned me money to pay my bills so that I could leave the campus with my creditors' blessing.

Looking back, I realize that I did not acquire much of a scholastic patina on the Farm. I was too busy. Had I faced today's rigorous scholastic competition I would have been rolled out after the first exam. So I'm thankful to have trod the Quad in the real Golden Age of Stanford, when the accent was on adventure of the spirit as well as of the mind.

# Science Yields a Humanitarian

## JOSEPHINE DOW RANDALL, A.B. '09, A.M. '13

*Josephine Randall has had two interlocking interests throughout her professional life—interest in the natural sciences and interest in the welfare of children. The Josephine D. Randall Junior Museum on Corona Heights in San Francisco bears her name in honor of her years-long struggle to establish a natural history museum for city boys and girls. Since her retirement Dr. Randall has headed a project for the planning of recreation parks in California, has aided in the work of the San Francisco Youth Association, and has made a study of recreational opportunities in sixteen European countries. She makes her home in Palo Alto.*

SEVERAL OF MY PROFESSORS and a few very special incidents while I was attending Stanford University have influenced my entire life and, vicariously, have been and still are of influence to hundreds of San Francisco children.

In 1903 I enrolled in the Zoology and Botany Departments at Stanford. I was especially interested in research work, much of which was done under the guidance of Professor Harold Heath.

Professor Heath was an inspiration to all his students. While we were attending the Marine Laboratory in Pacific Grove, he took us on never-to-be-forgotten field trips and introduced us to the tide pools and the life and beauty of their inhabitants. In classwork at the University I worked with him on a species of parasite found in a new genus of starfish which had been discovered in the deep sea of Japan. We named it Astrofilum Japanica (I do not now remember how it was spelled). Dr. Heath let me help name it, and we published a monograph describing it.

The zoology students and their professor often went on overnight camping trips. Sometimes Dr. Jordan would visit us in the evening and as we sat around the campfire would tell us stories of experiences he had had. Dr. Gilbert, our major professor, would also visit us.

In one of my classes with Dr. Heath I became interested in the nervous system of a lobster. I wanted to find out if a lobster had a brain—even a rudimentary brain (he has!). During the summer of 1912, after classes were over, I went to the laboratory, found my lobster, and was having a grand time following a nerve to an enlarged central ganglion when, to my surprise, Dr. Gilbert walked in. He asked me what I was doing and asked me if I was registered for a Master's degree. After asking the question, he looked over my work and walked out. A little later he returned and said "You are now registered for a Master's degree." The next year I received it. The title of my thesis was "The Innervation of the Crustacean Heart."

Professor and Mrs. Starks often invited a few students and professors to Pacific Grove for a house party during the Christmas holidays. I was fortunate in being invited at a time when Dr. Gilbert was there. From Professor and Mrs. Starks and from Dr. Gilbert I learned much of lasting value to all my future work.

A friend of mine who was taking a course with Professor Ira Cross invited me to go on a field trip to San Francisco with her class. We visited Chinatown first. Professor Cross, who seemed much worried, told the girls to walk close together and in the middle of the sidewalk, for girls were sometimes kidnaped and taken below the sidewalk to opium dens.

We expected to visit the county hospital next, but by mistake we arrived at the county jail. Professor Cross said that as long as we were there we might as well visit the jail and go on to the hospital. I was horrified at what I saw at both hospital and jail. That field trip, I believe, strongly influenced my future life work, for there seemed so much to be done in the world for human beings.

It was necessary for me to work my way through college, and so I carried several different jobs simultaneously in order to have a large enough income. I was secretary for Dr. Snow in the Health Department, secretary at the Student Guild Hospital, worked in the Registrar's Office, and worked for Professor Dudley in the Botany Department. When Professor Dudley went on collecting trips, he would send his collections back to me and I would press and label them. Often I would hunt up a janitor's cart, fill it with drying blotters and wheel them out to the Inner Quad, where I would spread them out to dry. It may suggest the "feel" of the Stanford of those days when I report that one day I met a jackrabbit strolling along the arcade, he no more disturbed by my presence than I was by his.

Professor Dudley was an inspiring man to work with. He told us about the beauty of the wilderness areas and the importance of saving them for future generations. He instilled in us the desire to do all we could to save our diminishing open space and to provide regional parks as close to congested areas as possible. That I am now on a Citizen's Committee for Regional Recreation and Parks in the San Francisco Bay Area is one of the results of my early association with Professor Dudley.

A hermit lived in the hills back of Stanford. Students sometimes visited him, and he always welcomed us courteously. His cabin and his yard were spotlessly clean, and the several trails near his cabin looked as though they had just been swept. His table was always neatly set for two. Once we asked him whom the second place was for, and he said, "Oh, for Isabel (I am not sure of the name). She went away one day, but she will come back. I always set the table and have tea for her, so it will be ready when she comes." Then he walked a little way on the trail and looked into the distance. "She will come back some day, and I shall be here waiting for her."

Because of unexpected circumstances, I was in the recreation field from 1913 to 1956. My work in recreation started in San Diego as playground director. With the advent of World War I, I entered on War Camp Community Service. From 1920 to 1924 I was a field worker for the National Recreation Association, and from 1924 to 1926 I made a survey of recreation facilities, both public and private, in San Francisco. In 1926 I was appointed Superintendent of the San Francisco Recreation Department, a post I held until my retirement in 1951.

When I took charge of recreation in San Francisco, I felt sorry for many of the children. They no longer had woodsheds where they could "make things," they had no place to house collections or make a garden and no way to learn about the birds and insects and small animals that country children know so well. I felt that the finest form of recreation I could provide for the city's children was a place where they could work at all kinds of crafts; where they could handle small animals, have their own gardens, and learn about many forms of living things. A Junior Museum seemed to be the answer.

In 1936, ten years after my appointment, the Recreation Department purchased a space of nearly sixteen acres in the center of San Francisco just below Twin Peaks. In 1947, $622,000 out of a $12,000,-000 bond issue was set aside for a junior museum.

The purpose of the Junior Recreation Museum, which was opened in February, 1957, is to give young people the opportunity to participate in study of birds, plants, reptiles, insects, and minerals. The children are shown proper methods of collecting, mounting, and classifying material—also of caring for live specimens in terrariums and aquariums.

My Stanford scientific training has been valuable to me not only in relation to the Museum but in all my work, as have also the leadership and the insights it was my privilege to enjoy from Professor Dudley, Professor Heath, Dr. Gilbert, Dr. Jordan, and, in fact, all my professors. What I learned I have tried to pass on to my staff in the various positions I have held.

And thus Stanford, through its faculty, has left a valuable inheritance to the children of San Francisco; an inheritance that will be handed on from one generation to the next.

*Alexander the Great . . . sighed for more worlds to conquer. But other worlds he knew nothing of lay all about him. The secrets of the rocks he had never suspected. Steam, electricity, the growth of trees, the fall of snow—all these were mysteries to him.*

DAVID STARR JORDAN
*The Higher Sacrifice*

# Four Years in Four Sentences

## WILLIAM PARMER FULLER, JR., A.B. '10

*Parmer Fuller retired from the chairmanship of W. P. Fuller and Co. in 1949. He has participated in many civic and national activities, has served as a member and later as president of the Stanford Board of Trustees, and is on the Board of Trustees of Mills College. He is married to the former Adaline Wright, '10, and has three sons who graduated from Stanford—William Parmer Fuller III, '34; George Fuller, '35, A.M. '36, Ph.D. '39; and John Fuller, '41, MBA '47.*

*When asked for some reminiscences of his undergraduate years at Stanford, he provided the letter given below. It is reproduced here by permission of the Stanford University Press.*

DEAR SAM:

You ask for a resumé of my college days, Sam, and here it is. I entered as a freshman in 1906. I was suspended twice, expelled once, ordered out of the editorship of the *Daily Palo Alto*, and graduated with my class. What more could anyone ask?

# Idyllic Days

## MARY CURRY, A.B. '15, A.M. '16

*Mary Curry (Mrs. Donald Bertrand Tresidder), the wife
of Stanford's fourth president, makes her home in Yosemite
Valley, where she and her husband lived until his election to
the presidency of Stanford University. She keeps also a residence on the Stanford campus.*

*She is the author of a book,* The Trees of Yosemite, *and
president of the Yosemite Park and Curry Company.*


FROM 1899 ON my family lived in Palo Alto, and of course the Stanford spirit and campus doings spilled over into the small college
town of those days.

In the autumn of 1912 I entered Stanford, an eager but diffident
member of the "500"—the number to which Stanford women had been
limited by Mrs. Stanford's decree. The entire student body probably
reached about 2,000. There were still a good many of the "Old Guard"
active in the faculty, and the problem of buildings versus faculty
salaries was not forgotten, especially in view of the blow dealt a few
years earlier by the earthquake of 1906.

The Art Department of that time was very limited and a department of music was nonexistent, aside from the organist of Memorial
Church and the Stanford Band. Indeed, the San Francisco Symphony
itself was barely getting under way; I remember going up to "the
city" a little later for an occasional program, under "Papa" Hertz, and
for an opera or two as time went on, expeditions which might include
dinner with "Dago red" at one of San Francisco's Italian restaurants.
There was no Department of Speech and Drama then, either, though
the sophomore farce, the junior opera, and the senior play were outstanding events each year.

Automobiles were few on the campus. I don't recall that any of
my friends were proud possessors in their own right, though a few
may have sported the family car on special occasions. The trolley car

71

still bumbled back and forth to Palo Alto, but on and about the Quad feet and bicycles were the modes of transportation, or one might rent a "buggy" for a trip to King's Mountain or La Honda in a rare celebration. I can't remember ever seeing a taxi in those days. By the end of my graduate days automobiles must have doubled or trebled, it seems to me, in spite of the First World War.

Those were idyllic days, however, in many respects, when one looks back from the crowded schedules of the present. The war clouds were still in the distance, and the difficulties in the upper echelons of administration and faculty, and the transition—Jordan to Branner to Wilbur—had no impact on our student world.

Don Tresidder (my future husband), a pre-med student from Indiana, came to Stanford in the fall of 1915 as a sophomore. He had worked in Yosemite the previous year, so ours was not a Stanford romance in its origins, though it held many Stanford memories. I must confess that I wasn't even his major interest at that time, but we had friends in common and most of us were lovers of the out-of-doors. I have many recollections of breakfasts among the redwoods of Jasper Ridge and of roaming across its upper slopes, looking half-fearfully for "the hermit" who had lived there and was reputed to take a dim view of intruders in his bailiwick. Morning fog drifting through the eucalyptus trees, the pungent smoke from their burning leaves, picnic suppers on Pine Hill or along the creek near the "Isolhof" (the Isolation Hospital)—such fragmentary pictures stay on through the years. When we returned to Stanford in the Forties, in the days of Don's presidency, our horseback rides in those hills and the student hikes he encouraged and accompanied occasionally were a double pleasure, both for the day and for the "remembrance of things past".

Some of the warmest memories of my Stanford days cluster around what was then "English Corner"—the northeast corner of the Outer Quad—and particularly about Theresa Peet Russell and her "Gridiron" class, English XII.

This was a course in advanced composition, where the students produced what they would, in verse or prose, essay or drama or short story. There may have been some assignment of form or subject, but I don't recall it. A Board of Editors selected the resultant masterpieces to be mimeographed and issued as the "Gridiron" every two weeks. (We used pen-names, but by the end of a semester—no quarters then—the disguise had usually worn thin.) The "Gridiron" pieces were subjected to merciless discussion by the class. Criticism was frank and ruthless, from exceedingly different points of view, under Mrs. Russell's dispassionate and witty control.

Mrs. Russell was a Radcliffe graduate; her husband had been an archaeologist in the Southwest. After his death, a chance meeting with William James, who was then on his way to Stanford for a semester of lectures—a semester which, as fate would have it, included the 1906 earthquake—interested her in the University, still new enough to be a conversation piece. I have always been grateful for that chance.

For purposes of this "reminiscence" I dug out some of the first semester's "Gridirons" from the trunk in which they were buried and looked through them with mingled nostalgia and chuckles. Lines from one of the poems had always haunted me—partly, I think, because I couldn't quite remember one of its adjectives. I will quote from "The Last Laugh" briefly:

> "I am dead, and I did it myself.
> I lie deep in the cordial earth
>
> . . . . . . . . . .
>
> Death is sweet; I am proud of myself . . .
> Poor God has a sick world on his soul,
> Bubbling with anathema—I
> One small glad-purring death . . . On the whole
> 'Tis less sweet to be God than to die."

"Glad-purring," with its incongruous juxtaposition, was the word which escaped me. Controversy raged about that poem, its subject and the treatment of it, the metre, the words. (Later the rumor circulated that the girl who submitted it had had benefit of the pen of a boy friend with a macabre turn of mind; I don't know the truth of this, but the supposed author was certainly far from the type which would be expected to produce it.)

Mrs. Russell's Sunday afternoon teas, when she lived in Palo Alto with Betty Buckingham, another member of the English Department, gay and whimsical and moody by turns, are another of my pleasant memories. They afforded an informal meeting-place for faculty and students where provocative discussion flourished.

Further associations linger about the neighborhood of English Corner. English Club (now long defunct, alas!) held interesting meetings. Margery Bailey might yield to entreaty and sing some of her chanteys or folk songs; *Shenandoah*, with its dark undertones and its magic closing line "Across the wide Missouri," or the mock-tragic

>"There came to the Cape
>A lady in crape
>Of whom you may not hear"

are a couple that I recall. There might be argument, high, wide, and handsome, or a hilarious skit, or the reading of some play. One year English Club put on an outdoor drama in the Arboretum, near the Mausoleum; I remember it as being charming, with a wandering minstrel—perhaps the page of Richard the Lionhearted, seeking his master—and snatches of the page's song still go through my mind occasionally, though I can't remember the name of the play nor its author.

I was proud of a season on the staff of *Sequoia*, a literary magazine where one of the joys was grubbing through early numbers that carried me back to Charley Field's rhymes about "the days of grapes, the days of scrapes, the days of Ninety-one," which then were not so long gone by.

I had an unsuccessful fling at a public speaking class, and have always regretted that I didn't grit my teeth and go through with more of it. I fervently wish, too, that I had studied botany, but that desire is derived from interests developed later. My course was noteworthy in its escape from the laboratory sciences, of which at least one was even then supposed to be included, but as I completed my undergraduate work in three years, thanks to some extra Greek credits, I somehow slipped past that requisite, for I greatly preferred the library to the laboratory. In one of my graduate years I did make a stab at taking "Physics for the Feeble-Minded" (as a survey course on the subject was then known), but the semester was broken off by external events and I never completed it.

A dedicated bookworm, I haunted the stacks of the old library, which was then on the Outer Quad. When, later, I did graduate work at Columbia, I was greatly disappointed by the restrictions placed there on admission to the holy of holies. Yale, my next way-station, was much more lenient and agreeable in that respect. Yale was more akin to Stanford not only in this but also in an atmosphere of give-and-take as between students (graduate students, at least) and faculty.

Being tapped for Cap and Gown was one of the happiest surprises of my Stanford days, and it really was a surprise. BWOC wasn't a current phrase then, but I certainly would have considered myself far from rating it, as my modest accomplishments were all bookish. I still remember my gasp of astonishment when the gay and friendly girls trooped by to gather me in. I have continued to enjoy its meetings when I could through the years that have passed since then. I envy the girls of today the ease and fluency with which they tell of their diversified activities or preside over a group. I envy them the far-flung campuses where they may have a glimpse of other worlds than ours. I speculate on how I would come out if I were thrust into the hopper at this point instead of fifty years ago.

*Government imposes upon us general rules, dictated, it is hoped, by the general will and general interest. Science seeks general laws, and morality general principles. Religion expounds the universal truth. Art alone asserts the uniqueness of the individual.*

ALBERT LEON GUÉRARD, Professor of General Literature

# "Yes, But I "DON'T WANT TO."

FRANK ERNEST HILL, A.B. '11, A.M. '14

*Frank Hill has been a teacher at the University of Illinois, at Stanford, and in Columbia Extension. In New York he became an editorial writer on the* Globe and Commercial Advertiser, *then on the* Sun, *and then, for six years, editor-in-chief of Longmans, Green & Co. He is the author of many books, both poetry and prose. His interests have ranged from consideration of current events to Chaucer's* The Canterbury Tales, *which he translated into modern English. In recent years he has been working with Allan Nevins on a three-volume history of the Ford Motor Company, the final volume of which is now completed and will appear shortly.*

When I arrived at Stanford in the fall of 1907 to begin my undergraduate work, the University still had an air of pioneer days about it. To be sure, it had had already seventeen years of activity and had attained to a reputation. Its character was fairly well established, and early graduates such as Will and Wallace Irwin had distinguished themselves in the literary world and had become legends. Still, the place was relatively simple. It was, in addition, isolated. No automobile could invade the campus. No bus or streetcar ran there. If you *must* go to Palo Alto, you walked, bicycled, or paid a ten-cent fare (rather an extravagance) to ride in one of the numerous carriages which loitered around the entrances to the Quad.

When, in 1940, I made my first and, so far, my only return to Stanford, this sense of space and the unfinished was gone. We of 1911 had seen the streetcar line come in, but now in addition there were automobiles, and the campus had shed the look of something in process and acquired the look of something finished. I remember feeling that it looked like a well-settled portion of Hawaii, and I regarded it skeptically if not pessimistically.

Actually, I think the spirit of the earlier University still persisted, and so far as I can judge from a distance, it persists today. This spirit, it seems to me, was born as the University came into being, a result of the conditions it faced, the man who headed it, and the first students who came to it, attracted by a certain challenge the institution presented. For Stanford became at birth the rival of the University of California, a University which at that time seemed adequately to fill the needs of the state.

What did the new place of learning have to offer? Mainly, it was something in the pioneer tradition—an emphasis on individual effort and the individual's right to succeed on his own terms, a much larger amount of academic leeway than its great rival permitted, and an energy which sprang from the circumstances of its birth and its need to win success. Of course, as universities then went, Stanford was one of the wealthiest, but this was of importance only in giving those associated with it the sense that the bid they were making for success in the academic world had a solid support behind it.

As a new student at Stanford I quickly understood what was expected of me. It was expected that I would enter into curricular and extracurricular life with zest—that anything I did (study, debating, writing, athletics) would be done vigorously and fully. This was the assumption, I think, of all Stanford students. If study were your chief object, you were respected if you studied hard, although, to be sure, you were a "dry" and not so highly regarded as the man who went out for the football team. Similarly, if you were a writer, as I aspired to be, you were on a lower plane than a track or baseball man, but again it was accepted that this was your field of operation, and you could win respect by performing well in it. Even a football player liked to think that his University could produce good debaters and poets. This general expectation that you would stretch yourself in whatever you undertook had its effect upon me. I liked to think that such an expectation still exists. It is a good thing to be imposed upon any young man or woman.

I came to Stanford as the author of a published book of poems, *Zoroaster,* which I had the good sense never to mention. I did not do so even when, as a freshman, I became one of the two winners of the prize song in the first month of my residence—a song which was sung exactly once and which brought each of the two of us who composed it the large sum of $2.50.

My campus life in literature was a rich one, both because of teachers who conducted stimulating classes and because of a group known as the Round Table, composed of about a dozen young men, which met monthly at the house of Dr. Henry David Gray to read something they had written and get honest criticism from Gray and fellow members. In this group sooner or later were Bruce Bliven, Frank Weymouth, Ernest Jerome Hopkins, Maxwell Anderson, and others.

At the time I first knew Stanford, the first president, Dr. David Starr Jordan, was still very active. A man of huge stature—well above six feet and filled out in proportion—he was not in appearance an intensive person. Rather, he seemed relaxed and philosophical. But he was one of a number of men in his generation who had a personality of extraordinary breadth and creative force. Primarily he was a scientist and specifically one of the great authorities on fishes, but he was also interested in literature, sociology, and politics, and wrote essays which showed an immense range of reading and an ability to simplify whatever he had to say. In earlier years he had been a notable baseball player, but he never played to my knowledge after I arrived. Still, the fact that in the faculty-alumni games which had been annual events before my coming he would usually knock a home run was well known among the students.

Dr. Jordan was also a public speaker of note; almost every sentence he uttered set his listeners to thinking. I was impressed by one trick of style in his speaking which may have been accidental and which apparently has gone unnoticed. It was this: If he had a point to make which required emphasis, he would not intensify what he said but louden it. For example, if he had said, as he well may have, "The world cannot afford another war," it would come out as "The world CANNOT AFFORD another war." This habit I became aware of, and I listened with expectation to the loudening of his voice (quite without emphasis otherwise) which marked some notable utterance.

In my senior year Dr. Jordan with Dr. Edward H. Krehbiel gave a course on international peace which was attended by perhaps a hundred and fifty students. I did not take it, but my roommate, R. Justin Miller, filled the post of secretary for International Concilia- tion, as the course was called, and I heard much about it. All of us (that is, the Stanford intelligentsia of that day) were fully convinced that war was on the way out, since a major conflict would be both too bloody and too expensive for any sensible nation to fight. (The nations proved soon not to be sensible.) Dr. Jordan's best writing was perhaps contained in a book against war—*The Human Harvest.*

I was barely acquainted with Dr. Jordan while I was still a stu- dent. When I returned to Stanford to teach, he had retired from the presidency and was chancellor of the University. I saw him several times during this period and well remember his replying to my ques- tion if he knew a certain man, "I know EVERYBODY." This was said with a smile. He also showed me a letter he had written to one of the hundreds of persons who sent him poems. It seemed to me the perfect letter for most such persons, and read in effect: "Dear Sir: I have received your poem. It is a remarkable poem. Sincerely yours, etc." Was a more expert evasion ever invented to meet such a situ- ation?

My doctor in San Jose told me of an occurrence which I think sheds some light on Dr. Jordans' personality. Jordan had consulted him and was to return the following Tuesday for another visit. The Chancellor (as he was then) took out a little notebook and labori- ously made an entry in it. His wife reproached him softly, "Why, David, can't you remember *that?*" The big man looked down at her with a gleam of a smile and said with the loudening effect I have mentioned as characteristic of his public speaking, "Yes, but I DON'T WANT TO."

The Stanford I knew, of which Dr. Jordan was an important part, has long since vanished. But I like to think that something of the instituiton as it then was and of its first president survive in the Stan- ford of today.

# Values Which Last

## MABEL NEWCOMER, A.B. '13, A.M. '14

*Mabel Newcomer was professor of economics at Vassar College from 1926 to 1956. In 1944 she served as the only woman delegate to the United Nations conference on international finance, which set up the International Fund and World Bank. She also received the first AAUW achievement award in the field of the social sciences. Though most of her research and writing has been in the field of government finance, she is also known for her book,* A Century of Higher Education for American Women, *published in 1959.*

I went to Stanford as a matter of course. My father was a member of the faculty; I had lived in the community ever since I could remember; and most of my friends were entering Stanford. I was probably fortunate to get into college before admissions committees were taking motivation and goals into account.

Chance, not planning, guided my academic progress. I majored in history because my favorite high school teacher had given me a liking for it. And I discovered my interest in economics because the introductory course in this was required of history majors. I deserted history for economics in my sophomore year, and would have deserted economics for chemistry in my junior year if such a move would not have delayed my graduation. At that period of Stanford's history the free elective system was at its height, and with no fixed goal and a good deal of intellectual curiosity I sampled an amazing variety of subjects. Even when I lacked the important prerequisites for a course I was allowed to try. Today, as an educator, I cannot defend the aimless, patternless array of my elections. But I survived very happily, and after my aims and interests stabilized I was able to pursue graduate studies without regrets for earlier lack of direction.

Much of the factual material of my courses has been forgotten, and would probably be irrelevant in today's world in any event; but it stimulated my interest at the time and sent me on to further study. In the long run, the courses that I valued most were those in basic techniques and theories. Everett Smith's training in writing, for instance, taught me the virtues of simple and direct expression. Percy Martin's course in history training, taken in my freshman year, gave me an understanding of research methods that most students acquire the hard way when they are faced with graduate theses. Albert Whitaker's drill in economic theory made my later courses in theory seem like child's play, even when the specific theories were different. And Victor West's courses in political institutions aroused an interest in current social problems that shaped my lifelong career.

This is, of course, the judgment of a college professor looking back over fifty years. It is only fair to say that as an undergraduate I regarded association with my fellow students as more important than study. I cared more for the approval of classmates than professors; and I considered my election to the women students' governing board as more important than my election to Phi Beta Kappa. But it was the academic work that counted in the end, and would have, I believe, even if I had left the academic world for good on graduating from Stanford. And I often wonder, when today's educators deplore the fact that students are more concerned with what their peers think than with what they are learning in their studies, if this is really a condemnation of our educational system. The important thing is not what sways the undergraduate at the moment, but which values last.

*Many students do not care for church services. But the church cares for them. I visit these delightful drifters in hall and frat. I catch them in the hospital. I invite them to my home. Office hours provide daily opportunity for friendly consultation. Sorrow, sin, and shame are not absent from student life. The parson is the friend of all—not alone of the pious.*

D. CHARLES GARDNER, University Chaplain until 1936

# That Microcosmic World

## ROBERT JUSTIN MILLER, A.B. '11, J.D. '14

*Justin Miller has been professor of law in five university law schools and dean of the law school in two others. He has filled the presidency of the Federal Bar Association for two years; was general counsel for the National Association of Television and Radio Broadcasters from 1951 to 1954; and has served on numerous commissions, both state and national. He is the author of several books and of many articles in legal and other periodicals. He now practices law in Los Angeles, is married, and the father of two children.*

My time at Stanford spanned the years from 1907 to 1914. When I first saw the campus the wreckage of the 1906 earthquake was still apparent. The usable portion of the University buildings was confined largely to the Inner and Outer Quadrangles, together with Roble and Encina. The rest of the vast campus was indeed a "farm," or in the California vernacular, a ranch; ideal for hiking, with few roads and little traffic of any kind. Automobiles were not allowed on the campus; indeed, there were few of them anywhere. I remember hiking with Geoffrey Morgan, one evening, down El Camino Real to San Jose, where we attended a vaudeville show. We walked in the dark most of the way. I have no present recollection of seeing a single automobile along the way.

I was a perfect example of the "working my way through college" student. My financial resources in September 1907 were $32. Of this, $16 went for registration and incidental fees—quite a contrast to the toll charged for entrance into higher education today. My first job consisted of cleaning up the scattered lumber and rubbish around Madroño Hall, where a reconstruction project had just been completed. My next one was with the *Oakland Tribune*, delivering the paper, collecting for subscriptions, and—when I could—securing new ones. This necessitated my living in Palo Alto. Consequently, my contacts with the life of the University were at that time very limited.

During my freshman year I was summoned to the treasurer's office where I met Mr. Charles Lathrop. He informed me that I had been awarded the Leland Stanford Junior Scholarship. I had made no application for the scholarship—in fact, did not know that it existed. Apparently, some friends had intervened in my behalf.

The scholarship was a godsend. It provided a room at Encina Hall and an "expense account," covering board at the Stanford Inn and other necessities for which I rendered an itemized report to Mr. Lathrop each month. I became a full-time member of the student body; I participated in minor sports, belonged to Nestoria debating society, had a minor theatrical role, became a member of the English Club, engaged in class politics and in the other exciting adventures which characterize the life of the college man. I learned quickly, however, that good grades were incompatible with the "flunk-out" tables—where some of the boys played pool—and with the houses of cheer, located at Menlo and at other spots around the periphery of the campus.

My undergraduate courses fell into that amorphous classification, "prelegal," which consisted of several required courses but gave wide freedom of election as to the rest. My favorite courses were in the English Department, particularly those given by Professor Frances Theresa Peet Russell. She was unquestionably the most inspiring teacher of my whole student life. It was she who introduced me to satire. I soon visualized myself as a professional satirist and looked about for subjects to work upon—and I had not far to look.

The Student Affairs Committee of the faculty had recently declared "out of bounds" the resorts which edged the campus, and had also decided that liquor should not be used in student quarters. There were rousing protests, noisy night-time parades, and other manifestations of student unhappiness. The chairman of the committee, Professor A. B. Clark, wore a beard and had a habit of smiling at times when he was imposing disciplinary penalties. One day I heard one of the "roughs" telling of a dream—a veritable nightmare—which had been dominated by a large, evil face, consisting of "whiskers and a grin." I adopted the phrase, as the title of a theme depicting the mood of the man who had suffered the nightmare. The result was a shocking "C" and an admonition from the "reader"—not Mrs. Russell, I am sure—that my theme constituted most unbecoming conduct on the part of a hitherto superior student. The admonition persuaded me to abandon satire, thenceforth, in my English themes.

Nevertheless, I was not yet persuaded to abandon the sharp-tongued weapon as a professional career. My next experiment was in a contribution to "Chappie," a bit of doggerel entitled "Rough-neck's Lament." The first lines introduced the subject as follows:

> "How dear to my heart are the memories of Menlo,
> When beer-bustless nights are a prey on my mind
> And I long to be back with a big rolling schooner
> Of foaming old lager to ease up the grind."

The publication of this casually concocted bit of satire produced —to me—startling results. Apparently, everyone who read it assumed that it was a presentation of my own point of view. The "roughs" were jubilant. In an election of Encina-governing committeemen, held shortly thereafter, I was high man.

Then came the delayed reaction: a summons from Treasurer Charles Lathrop. This required a little flashback. Uncle Charlie, as he was known familiarly to the students, was a brother of Mrs. Jane Lathrop Stanford. He lived in a big house atop a hill overlooking the campus. He was reputed to have been once too well acquainted with John Barleycorn and had a very sensitive nerve concerning that subject. I learned these facts—or rumors, whichever they might be—after publication of the "Lament." Mr. Lathrop had been, up to that time, apparently well-pleased with my conduct. He used to greet me cordially when I presented my monthly expense account. But this time he had the manner of a disappointed parent. He told me, in substance, that he was sorry to withdraw the privileges and perqui-sites of the scholarship; but that he was sure I could, now, make a go of it by myself.

This decision changed my status as abruptly as had the awarding of the scholarship in the first place. I was reduced, again, to the classification of unskilled laborer and, again, began to look for jobs—washing windows, pick and shovel work, selling books, taking magazine subscriptions. Through the kindness of James Errett Shelton and his brother Cortez, the managers of the Stanford Inn, I became a "hasher" at that caravansary, where before I had been a paying guest. "Hashing" was, as it still is, an honorable occupation at Stanford. It provided substantial food and caused no loss of prestige.

About this time there came, as a visitor to the University, Ida Tarbell, who had recently achieved best-seller fame as the author of a history of the Standard Oil Company. Miss Tarbell's writings and those of other authors of her time laid the foundation for investigation of monopolies and of other business practices; these, in turn, led to extensive legislation expanding government controls over American industry. Here was a form of writing more powerful than the indirect attack of satire. I was intrigued, of course, and began to look about for a subject, near at hand, for similar scrutiny.

What resulted was my investigation of a secret-secret society called Scaraboea, or—in the language of students—the "Bug." My investigation uncovered evidence of such an organization, operating under cover, which was reputed to be exercising a malign influence in student affairs and in student-faculty relations. I collected such information as I could from sources which dried up quickly as my purpose became evident. When the article was published, it was followed by editorials and communications, increasingly bitter and recriminating, until the whole controversy burned itself out.

The "Bug" controversy was one of my most valuable educational experiences. It taught me that one who seeks change—even demonstrably an improvement—necessarily disrupts the vested interests of those who are dependent upon or exploit the *status quo*. My friends classified themselves in their reactions to my activities. Some backed me strongly. Some agreed that I was on the right track but was too much inclined to stir up trouble. Some became taciturn, resentful. The "Bug" members revealed themselves by their open hostility. Here, on the Stanford campus, was a microcosmic world dominated by its "opinion makers," disturbed by conflict, anxious to live and let live, disapproving of inequities but unwilling to challenge them specifically. How many times in later life have I seen this pattern of life emerge; how many times have I seen the necessity of compromise; how many times have I quoted from Benjamin Franklin's last speech at the Constitutional Convention: "Thus I consent, Sir, to this Constitution because I expect no better and because I am not sure that it is not the best. The opinions I have had of its errors I sacrifice to the public good. . . . On the whole, Sir, I cannot help expressing a wish that every member of the Convention who may still have objections to it would with me on this occasion doubt a little of his own infallibility, and to make manifest our unanimity, put his name to this instrument."

As my memories of Stanford mellow with the years, they come to concern individuals more than events. It would take a volume to record my impressions and my appreciation of men like Duniway, Adams, and Bolton of the History Department, Whitaker of the Economics Department, Angell of the Psychology Department, and of Woodward, Cathcart, Bingham, and Huston of the Law School. They are the ones who gave me the foundation upon which my professional work has been based. Except for two or three first-year lecture courses, classes at Stanford were small. We became acquainted with our teachers on a basis of friendly association, and thus gained an understanding of values and a lift of spirit far beyond mere classroom performance and scholastic grades.

My three roommates, Bruce Bliven, William S. Porter, and Frank Ernest Hill—each in his own way—made a contribution to my intellectual and emotional development far greater than they or I realized at the time. Of the three, my closest associate was Frank Hill. We "batched" together, hiked together, and worked together, solving many important problems—to our own satisfaction, at least. The separations which follow graduation are, frequently, unhappy; but I think I have regretted them more in Frank's case than in any other.

In all my years at Stanford, the man who made the most lasting impression upon me was David Starr Jordan. Each time I heard him speak he opened new vistas to me; each time I gained little gems of practical working philosophy. For example, one evening a group of us were engaged in a "bull session" at Encina; Dr. Jordan wandered in unannounced, as was his custom, and joined in the discussion as if he had been just another student. As the discussion went on, someone inquired: "Dr. Jordan, what is your definition of success?" He hesitated a moment, then replied: "I should say that success consists in doing what you most like to do." He paused, and then continued: "And doing it well enough so someone else will pay you for doing it." No striving for effect; just a simple, common-sense, working rule of action, which I have used many times to guide me at the crossroads and have passed on to others who asked the same question.

My first experience with "ghost writing" happened in connection with another incident involving Dr. Jordan. One phase of the secret-secret operation previously mentioned was a conspiracy to discredit him. About 1910 or 1911, the work of the conspirators took form in an attack based upon what was claimed to be too much absence of the President from the campus. I suggested to Laurence Hill, editor of the student *Daily,* that this called for an editorial defense of Dr. Jordan, one explaining the need for presidential contacts with other universities, research and educational programs, in anticipation of Stanford's growing needs for top-quality talent and scientific facilities. Hill, unsure of the implications of such an editorial, finally proposed that if I would write a "letter to the editor" upon the subject, he would publish it. I did, and he did; but to my surprise, he ran it without change as his own editorial. Of course it had much greater effect as an editorial—presumably reflecting studentbody opinion—than would a letter to the editor.

The only course I took with Dr. Jordan was one in which I acted as his student assistant in a course concerning war and peace. At the end of the course he offered me a fellowship, to work with him in developing the subject and looking toward a career in international relations. I told him I preferred to go ahead toward the practice of law as the best entrance into public service. In view of what has happened in the intervening fifty years, this is the one "road not taken" about which I have most seriously questioned the wisdom of my decision.

Another "road not taken" is evidenced by a letter in my files from

Professor Lee Emerson Bassett, suggesting that I become an assistant professor in the English Department. My association with the English Department had been a happy one, and I reread Professor Bassett's letter occasionally with a very real nostalgia. Ironically—considering my declination of these two teaching opportunities—seven years later I left law practice and public office to return to teaching, where I spent fourteen years, the longest uninterrupted segment of my professional life.

Every experience in my professional life has reflected Stanford's influence. Lawyer, teacher, writer, government executive, judge, administrator—I found inspiration for all of them from Stanford's gift so richly given. I could wish for no greater opportunity, on behalf of youth today, than for them to enjoy a similar share in the Stanford heritage.

*Upon every citizen in our democracy rests a solemn obligation to inform himself, so that he may shape American foreign policy—his foreign policy—along constructive and far-sighted lines.*

THOMAS A. BAILEY, Professor of History

# A Freshman at the Stanford Press

## HARRY W. FRANTZ, ex-'17

*Harry Frantz has been a writer and editor of international news since 1920, when he joined the foreign department of the United Press in New York. Transferred to the Washington bureau in 1922, he writes for foreign clients of United Press International.*

*He has the peculiar distinction of having written for newspapers in 80 countries while rarely contributing to the United States press, the result of his writing in the condensed and selected style required for cable and radio transmission.*

*During World War II he was director of the press division of the Office of Inter-American Affairs. In 1945 he worked as a writing aide for the State Department at the Chapultepec Conference in Mexico City and the United Nations meeting in San Francisco. Recently he has assisted in development of news service to African countries.*

*He lives in Bethseda, Maryland; is married, and the father of one daughter.*

Within a few weeks after enrolling at Stanford University in September, 1913, I found myself working on a doctoral dissertation, a distinction probably shared by no other freshman in Stanford history.

I hasten to explain that I was not writing the thesis, but merely correcting the proofs which would hasten its long-retarded publication. This and subsequent similar tasks opened the doors to acquaintance with many distinguished scholars of the period whose work awaited the efforts of myself and other printers at the Stanford Press.

As a "workaway" on the Stanford Ship of Knowledge, my freshman year was spent largely on correction of a large accumulation of "dirty" proofs which earlier operators of the Model 5 Linotype had abandoned as an almost hopeless task. Some of the jobs required additional composition for completion or revision.

My introduction to Stanford scholarship really began with an eventually successful effort to clean up the multilingual proofs of *The Birds of the Latin Poets*, by Ernest Whitney Martin, associate professor of Greek. I reset type from "Acalanthus" to "Vultur."

This was a dissertation submitted in 1910 to the faculty of Leland Stanford Junior University for the degree of Doctor of Philosophy and was dedicated to Henry Rushton Fairclough, professor of Latin —"true friend and teacher." It was finally published by the University in 1914, and I felt a satisfaction at completion of this publication probably second only to that of its brilliant author.

For four years before entering Stanford as a "special student" (one lacking the prescribed entrance requirements), I had worked in newspaper composing rooms and other printing establishments in the United States, Canada, and Mexico. I was therefore competent to handle many of the difficult typesetting jobs which are normal in a university press.

My nightly eye-tiring half-shift at the Stanford Press automatically precluded any distinction as a student, socialite, athlete, or "Man about the Campus." But several years of typesetting on such diverse publications as Dr. David Starr Jordan's studies of ichthyology, University catalogues, Dr. Branner's seismological journals, psychological treatises, and various books of verse gave me a peculiar interest and appreciation for the work of first-class scholars.

The experience would contribute later to a modest success in four decades of international correspondence devoted primarily to "heavy information"—known professionally as "bread and butter news."

Through the 18 months of the International Geophysical Year (1957–58) I wrote a story daily about one or another of the 12 physical scientific "disciplines." What I lacked in technical education was offset by an insight into the mentality and methods of the scientists who talk with reporters. Since 1928 I have interviewed countless scientists about their work in Antarctica. I have probably spent more time in the statistical reference section of the Census Bureau than any reporter in Washington. My most recent assignment was to the FAO International Conference on Fish in Nutrition.

I worked part-time at the Stanford Press between September 1913 and May 1916, subject to interruptions caused by journeys to Hawaii, Japan, the Philippine Islands, and the China Coast. In those years the Stanford Press was owned and operated privately by J. A. Quelle, a fine printer, a gentleman, and a scholar. He gave part-time employment to many students. The Press was taken over by the University during World War I.

The Press was in a one-story wooden building, at the end of the car-line from Palo Alto. When the Stanford Union was built, it was so close to the Press that, by night, one could hear dance music along the Row and harbor thoughts of envy or loneliness. After all, however, there still were ships running to Honolulu, and the Orient beckoned! The friendship and hospitality of Dr. Payson J. Treat, professor of Far Eastern history, and his gracious wife were to guide my wanderlust toward a journalistic goal.

There were some wonderful compensations in the divided life of a printer and an undergraduate. I remember the gentle and careful manner of the scholar-poet William H. Carruth when he came into the office to check proofs. I set type for *Each in His Own Tongue,* which became a classic. I was flattered when Dr. John E. Coover, author of a notable two-volume monograph on telepathy, clairvoyance, and similar phenomena, asked my reaction to some of his conclusions.

Dr. Jordan once invited me to his home. His frequent compositions about international affairs were often on my "copy board" and a source of inspiration.

Dr. Murray Wildman of the Economics Department, my major professor, was intrigued by my unusual background concerning labor troubles and itinerant employment. I was a member of the International Typographical Union.

At times I set overnight copy for *The Daily Palo Alto,* and thus became acquainted with its editors and reporters. These men, in fact, became my chief friends and acquaintances in the student body. Some of them later had distinguished careers as writers or newsmen, as Frank J. Taylor, E. D. Kneass, and Earl Behrens. The print-shop thought that Miss Anita Allen, woman's editor in 1915, was the most talented and gracious member of the *D.P.A.* staff in those years. Alice Rogers, then on the campus, was to become the foremost woman writer on worldwide aviation.

In 1914 the Stanford Press published a small book by the celebrated Brazilian historian and diplomat, Manoel de Oliveira Lima, entitled *The Evolution of Brazil Compared with that of Spanish and Anglo-Saxon America.* I do not remember whether I set type for this publication, but the Stanford tie later led to a warm acquaintance with him through many years, at New York and Washington. While I covered "Diplomatic Row," he informed me of countless topics of interest to Brazilian newspapers. I occasionally consult the wonderful collection of 45,000 books about the Portuguese Colonial Empire which Dr. Lima presented to the Catholic University in Washington.

I profited by the valuable acquaintance and occasional hospitality of Dr. Vernon Kellogg.

Lacking authorship of any doctoral thesis of my own, my greatest pride as a compositor is still directed to *The Pronoun of Address in English Literature of the Thirteenth Century.* It was a dissertation by Arthur Garfield Kennedy, instructor in English philology, submitted for the degree of Doctor of Philosophy, and published in 1915. Its 91 pages were devoted to the pronoun of the second person in Middle English.

This composition involved the frequent insertion of Middle English alphabet matrices in the linotype assembly box before casting. Accurate proofs on this complicated job probably represented my most praiseworthy achievement during Stanford years.

*Nations, like dogs and people, usually respond favorably to friendly gestures. Conversely, name-calling begets competitive name-calling, and bitterness mounts in an ever widening circle.*

THOMAS A. BAILEY, Professor of History

# Freshman, '08

## NEILL C. WILSON, A.B. '12

*Neill Wilson did newspaper and advertising work in San Francisco from 1912 to 1944, producing in the same time three books:* A City of Caprice *(verse about San Francisco);* Treasure Express *(history of Wells Fargo);* Silver Stampede *(history of a Death Valley region mining camp).*

*Since 1944 he has written two novels,* The Nine Brides and Granny Hite *and* The Freedom Song. *With Frank J. Taylor, he has published* Southern Pacific *(a railway history) and* The Earthchangers *(a study of international construction companies). Between 1946 and 1961 he has written and had published twenty-six stories in* The Saturday Evening Post. *He lives in Sebastopol, California.*

There were 1,700 men and 500 women students in those halcyon days of 1908–09. This was satisfactory to the boys and a romp for the girls, and it was conceded that, by and large, the registrar had chosen with an inclination toward beauty. Besides old Roble Hall for girls and Encina for men, there were a dozen fraternities and six sororities to house the students.

Competition among the houses of the "Row" was intense and no holds barred. The yellow frame railroad station under the oaks at Palo Alto saw unseemly scuffles for likely-looking freshmen's suitcases. I was not particularly likely-looking, weighing but 145 hungry pounds including suitcase and being garnished with glasses, but my baggage was snatched by a Delta Tau Delta man I'd met during the summer, my hat by a Delta Upsilon; I followed my suitcase as being the more valuable article, and by the following dawn, after reasonable resistance to pressure, I surrendered and was pledged a Delt. The house was on a hill far behind the campus. Life was joyous up there, but it was a fearful walk to an 8:15 class down on the Quad.

The University had opened with David Starr Jordan its first president. He was still its president when I entered. He was a big man physically and mentally, a tremendous figure in the academic world both as an educator and leading ichthyologist. My first and most impressive encounter with him was when, a raw freshman with a tiny red-buttoned freshman beanie on the top of my cowlick, I saw him approaching under the arcade of the Quad. I was not sure what to do, so did nothing. When we were almost abreast, he removed his wide-brimmed hat with a flourish and bowed to me. I snatched for my beanie and couldn't find it; all I got was hair. David Star Jordan passed on, like a full-rigged ship passing a canoe and swamping it.

During my freshman year part of the student body was badly at outs with collegiate authority. There had been a big dust-up the spring before over a ribald parade put on in protest against the efforts of a newly-appointed Student Affairs Committee to put down drinking among members of the student body. Following the parade, forty-one upperclassmen, several prominent athletes among them, were suspended and a number of others had hours added to their requirements for graduation. Undergraduates were still simmering in the fall, but the president had been away at the time of the parade. Though he strongly supported his appointees, his absence deflected from him most student criticism. Whether through good fortune or through his sheer greatness, nothing long disturbed the admiration students had for him. Other people might be hated; he continued on his own high plane, a kind of friendly reasonableness spreading around him.

Stanford at that time was a pastoral place. It was surrounded by fields of barley and grass, by orchards of prunes and apricots. There was a vineyard of size close to the campus and a winery farther off, though its great casks had long been empty. Palo Alto, a long mile off, was reached by two-horse carriages at ten cents a head. In the packed loads of passengers inside the carriages acquaintances ripened fast. Everybody knew everybody or said hello, anyhow.

There were not many graduates as yet, and for undergraduates the general color of life was red both symbolically and in fact—the cardinal of football jerseys, the red of the berry hedges that framed the oval in front of the Quad, the red roofs of the Quad itself.

The one important football game was with California. For a number of years, including my first at Stanford, the game was rugby. My place was only in the rooting section, but when Cal was smashed to earth in that year, my satisfaction and the satisfaction on the campus was so intense that you tasted it.

Such was the first of the four wonderful years which ended in May, 1912, with Dr. Jordan's handing me a beautiful young lady's diploma, and mine to a brilliant Japanese student, on the stage of the old Assembly Hall. Four years of an era that knew not war, income tax, smog, nor even tuition bills, nor anything whatever to irk us except perhaps Professor Clark's Student Affairs Committee.

*. . . the preparation for life, the outlook upon life, the power to hand on the lamp of fire, which are acquired here: In these consist the Stanford Spirit—a term which, like other great abstractions, such as culture, civilization, God, is indefinable and liable to abuse.*

MELVILLE BEST ANDERSON, Professor of English

# Three Pairs of Spectacles

## ELINOR COGSWELL, A.B. '16, A.M. '17

*Elinor Cogswell was editor of the* Palo Alto Times *for sixteen years. For the five years prior to her retirement in 1960
she was editorial writer and columnist for Peninsula Newspapers Incorporated. Since 1960 she has been "trying to find
my footing as a free lance writer."*

*Her present home is on Westridge Drive, halfway be-
tween Menlo Park and Stanford.*

In forty-eight years spent where the rolling foothills rise, I have
looked at Stanford through three pairs of glasses, each with its own
particular tint.

A small-town girl with almost no money, I was the greenest of
freshmen that fall of 1912—and saw everything through the rosiest
of spectacles. To me, Stanford was a subdivision of paradise; professors were saints and sages.

As I became more discriminating, I learned that faculty folk were
human in a variety of ways, some of them quite delightful. Many of
my teachers became—and remained—my friends.

Oddly enough, the one who influenced me most in my freshman
year was a man who did not even recognize me outside the classroom. I think Van Wyck Brooks did not like teaching—he quitted it
after a year or two—but I am grateful that he endured it through
1912–13. He showed me for the first time that it was not enough to
digest lectures and books, even though I demonstrated in bluebooks
that the digestion had been thorough. He somehow got across to me
the excitement of taking off on my own.

We Stanford women formed "the 500," joyously outnumbered
five-to-one by the men. We sat upstairs at assemblies. Never shall
I forget the emotion, joyous and painful, too, when "Hail, Stanford,

"Hail" was started by the men's voices down front, rolled back row after row, and finally caught up the sopranos and altos around me.

But student activities did not loom large in my program. I lived in Palo Alto and either walked out Palm Drive to Quad or rode the red trolley car. Automobiles were no problem in those days. A date in San Francisco meant a ride on the train and a post-midnight hike to the campus after the last trolley had gone to the barn.

A highlight of my junior year was election to English Club. Among its recent alumni were Maxwell Anderson, Bruce Bliven, Robert Duffus, and Frank Hill. We produced "Sherwood" in a forest setting on the Stanford Estate. Naturally, it rained on us and our small but valiant audience.

A later Golden Age of the club was to produce John Steinbeck, Rosemary Drachman, Archie Binns, and other now-successful writers. As an Old Grad, I was allowed to share in the fun.

But most of my social needs were met by a group of friends who, like me, could enjoy themselves without money—hiking, picnicking, endlessly talking. These ties have never been broken; we do little hiking now, and we hold our picnics in patios. But we can still talk for hours without boredom.

David Starr Jordan, long one of my idols, was withdrawing from active participation in University life, becoming more and more entangled in world affairs. I was not aware of this, however; his great personality still dominated and his great bulk was a familiar sight on Quad. Presidents might change—first came John Casper Branner and then Ray Lyman Wilbur—but it was still Dr. Jordan's school to me.

As I look back on it, I can't understand how we were so untouched by the trends and events that obsessed him and that were so soon to lead the world into war. At least, we were angry over the mistreatment he suffered in the East for his lectures on peace, and I am proud of our exuberant rally to his support on his return, even though it was inspired less by understanding than by a desire to defend our own.

Up to the moment the United States entered the war—the spring of my graduate year—our participation in the overseas tragedy had

been little more than another college activity. There were the Belgian
Relief fairs, the organization of ambulance units, the enlistment of a
gallant few in the Lafayette Escadrille. The first Gold Stars on Stanford's Honor Roll pointed up the drama; to only a few did they represent personal tragedy.

If we were stunned when our own country was drawn into the
conflict, we were not immediately diverted from normal campus life.
We merely added the gallant activities involved in making the world
safe for democracy.

But wartime changes were beginning when I packed my M.A.
sheepskin into a trunk and left Palo Alto—forever, as I supposed. I
was not around to see the real war years, when most of the men left
on campus were in uniform and stern rules were adopted to protect
Stanford women from soldiers at Camp Fremont. The growing casualty lists brought war closer then. . . .

I donned my second set of colored lenses when, after a year in the
Hawaiian Islands, I joined the staff of the *Palo Alto Times*. Through
them I sometimes saw my alma mater in a jaundiced light, for as a
reporter I was often frustrated in efforts to get from Stanford sources
the information I considered necessary. And as editor in later years,
I was inevitably identified with the town when it felt adversely affected by University policies. Sharpest of these disagreements came
over the refusal to permit enlargement of the Palo Alto Hospital on
land leased from Stanford.

Yet in spite of frustrations and disagreements, it was exciting to
watch from a good vantage point as Stanford grew in stature and
strove to meet increasing challenges. . . .

For two years now I have worn the third set of spectacles, those
of the retired alumna serving as a volunteer worker for Stanford. The
coloration is golden, for money-raising is the immediate goal of the
volunteers. But we get an exceptionally clear and close-up view of
the University's real problems and real accomplishments.

With all its changes, the Stanford campus has lost none of its
appeal for me. New streets and new buildings have settled into the
pattern, and tarweed is still autumn's most pungent perfume.

That intangible which is the real University is a composite of the

Stanford dominated by David Starr Jordan; the Stanford adjusting jerkily through the years to new demands and new personalities and new fields of knowledge, and the great University emerging through travail and courage—taking its place as the "university of high degree" envisioned by the Founders, but in a world which their forward look could not foresee.

*I have often thought that women who use perfume to catch men (if they do) have overlooked some opportunities. Tarweed essence would have appealed to me.*

ROBERT L. DUFFUS, '10

# Athletics at Stanford

## ROBERT LYMAN (DINK) TEMPLETON, A.B. '21, LL.B. '24

*Dink Templeton was track coach at Stanford from 1921 to 1939. While at Stanford he played five years of varsity football, rugby and American, and spent four years on the varsity track team as a high jumper and broad jumper. Since 1939 he has been a sports columnist and radio commentator —and, as his articles show, has acquired and kept an unmatched knowledge of Stanford athletics in all its various forms. He lives in Palo Alto, is married to Catherine Elisabeth Williams, '19, and has two daughters.*

### 1906–1918

The gods of my boyhood days were Leland Stanford Scott, Bill Pemberton, Mow and Stan Mitchell, John O. Miller, Mickey Reed, Carlos Sampson, Babe Crawford, Harry Horton, and Bill Theile, incomparable Stanford athletes whose luster has not been dimmed by time.

Scott was a star on the football, baseball, and track teams, twice startling the nation by breaking the world record in the pole vault at 12-10¾ and 12-11⅛. Bill was the football captain of the 1909 team, a giant of a man who was sought by prize fight managers everywhere to become the White Hope to lift the heavyweight championship from Jack Johnson; he was a man whose vitality was so great that on rally night before the Big Game, Bill broke away from the team to lead the serenaders wildly whooping it up around the giant bonfire. Mow and Stan were brothers who started and finished the brilliant passing rushes that scored so many points for Stanford, great running backs and baseball players. John O. was the tall, bow-legged, pigeon-toed middle distance runner and wing forward who would have beaten the world in any era he happened to be trained in. Mickey Reed was the sprinter and wing three-quarters whom Coach Dad Moulton compared with the great pro sprinters of earlier days,

100

always a certain winner with his tremendous burst of speed. Carlos Sampson was the home-run hitter and brilliant shortstop in the days when the old diamond was on the spot where the library is now located. Babe was the strong quiet man, a giant both in football and putting the shot. Harry Horton was the American football player who was finally won over to rugby, known to have calves the size of a ten-pound lard pail, yet a star low hurdler besides.

And of course, Bill Theile, the greatest pitcher ever known on any campus including Christy Mathewson, so we believed, who gave up a career in the majors to practice law in Salinas.

There were dozens of others, of course—Sam Bellah, Herc Cheda, Kenny Fenton, Dutch Koerner, Cub Mintern, Jasper Holman, Tom Coleman, and a little later George Horine starting a world-wide controversy by breaking Mike Murphy's "unbreakable" record in the high jump, 6 feet 5⅝ inches. George cleared 6-6½ by a full six inches, later cleared 6-7, and the East roared back in headlines that he must have done it with an illegal dive.

But long before 1907, when I arrived at Palo Alto as a 10-year-old, Stanford had become known for its athletic achievements, and was famed for the tremendous Stanford Fighting Spirit.

Starting from scratch without a coach, in the spring of 1892 the first Stanford football team beat the proud old Blue and Gold of Berkeley by the score of 14 to 10, and not until the eighth game of the Big Game series, in 1898, did Cal win its first victory over Stanford.

For years the Farm and Palo Alto, too, told and retold the tales of the Stanford fullback, Bull Chalmers, the Ernie Nevers of the pre-rugby years and a great baseball player besides. And of Tip Vandervoort, American and rugby player as well as the broad jump record holder, who never played on a losing team.

Those had been the days of Jim Lanagan, great graduate coach, whose teams never lost to Cal in the six years before he left coaching to enter law practice. In 1903, Lanagan's first year, the Big Game was a 6–6 tie. The next two Stanford won, and then the two presidents, David Starr Jordan and Benjamin Ide Wheeler, changed from American football to rugby. Lanagan traveled to Australia in the summer of 1906 to learn the game of rugby, and did it so well his Stanford teams won the first three Big Games of rugby from Cal.

Until 1914 rugby grew and prospered in California, and folks in these parts believed it would eventually take over for the slower, clumsier American football on a nation-wide scale.

But in 1912 the Waratahs of Australia toured the Bay Area, and one of their stars, Danny Carroll, liked Stanford, decided to stay, and was one of the main reasons why Stanford beat Cal 13–8 in the thrilling Big Game of 1913. At Berkeley they fried, decided the freshmen must go, passed a rule against their use on varsity teams and asked Stanford to agree. Fat chance of that! Stanford replied that it took 15 B credits from high school to get into Stanford, which made it impossible for any freshman to be a ringer.

In the meantime, the finest athletic team of any kind I've ever seen, before or since, the New Zealand All Blacks, toured California in 1913, and this time Jim Wylie, greatest of all the game's forwards, decided to stay at Stanford where the Farm hospitality was the only proselyting needed.

So Cal changed its rule back, using freshmen in the Big Game, but it was no use. The Stanford forwards, with Jim Wylie, had learned the deadly passing rush of the All Blacks, short passes with big, powerful men handling the ball at full speed. Frank Rehm to Wylie to Bill Bloeser and right down the line until it went to backs such as Charley Austin and Otto Lachmund, perhaps the best open field runner in all Stanford football history. It was the peak of rugby perfection ever achieved on the Coast, and I still feel that any American football coach who can drill his whole team in the art of lateral passing can revolutionize the game.

But it was also the beginning of the end of rugby. The Stanford rooting section rubbed it in heavily during the game, singing a special parody of the song "Don't you remember, California in September," which reminded Cal of their weakness in canceling their own freshman rule. As the score mounted to 26–8, the Berkeley people burned. This time the freshmen had to go. In the spring of 1915 they sent an ultimatum to Stanford, "Unless you pass the freshman rule, we will abrogate relations."

A student body meeting was called in the old Assembly Hall to discuss the matter, and for perhaps ten minutes the meeting was quite orderly. Suddenly from the middle of the crowded hall there arose long Johnny Norton, crack hurdler, since nationally known as a great educator at Columbia. His eyes blazing and mad through and through, Johnny shouted the immortal words, "I say, To Hell With California!"

To say that pandemonium broke loose is putting it mildly; the student body nearly blew off the roof in unanimous acclaim. That was the message sent to Cal, and during the summer, U.C.'s graduate manager, Johnny Stroud, announced that all relations had been severed with Stanford, and Cal would play American football starting that fall.

Those rugby days are fading into the distant past, but no one who ever saw him could forget fullback Bennie Erb, the first punter to master the art of curving his kicks in either direction, to the left, or turn the ball over in flight to go out of bounds to the right within a few yards of its finish. The last game the Waratahs played in America, at Golden Gate Park, he won by drop-kicking a 55-yard field goal.

My brother, Rick Templeton, was the finest place-kick goal kicker I have ever seen and, at 150 pounds, kicked the longest drop-kick field goal of all time, 67 yards on the old Santa Clara turf.

But it wasn't only football that brought achievements from Stanford athletes. Early in the century Fred Lanagan broke the world record in the pole vault, just under 12 feet. The next year Norman Dole became the first man ever to clear 12 feet. His record was 12 feet, 1 and 32/100 inches, and he became the only Stanford athlete, before or since, to be presented with a silver loving cup by the students of the University of California! And if his record seems ludicrously low in this day of 15-footers, I doubt that any of the moderns could clear 12 feet with the equipment Norman Dole used that day, especially with no slide to put the pole into.

The Stanford crew went to Poughkeepsie in 1916, and the experts had a ball kidding the members about their clumsy style. But in the four-mile championship race they were leading but didn't know the finish line. Cornell managed to nip them at the finish because Stanford thought it had a half mile yet to go.

The headlines in New York papers and across the nation, though, were not about Cornell but about Stanford's amazing showing. From that race Rix Maurer was selected All-American stroke.

Then there was Lin Murray, half-miler and left-handed tennis player, who won the national singles championship from Bill Tilden in 1918.

And the baseball team of 1913, captained by Zeb Terry, and coached by law student Nig Peters, who had given up a brilliant major league career for law, swept through the season's opposition and spent the summer touring Japan, the first American team to show in that country.

What a ball club that was! Pitcher Ray Maple, whose "nickel curve" of those days turned out to be the slider of the modern pitcher. Bubba Dent, the tall, gaunt, dedicated catcher. First baseman Tom Workman, who turned down a bonus offer from John McGraw of the Giants. Louie Cass, second baseman and star rugby halfback. Terry, who was the Chicago Cubs' regular second baseman for many years, at shortstop. Pete McCloskey, the stylist with the rifle arm, at third. And in the outfield, Wally Argabrite, Artie Hahn, and Heinie Beeger. They stand out in my mind as though it were yesterday, for if there has ever been as good a college ball club since, I've never seen it.

Two of the athletic thrillers of all time came in the Big Meets of 1913 and 1915. The '13 meet was held on the small, tree-shaded track at Berkeley, a little less than a fifth of a mile, with a brook running through it and a wooden bridge to cover it on the far turn of the 220. Cal was favored, but Stanford freshman Herb Whitted came through with two brilliant upsets in the hurdles to defeat Cal star Eddie Beeson. Paul McKee won the 100 with Cap Campbell second, and in the 220 the two Stanford speedsters reversed the positions.

In those days, however, each University named one place judge for each place, and the Cal judges picked Fui Wood for second. That made it a tie for second place, two points apiece, and gave Cal the meet. The decision was so raw, however, that Stanfordites continued to argue long after the rest of the meet was over, and challenged Cal to rerun the second place.

So, fully an hour after everything else was over, McKee and Wood took the marks for the rerun, in lanes, around the curve, and the tension in the crowded bleachers was almost unbearable. Wood, on the outside, held the lead down the straightaway, around the turn, right to the wooden bridge. But coming into the finish, suddenly McKee was ahead by four feet. Paul was a beautiful sprinter and he maintained it as the Stanford side went absolutely crazy. Never had there been a greater Stanford hero than Paul B. McKee.

Two years later, at the dedication of the new Cal track, there was another such finish, only more so. Big Stanford crewman Derrol Chace had beaten Cal's captain, Jimmy Todd, in the 440, and Jimmy had been violently ill right up to the time of the relay and was half carried to the starting post, his head swathed with iced towels. Stanford needed only one point to win and had saved out Ed Beale to have a fresh man for the anchor lap. It looked like a cinch as the first three Stanford quarter-milers built up a twenty-yard lead. How silly it looked to see the tortured Todd sprinting wildly up the back stretch after Beale. But he kept sprinting around the turn, actually caught Ed at the head of the finish stretch, and for the last 100 yards they battled it out, dead even, neither gaining a fraction of an inch. At the tape Jimmy Todd managed to throw his chest out just enough to get the call. He'd won the relay and the meet under absolutely impossible conditions. No one could sprint a 440, said the absolute law of track. But Jimmy Todd had done it. Furthermore he had done it while so ill he could scarcely stand by himself.

Nowadays you do not see a student body rooting section turn wild as they did in those days. The Cal side of the stadium emptied onto the track in a jiffy and started the victory serpentine around the track.

In the meantime some lightning thinking by my brother, Rick Templeton, was to change everything. Rick had won the high jump and taken third in the high hurdles, but early in the afternoon he had taken one jump in the broad jump just for a warm-up, and then forgotten all about it. He rushed over to the broad jump officials, and the records showed that he had actually qualified for the finals with that one jump. The Cal officials said he had forfeited all his later jumps by not showing up. But the rules were clear, and the Stanford officials, Jumbo Morris and George Presley, pointed them out. He forfeited all but his last jump. He had one coming.

The Cal serpentine stopped on the track. Trainer Dad Moulton started giving Rick a 15-minute rubdown. Jumbo Morris carefully and plainly marked off 22 feet, the distance Rick would have to jump to get the third place and win the meet. But Rick was not a broad jumper. He'd be lucky to get even his step.

Finally everything was set for the big attempt. Down the runway came Rick, flying. As if by a miracle he hit the board exactly, leaped in the air like a good high jumper. And came down exactly on that 22-foot mark. Anyone who failed to see him land could have had no doubt about it, as Jumbo Morris leaped almost as high in the air, sailing his senior sombrero far across the field and letting out a victory cry that sent the Berkeley rooters slinking off the track, back into the bleachers, as the Stanford side took over the field in a triumphant victory march. The score was Stanford 62, California 60, and never in any Stanford-California athletic meeting has there been a dramatic finish to compare with this one.

*It is as important for a man to have a philosophy of recreation as it is for him to have a philosophy of work.*
                                                                    RAY LYMAN WILBUR, '96

# FOUR

". . . you cannot put a five-thousand-dollar education on a fifty-cent boy. The experiment has been tried thousands of times. All our colleges are trying it over and over again, and it generally fails."

THE WORDS are Dr. Jordan's, but the spirit of them was the motivating force behind Ray Lyman Wilbur's lightning swift alterations of "things as they are" so soon as he took charge at Stanford. Nearly all of Dr. Wilbur's life had been spent in close connection with the University. In the course of that thoughtful and observant life, he had undoubtedly formed many opinions, worked out many tentative plans. Now they were to be put to the test.

He wasted no time. In quick succession, the pluses and minuses of early report sheets gave way to letter grades. Grades were accompanied by grade-points, B earning one point less than A and so on down the scale. Number of grade-points must equal number of units of work taken or the student would be denied graduation—if, indeed, with a sagging record, he had managed to stay in Stanford at all. Lest any be forgetful of his standing, the student's name, the units, and the grade-points he possessed were printed in a college directory, open to all—in local vernacular, the Bawlout. It was undergraduate mythology, accepted by many as fact, that professors consulted the Bawlout before deciding on grades. Let a man be low on the printed page, and he would be marked low everywhere. . . . Entering students found no department open to them. Their first two years were spent under guidance of a committee drawn from all departments. A substantial part of their courses during those years were required of all, thus making sure that underclassman was measured against underclassman. . . . Clearly, the fifty-cent boy was in for trouble.

The changes stirred up controversy, of course, some of it emotional only, some of it soundly based, since, as every teacher knows,

# 110

the boy valued at fifty cents in required courses is now and then a near-genius in his specialty. Petitions went from the alumni to the Board of Trustees—went there and died there. The President had made sure of Board support before he took office.

His explanation of his purpose was curt and clear:

"Quality and not quantity is the Stanford ideal. The level of work should not be set by the mediocre student. . . . Whether we like it or not, every phase of human life is competitive. Certainly it is at least as important to know what the score is in the academic or scholastic field as it is in athletics."

Curricular changes were, of course, not the only ones. Military training was re-established. . . . Freshmen entering in any term were limited to a given number—a precaution against the University's over-rapid growth which World War I was to render temporarily superfluous. . . . New buildings went up in defiance of sharply rising prices. Use of old ones was augmented: first, by the scheduling of classes for Saturday morning (a change which "was not appreciated," in Dr. Wilbur's dry estimate, by the undergraduates who were to carry them); second, by a shift from the semester to the quarter system, thus allowing four terms in a year instead of two. . . . Hazing, which at Stanford took the form of tubbing, had been abolished by student body fiat in 1906—when, as it happened, the freshman class was the largest yet to enter and capable of vigorous self-defense. Like other abolished things, it had crept back in. Dr. Wilbur's objection to it took a form other than fiat; he removed the tubs and substituted showers in student residence halls. . . . Like every other American college president and like his predecessors, he waged continuous war against the drinking which was almost as much a tradition at Stanford as at institutions longer established. Though with a different set of values—as for example, the value he placed on competition—he was as sternly moralist as Dr. Jordan himself.

What did the faculty think of the new Stanford in which their teaching was to be done? The newer members usually conformed, often with full approval. Grades, grade-points, attendance checks— all they meant was that the upstart university of the West was itself conforming, drawing nearer in practice to the institutions by which their own degrees had been granted.

The Old Guard, on the other hand (the term had become more inclusive with time)—the Old Guard neither conformed nor refused conformity. Its members simply went on, each in his accustomed way, whatever that way had been. From this group the President, with his customary good sense, turned his eyes away. Stewart Young in Chemistry, Anderson in English, Albert Leon Guérard (a slightly later comer) in General Literature, Harris Ryan in Electrical Engineering—where one of these presided over lecture room or laboratory, there, he knew, scholarship would be advanced, no matter what the method. Even the fifty-cent boy, given such mentors, might somehow push his value up to a full dollar.

*There ought to be a poet submerged in every novelist; that is part of what his sensibility amounts to. And in addition—he needs a memory that spills easy, a memory with a loose top, so that any chance can tip it and send rolling the vast and invaluable supply of what the writer did not know he knew, the store of perceptions he did not know he had recorded.*
WALLACE STEGNER, Professor of English

# Random Reminiscences of Stanford Presidents

## Russel V. Lee, M.D. '20

*Russel V. Lee was a Christmas freshman at Stanford in 1912. In the course of working his way through the University he met the remarkable Dr. Hans Zinsser and, as a result, changed to a pre-medical course and became a doctor. Following a term of service during World War I he established practice in San Francisco, later moved to Palo Alto, where he founded the Palo Alto Medical Clinic. In World War II he joined the Air Force, became a colonel and Chief of Preventive Medicine, and was awarded the Legion of Merit.*

*Both founder and long-time president of the now enormous Clinic, and founder of Channing House, a retirement home now under construction, he has found time to serve on President Truman's Commission for the Health Needs of the Nation (1952) and on many national commissions and boards concerned with the nation's health.*

*He is the father of five children, all of whom were graduated from Stanford and from the Stanford School of Medicine, and all of whom are physicians.*

The eminence that Stanford has attained and the wide recognition of its achievements have tended to obscure the essential youthfulness of the institution. There are people alive today, like Mr. Hoover, who registered in the first class and who knew intimately every important person associated with Stanford. Even the author, who does not regard himself as of great antiquity, has had the honor of attending as a physician every president of Stanford except John Casper Branner.

It is my intention to draw upon this personal association for certain random reminiscences which may or may not shed light upon the characters of these unusual men, whose genius was largely responsible for the greatness Stanford achieved in so short a time. Each of them was a distinguished man. But each differed markedly from all the others. Certain things they had in common. All were large men, of striking physical appearance, vigorous and energetic. Three of them were doctors of medicine, one a great practioner. They had the common heritage of poverty in their youth and all were men of tremendous drive and of great achievement aside from their careers as administrators of a university. But each had his own distinct and vivid personality.

David Starr Jordan was an immense man, an athlete, an orator never at a loss for a word to be thundered out in his great booming voice that needed no microphonic amplification. He was brought up in the Victorian tradition, but he had the benefit of a scientific and a medical education. He understood and at times, I am sure, reluctantly, deferred to the prevailing attitude toward certain aspects of human behavior. But in a period when Darwin was an agent of the devil, Dr. Jordan was a vocal advocate of biological evolution and, in his monumental work on the classification of fish, a doughty supporter of the best scientific methodology. To be sure, he believed in mass and number. When someone reproached him with the fact that ten of his classifications (out of many hundreds) were wrong, he thundered, "Very well, how many were right?"

By all accounts he was not a great administrator. But he handled Mrs. Stanford with finesse and success, and this was no mean feat. Moreover, he had in an amazing degree the most valuable asset of any executive and this was an almost uncanny ability to recognize men of promise when they were young and unproven. Under forty, himself, when he took the Stanford challenge, he surrounded himself with young men who only he knew were men of genius. Twenty years later no less than twenty of them had become or were presidents of their respective learned societies. The list included "Daddy" Marx, "Daddy" Ryan, E. C. Franklin, and many others of tremendous ability and distinction. And he hardly missed in any of his choices.

He was an evangelist and he became an apostle of peace, in his later years going all over the world preaching the insanity and immorality of war. Would to God the so-called practical men had listened!

I remember September, 1914; the Great War had just begun and caught Jordan in Europe. He returned to address a jammed Assembly Hall eager to hear what the great man of peace would say about the Great War. In a booming voice that filled every part of the hall, "My dear students, I have just returned from Europe where I have been for six months on a mission of peace. (A little titter.) We have been so far successful that all the nations of Europe except Italy—and she soon will be—are at war. We were not successful; we were merely right." Fifty years have shown how right he really was.

Jordan lived too long. In his last years his great mind was dimmed, but the light always glowed. The cruel disintegration of slow years set in. He would wander into my office and terrify a poor woman by growling, "Well, will you get out or shall I?" But always with kindness, with humor, and with real love of mankind.

I had a few contacts with John Casper Branner, a great scholar, a handsome, bearded man, reserved, perhaps a little cold. My one real contact with him consisted of a reproof and an admonishment when, as a young lab assistant, under orders from my professor, I had flagrantly defied regulations to buy a hundred microscopes which had not been in the budget. "Young man, this is improper and irregular and strictly speaking you are responsible. The amount (some $2,000!) should be withheld from your salary." (It was $35 a month.) "But," (with a twinkle) "we will not enforce this imposition at this time." But he made it abundantly clear that his orderly, disciplined, direct mind deplored such sloppy tactics.

Although I was associated with Ray Lyman Wilbur in many things over many years, I never felt that I knew him well. We were both physicians and as a physician I attended Mrs. Wilbur and Dr. Wilbur as well. Our communications were good; we agreed on most matters of Medical School and University policy; we worked together and got things done; but we were never really close. He had a group of very intimate friends, most of them contemporaries from his Stanford student days—Herbert Hoover, of course; my rugged partner, Dr. Tom Williams; Alonzo Englebert Taylor, the great food expert; Fred Smith, who ran a sporting goods store, and a few more. With these he was very close, but with people generally he was not a cozy man. He was tall, of striking appearance in a rather Lincolnesque way, a great homespun humorist, a really good speaker with some of Dr. Jordan's ability as a coiner of epigrams. I took a group of green-horns up to his camp on Wooley Creek to fish for steelhead trout, an activity in which Wilbur was said to be a master. He was leaving as we arrived. The opportunity to get some valuable tips on steelhead fishing seemed fortuitous. "Dr. Wilbur, you are a great fisherman, how does one go about catching steelhead?" From the great educator all we got was, "One studies the habits of the steelhead."

Dr. Wilbur knew and, in behalf of Stanford and the national government in which he was Secretary of the Interior, cultivated many men of importance and great wealth. For these men, who had made vast financial successes, he seemed to have no great veneration. Speaking of one of them he said to me, "Had I devoted the energy and brains to making money that I did to medicine, I could have outdone him." He believed this about himself and so did I. He did quite well, incidentally, in his own financial affairs. He was a very good administrator with a mind that could grasp the essence of things quickly and accurately. He annoyed many people by reading and annotating letters while they talked to him. They did not appreciate that he was perfectly capable of taking in all they had to say and annotating his letters at the same time. Part of this he learned from taking histories from patients, but mostly it was an evidence of a first-rate, well-ordered mind—though one disgruntled visitor was heard to remark that Dr. Wilbur had spent too many years telling people to stick out their tongues.

Dr. Wilbur had great ideas for Stanford. Very early he grasped the truth that a great university is so because of its creative production, and this meant less effort put on pedagogy for halfbacks and more and more emphasis on the upper division and the graduate school. The rah-rah alumni declared war on this concept and gave him a bad time, but they failed to disturb his equanimity or his conviction of the correctness of his views. Stanford, of course, has gone far now in this direction. Dr. Wilbur's influence on Stanford's direction was tremendous, and his reformation of the school's administrative procedures was masterly and greatly in contrast to the methods followed by Jordan. He loved power and exercised it well. The Trustees kept him on after the normal retirement age because no one with his stature was available.

Robert Eckles Swain was vice-president when Wilbur went to Washington and was acting president for four years. He was a pioneer in the study of air pollution and made a wide reputation in the controversial smelter smoke case in Utah. Swain seemed superficially to be a somewhat pompous, German-professor type. He was not. He was one of the warmest, most idealistic, and most unselfish of men, and held the faculty, students, and alumni closely together while still adhering to Dr. Wilbur's objectives. With him one could get very close indeed, and I felt I knew him like a brother. After thirty years of close association, I believe I knew almost every detail of his life and experiences. And I also believe he had never done anything of which he was ashamed. Few like Swain!

I thought at one time that I knew Donald Tresidder very well indeed. In fact, I thought I was perhaps his closest friend. But many others thought that, too. Don, handsome, laughing, cordial, had one of the most charming approaches to human relationship of anyone I ever knew. He made each person feel his intense interest in him and his ideas. But he was truly a complex man, and I believe now that no one person knew him completely. After talking to many people, he made up his own mind and had his own sense of direction from which he could not be swerved. He brought tremendous organizational changes to the president's office—a sort of general staff system replaced the old one-man personal direction. He himself became rather inaccessible, but the machinery moved very smoothly indeed. Don was a great outdoor man, a superb fisherman and camp cook, a great rider with a taste for spectacular horses, a friend and patron of many young Stanford students, who adored him. I am sure he had great ideas for Stanford which were interrupted by his untimely death. No one can say what the school would have been had he survived. No one who knew him well will ever forget him. He had in the most highly developed degree that quality known as "personality." With it all, he had a Horatio Alger career. He was a poor boy, kept house for the scholarly George Barnett and absorbed from him a great love of music and culture, worked in the summer in Yosemite Valley as a waiter and, in true Horatio Alger style, married the boss's daughter and became a rich man—all according to the book. Someone some day should do a biographical study of this fascinating, intricate man.

J. E. "Wally" Sterling is too close to us all for this kind of reminiscence. Like his predecessors, he is a great man physically. But he is completely different from any of the other presidents. Under him Stanford has achieved the highest degree of harmony in its entire career; and as a tribute to his prestige with all elements, no one has tried to make him quit even though the football teams seldom win. To many of us it seems that he came in answer to prayer with just the qualities the times require. But it is much too early to try an appraisal now. This will be for someone else.

*Golden days at Stanford! Adequate equipment, small classes composed largely of men who had worked their own ways to an education, complete independence in teaching and research.*
HANS ZINSSER, Stanford professor, 1910–13

# Beginner at Research

Sophie D. Aberle, A.B. '23, M.A. '25, Ph.D. '27

*Sophie Aberle (Mrs. William A. Brophy) went from Stanford to Yale, where, after receiving a degree in medicine, she became an instructor in anthropology in the Institute of Human Relations, then instructor in the Yale School of Medicine. Under grants from the Carnegie Corporation of New York and the National Research Council, she instituted studies of the health of women and children among the Pueblo Indians, and in 1935 was appointed by the Bureau of Indian Affairs to the superintendency of the United Pueblo Agency. She was founder and chairman of the board of directors of the Southwest Training School for Federal Service; on the national board of the National Science Foundation; fellow of the American Anthropological Association; and author of monographs and articles in scientific journals. Since 1957 she has been executive director of the Commission on the Rights, Liberties, and Responsibilities of the American Indian.*

Stanford to me meant the opening up of an entirely new world. I had transferred from the University of California with a fervent hope that after I got my medical degree at Stanford, it would perhaps be possible for me to find my way into research work. When, in my first year in medicine, Dr. Danforth suggested that I study the genetics of black-eyed white mice, I was overwhelmed. He took me downstairs in the old Anatomy Building, past vats of evil-smelling cadavers prepared for the next generation of medical students, and into a small room in a corner of the cellar—a corner lighted by one small electric bulb and with a ceiling so low that he had almost to double up to go in at all and even I, who am not tall, could not stand straight.

When my eyes became accustomed to the gloom, I could see rows of small cages with little white objects behind the wire. This room

118

and the cages of mice were to be entirely my own. The research project was to be carried out here.

To this day I have not forgotten the immediate thrill and the lasting excitement of being given an opportunity to watch, to study, and to make records of the performance of these tiny animals. My enthusiasm was not dimmed by time. Indeed, it increased as I accumulated material and learned, through watching, recording, and correcting my observations, not only much about my mice but also what research really means and what persistent following of a problem finally does to steady and clarify thinking.

Month following month, the chief part of my time and certainly the most important part of it was spent in that cellar corner. There was always more to learn, more connections to discover between my problem and others which were being carried on around me. In the end, I wrote my dissertation about black-eyed white mice, had it accepted, and came out regretfully from my cellar to go on to other places and other tasks.

There is, though, a postscript. At Stanford at that time, the accepted dissertations, bound and beautiful, stood in a row on a shelf not far behind the main desk in the library. Waiting at the desk for the attendant to bring me some books I had asked for, I saw two young women, far too elaborately dressed to be students, wandering along the row of dissertations, reading the titles and murmuring to each other with mounting amusement. "Look, here's one on beetles" . . . "This one's talking about railroads; anyhow, I know what railroads are" . . . "This one—oh, listen! 'Hereditary Anemia in Mice.' I should think the more mice had anemia, the better!"

*In my own education nothing meant so much to me as the contact with a few great men whom I knew face to face.*

DAVID STARR JORDAN

# Stanford Memories

## ROSEMARY DRACHMAN TAYLOR, A.B. '22

*Rosemary Drachman (Mrs. John Winchcombe-Taylor), as she explains in her reminiscence, was eagerly practicing writing throughout her undergraduate career. She continued the practice, combining it with various salaried undertakings, until her best-selling "Chicken Every Sunday," followed by an equally popular "Ridin' the Rainbow," allowed her to give full time to fiction. She and her husband, who is also a novelist, live in Tucson, Arizona, where Mrs. Taylor grew up and where she has found the material for many of her books.*

*She writes that her first rejection slip was received at the age of eleven when she submitted to* American Magazine *an article entitled "What Makes Marriage Fail."*

This year at graduation they'll be putting down the paving block and on it will be the brass numbers 1962. When I graduated the numbers were 1922. Forty years! It *can't* be true.

What you remember! What you don't remember! The day the letter came to Tuscon. I can still feel the sense of triumph. Stanford had accepted me! I'd made it. I was in. For in 1920 Stanford's women could number just five hundred. Something to do with Mr. and Mrs. Stanford's will. Of men there could be two thousand. A lovely ratio.

Although I do not see myself arriving in Palo Alto, it must have been by train. Was I met at the station? Did I go to the campus by taxi, in someone's automobile, or on that funny little streetcar? I can't recall. As an Arizonan, used to the desert, I was struck by the greenness of everything. I know this part of California has its times of drought and dryness, but in my mind I always see Stanford country as lushly green. And there is fog at night and the misty rain. And oh, those springs when the fruit trees bloomed in the Santa Clara Valley! Are the lovely orchards gone now, cut down for the subdivisions?

I lived in Roble Hall. I see clearly that suite—the two small bedrooms with a study between—on the second floor of C Wing which I was to occupy with Grace Pope, the tall girl from Montana. The Roble girls, for the most part, come into sharp focus. Not always their names, but their faces. Helen Burntrage and Peg Carlsmith, Marion Potter of the red hair and rosy cheeks. Kathryn Donald, Eleanor Parsons, the plump laughing person with the aristocratic nose whom we called "Aunt Kate." And there was a Mary Somebody, tall and dark and efficient, knowing all the answers. And "Happy" Grill, the bubbling freshman, who burst in upon me one day, wide-eyed and breathless, with a copy of *Jurgen* under her arm. "They say it's very, *very* wicked, and it's been loaned to me for just two hours. We can read it together." We did read it, but Mr. Cabell's double meanings escaped us. We found no wickedness. In fact it made no sense at all to us. Now *The Sheik* . . . that we could understand.

How did we dress? How did we do our hair? Middling long pleated skirts with blouses and sweaters usually. Our hair we had marcelled and then we "ratted" it at the sides into huge puffs. Then there came the Irene Castle craze and we were all cutting off our hair. Skirts got longer. I see myself going to a dance in a many-paneled white evening dress that touched the floor. I know it touched the floor. One of my partners stepped on a panel and tore it off.

I have no memory of what time we had to get in on date nights. Probably much earlier than the coeds do now. But I know the name of the girl at another dance who was caught smoking a cigarette and who was expelled. And there were three girls who went to a nightclub called "Babylon." They too were expelled. Other days, other ways.

For gymnasium our uniforms were middies and voluminous, but voluminous, black bloomers. In swimming classes our suits more than adequately covered us. I nearly didn't graduate because I couldn't swim the length of the pool. You couldn't graduate without your gym credits, and you couldn't get your gym credits without being able

122 STANFORD MOSAIC

to swim the length of the pool. But I finally made it, puffing and panting, using the old-fashioned breast stroke, and with Grace Pope shouting encouragement from the side.

I had three years at Stanford. My junior and senior—my first two years were at the University of Arizona—and then the year I stayed on as secretary to Dean Mary Yost. Dear Dean Mary, with her Virginia accent, her merry brown eyes, and that careless pompadour always falling down. Actually I had still another year on the Quad, as in 1928 I came back to be secretary to Edith Mirrielees when she wrote her book on the short story.

How fortunate for a would-be author to have had Edith Mirrielees as a teacher in creative writing, and then later to have worked with her on that book. And there were other wonderful teachers, too. Payson Treat with his thrilling courses in the history of India and the Far East, David Gray in play writing, Carruth in poetry, Tatlock in medieval English literature, and the man—his name has gone—who spread before me the delights of Chaucer.

Lucky years, wonderful years. Full of big joys and small joys. And hurts, too. But you forget the hurts. The time in class when Miss Mirrielees said, "Now I am going to read you a very good short story." And it was mine! Later it was published in *The Cardinal*, my first work in print.

I remember the trips downtown to Sticky's and the divine hot fudge sundaes. And the trips to San Francisco with Grace in her Model T Ford. We'd eat at that restaurant, the Fly Trap—is it still in existence?—and order their sanddabs and the marvelous salad with the garlic dressing. There were those midnight feasts at Roble. What fun to open the boxes from home! Those nut-filled cookies, those triple-layer cakes! I'm afraid I think too much with my stomach. The meals at Roble I can't recall at all. I imagine they were wholesome, nourishing, and completely uninviting. Miss Gertrude Gardiner was in charge. There was a song we used to sing which began:

"It was good for G. M. Gardiner,
It was good for G. M. Gardiner,
So it's good enough for us . . ."

Big joys were the Junior Operas, the librettos of which I helped to write—the first one, *Maid to Order*, with Dan Evans, and the next, *Up on a Ladder*, with Tom Kleckner. I also wrote a pageant for the Women's Athletic Association. It was called *Randalin's Crowning*, was set in Roman Britain, and I haven't the faintest recollection of what it was about. Also I did a skit for a Ram's Head show and I can't remember that, either.

But I remember the fun of doing the shows and the talented young people I worked with. Dan Evans, of course—what a loss that was when he was killed!—and Tom Kleckner, and Tom Carskadon, and Lester Seib—who changed his name to Lester Vail, and was, to my glad surprise, the director of *Chicken Every Sunday* when the dramatization of my book came to Broadway. And there was Lloyd Nolan and Arnold Bayley and Chick Midgley. And Foresta Hodgson and Helen Whitney and Dottie Marston. And Dick Malaby and Gordon Davis, and many, many more.

I was once in a class with John Steinbeck. I recognized his quality and I envied it. Walking on the Quad with Miss Mirrielees, I said sadly, "I'll never be able to write like that." "No," she answered, looking at me over her glasses with her kindly quizzical gaze, "no, you never will. But if you work hard, you'll be able to write as well as *you* can and that should be good enough."

As I've already said, after graduation I went to work as secretary to Dean Mary Yost. I sublet an apartment from Professors Theresa Russell and Elizabeth Buckingham of the English Department. They were going to Europe on a sabbatical leave. The apartment was one of several in an old house, no doubt now torn down, on Salvatierra Street. It was run by two spinster sisters. One was a librarian, with shining white hair and *the* most beautiful teeth. The story about her was that William Allen White had once been her suitor but she turned him down because he refused to give up smoking. Her sister, who was the housekeeper, was very deaf, and she was *the* most beautiful cook. Her homemade bread! She used to bring me slices of it, hot and buttered, along with apricot jam she'd made from the fruit of the tree in the back yard. Oh, yum! There I go, thinking with my stomach again.

I loved my apartment. It had a living room, bedroom, a small place to cook, and a bathroom. Hot water came when you put a quarter in a meter. How frustrating to have it fail right in the middle of primping! I soon learned to lay in a supply of emergency quarters. There was a fireplace in the living room, a green davenport, comfortable low chairs, and thousands of books. Such fun to entertain there! Best of all, in the apartment next to mine lived Edith Mirrielees, and I could impose upon her by asking her to read and help me with the stories I was writing in my spare time.

But there was not much spare time, for I was busy in the Dean of Women's office. There were the usual stenographic chores, and I was also Dean Mary's Girl Friday outside the office, helping her with her parties and teas, meeting parents at trains, going down to the hospital to comfort coeds laid low with poison ivy, being available, if Miss Yost was not, to let someone weep on my shoulder.

I enjoyed my job immensely and felt ever so important being in the midst of things and getting to know so many of the students and faculty. One constant visitor to our office was Dr. Mosher, Dr. Clelia D. Mosher, the Women's Medical Adviser. I can see her now, a cheery, solid woman, in her mannish suit and hat, and always steamed up about something.

I was involved in her water project. She had the idea that drinking lots of water was good for scholarship. She'd signed up a group of girls who promised to keep track of the water they drank and report to me. In the meantime I was to look up their grades and check these against the amounts of water imbibed. Alas, there was no correlation at all. Some girls drank a lot of water and got good grades and some drank a lot of water and got bad grades. The same with those who drank just a little water. $H_2O$ did not increase your brain power. Dr. Mosher was terribly disappointed.

I could go on with these memories for pages and pages, but I must stop. How lucky I was to have gone to a great University, to have been taught by great teachers, to have made at Stanford so many lifelong friends.

# Men Who Lighted the Way

## RALPH MORELL HEINTZ, A.B. '20

*Ralph Heintz, an inventor, is now engaged in automotive (anti-smog) engine research, and is the founder of Heintz & Kaufman, Ltd., San Francisco, California, and the co-founder of Jack & Heintz, Inc., Cleveland, Ohio. His private research laboratory, "The Ramohs," is in Los Gatos, California, where he lives. He is a Fellow of the Institute of Radio Engineers and a Fellow of the American Institute of Electrical Engineers. His son, Ralph Heintz, Jr., is a graduate of Stanford, Class of '43.*

You ask about my memory of Stanford; what I found meaningful; what has stayed with me. All was meaningful, and all has stayed with me, but, of course, certain experiences stand out more clearly than others. Come to think about it, my thoughts are mostly about people; a certain few warm, learned men to whom I am humbly grateful.

Even before transferring from U.C., it was my privilege to have the friendship of Stewart Woodford Young. In fact, it was my admiration for Stew Young that prompted my decision to transfer from U.C. to Stanford at the end of my sophomore year.

Stew Young was Professor of Physical Chemistry, which I made my major subject, largely because of my affectionate regard for him. In the light of present-day nuclear science, the physical chemistry of 1915 might seem primitive, but the groundwork laid down by men like Stewart Young helped provide the foundation upon which atomic science is being built.

In 1915 the electron was the smallest particle to be identified. Milliken had weighed it only a short time before. Understanding of atomic structure was still pretty vague, yet Stew Young sensed that lead exists in at least two forms, each with its own atomic weight.

They are "isotopes," a term comparatively new in inorganic, but old in organic chemistry.

Sensing the existence of the two and its importance, Stew Young set to work to prove his idea correct. By obtaining samples of lead ore from all over the world and submitting these to meticulous analyses, and then by making hundreds of molecular weight determinations, he proved that there was a "light" lead and a "heavy" lead. It had long been known that lead is the end product in the decay of uranium; so if there are two kinds of lead, there must be two kinds of uranium. There are indeed two uraniums, one having an atomic weight of 235, and the other an atomic weight of 238. Uranium 235 is fissionable!

Dr. Edward Curtis Franklin lived in the world of organic chemistry. This is a world of synthesis. It is not surprising, therefore, that he should choose to build another and different world from the one in which he lived, for he was an expert with atomic building blocks. Could there, perhaps, be a system having the equivalents of hydrolysis and dissociation without water being a part of the system? Dr. Franklin sought to find out. He built up two systems, one based on liquid ammonia and the other on liquid cyanic acid. As I recall it, equivalents were found.

Is it possible for intelligent beings somewhere in the universe to inhabit Dr. Franklin's world of ammonia, or must intelligence always inhabit an air-breathing body that is mostly water? Perhaps we should reread Franklin's papers.

I remember David Starr Jordan as a man of great intellectual stature with a body to match. His student gatherings were an inspiration, and words simply chosen were resounding in their intellectual depth. The talk ranged from literature to science, and from politics to fishes. It is told of him that on opening a can of "California Mackerel" he observed that the can contained not mackerel, but sardines; so the "Mackerel" canners had to change a lot of labels. Such was the discerning eye of a great ichthyologist.

I have a special reason for being grateful to two other men: Drs. Ryan and Durand. In 1917 I left Stanford to enlist in the army and did not return until 1920, bringing with me my wife Sophie and an uninspiring bank roll. When it came time to graduate, I still lacked four or five hours. I asked Dr. Ryan if he thought I could get an hour or so of credit for my war work in the Air Corps. He examined me rather thoroughly and without comment. I made the same request of Dr. Durand. Then both of these wonderful gentlemen departed on their vacations, both to unknown destinations.

With graduation day approaching, the strain became acute. Finally with a day to spare, the credits arrived. Why shouldn't I have special warm regard for "Daddy" Ryan and Dr. Durand? To these gentlemen and to Doctors Stillman, Swain, Mitchell, and Sloan, I reassert my sincere gratitude.

*Science is not only the essential base on which technology is built; it is also a great creation of the human mind, on a par with the finest painting or poetry or music. It is as part of our great cultural heritage that science deserves a place in the background of every generally educated person.*

LEONARD I. SCHIFF, Professor of Physics

# "Nimbus Beyond the Footlights"

## DELMER LAWRENCE DAVES, A.B. '27

*Delmer Daves started as a property boy to learn about films. He acted in eight films before deciding on a writing career. Since that time he has written over fifty screenplays. In 1943 he was made a director at Warner Brothers and has directed over thirty films. In 1954 the title of producer was added to his credits, and, at the present time, he is producer-writer-director of most of his screen work.*

*While at Stanford he was president of the Class of 1926, and was prominent in dramatics. His son, Michael Lawrence Daves, graduated in the Class of '61.*

In the first play I acted in at Stanford, I became aware of a nimbus just beyond the glow of the footlights, row 3 on the aisle—I came to know this white form to be the leonine head of Dr. David Starr Jordan, President Emeritus. He loved the theater, attended every play, sitting in Olympian grandeur (he was larger than life in many ways, external and internal) and applauded with gusto when he was pleased. If I received no other letter regarding the plays I acted in or directed, there would be one from Dr. Jordan. He was a kind man. Busy as he was, he always had the time to be thoughtful, to guide and encourage, to share of himself, his wisdom, but I didn't know all this my freshman year. I was far too awed by his appearance and reputation to dare present myself; I wrote him thank-you notes and hoped one day we would meet.

When the day of our first meeting came it had to do with ichthyology, not with the theater. As a choir boy I had learned to letter by copying the Gothic letters in the hymn books during the longer sermons; thus when I arrived at Stanford and took the course in lettering to "sweeten" my first quarter grades, I finished the course in a week and was invited to become an instructor then and there, surely the youngest one on the Stanford roster. Somehow Dr. Jordan saw some

128

of my penwork (I had gone into the bookplate business on the side) and sent for me. I hadn't the vaguest idea of why I was summoned and could only imagine that the great man wanted to discuss our drama program.

Instead, after I entered his large office near the Physics Corner and shook his hand, he looked at me gravely, then asked: "Young man, have you ever drawn a *fish?*" My answer, of course, was negative—I doubt that one one-hundredth of one per cent of college freshmen are given to fish-drawing. Dr. Jordan lifted his broad frame from his ancient roll-top desk and peered at me, asking: "Would you *like* to draw a fish?" While I had no compulsions along this line, I know that if Dr. Jordan had asked me if I'd like to jump off the campanile for him, I probably would have said "yes," as I did now.

He said, "Follow me." We went into his laboratory where a large, flat fish lay submerged in what smelled like formaldehyde with fishy overtones. He explained that he had found this new species, was writing a paper on it, and required a scientific pen drawing to illustrate the submerged flounder, or whatever it was. "Think you can draw that?" Again I responded, "Yes, sir." With that he admonished me: "Don't leave out a scale or a fin—that's what makes 'em different."

This, then, was the beginning of a friendship between an "eager beaver" freshman and the Great Man—for through all my years at Stanford, here was a hero who always grew in dimension, who became my guide and mentor. A typical evening at his Thursday night talks at his open house would start with: "Well, what will we talk about tonight?" The whole world was his—and he made it ours, too. He made a "curioso" out of me—for he was a man who found everything on earth of interest, and his profoundly wise mind lit unextinguishable fires of curiosity in all who sat at his feet.

But the most unforgettable hours were those when he sat working at his mammoth roll-top desk and I sat close by carefully drawing another fish; during these hours we discussed a multitude of things—but the most fascinating of all subjects was one we returned to, time and time again: "How did it begin?" And these conjectures had to do not only with the earth and the things on it, but with the beginnings of religions and arts and communication—the beginnings of anything that came to mind. Such conjectures! Such stimulation! To this day I add to the volumes of them in my library, and I should dedicate every page to Dr. Jordan—because he lit the fires. He did more than that. He decided my future, my work, my life.

My "moment of decision" came during my fifth year at Stanford. While my major was law, increasingly my time and devotion had been turning to the drama; I had earned my way through Stanford at what now seems a bewildering variety of activities: painting posters, designing Christmas cards and bookplates, acting as draftsman for the city of Palo Alto, teaching engineering lettering and drawing, managing the Glee Club, acting as art editor of the *Quad* for two years, while simultaneously acting as dramatic manager for the same length of time—which meant managing as many as ten productions a year, not to mention acting in or directing many of them, as well as being president of my class. The crisis came in the spring of 1927 when I was playing the lead in *Macbeth* while trying to carry the above additional burdens and study law as well . . . Small wonder that Dean Kirkwood sent for me. His advice was earnest, crisp, and simple: he said I must give up scattering my energies and concentrate on the law during my last quarters, for these were of the essence to my future career as a lawyer. The Dean was kind, but firm; one might almost call his statement an ultimatum. I thanked him, said similar realizations had dawned on me of late, and left his office.

Professor Arthur Cathcart, who had taught me in many of my law classes and who was as beloved as any man on the Stanford faculty, peered over his glasses at me as I emerged, beckoned his finger to me silently, led me into his office, closed the door and asked: "What did the Dean say to you, Delmer?" I told him. He nodded. It appeared that I had been discussed at a faculty meeting. His fine, bright eyes gazed at me through the gold rims of his spectacles and he asked quietly: "Are you in the mood for any more advice?" I told him this appeared to be my day, and I would very much like to know what he had to say. He said crisply, and with some feeling—for he, like Dr. Jordan, had been friend to me as well as mentor—and this came from his heart: "There are too damned many lawyers in the world right now, there are too few men who have the gift to make people laugh and cry and forget their troubles—you have that gift. My advice is to forget the law."

I thanked him (as I thanked him again, many years later when he became emeritus) for helping me crystallize my life and future. I knew in my heart that his advice was the advice I truly wanted to hear, but for final decision I crossed the Quad to the office of Dr. David Starr Jordan.

He listened to my report of what had happened as well as to my own doubt that my father would be joyous at the idea of my putting aside eighteen years of schooling to start at the bottom, probably as a manual laborer, in the motion picture industry which would become my new world. I told Dr. Jordan, too, that the thought of leaving Stanford and friends like Professors Cathcart, Treat, Allen, Hulme, Davis, Bailey, and all the others, would be like turning myself into a castaway on an uncharted sea. I confessed to him that I considered him my ultimate mentor and would he help me at this time of decision?

He gazed at me calmly, for a long time, then pressed the buzzer on his desk and asked of his secretary: "Please bring Delmer that picture we didn't know what to do with." She brought in a large photograph of Dr. Jordan seated at this same roll-top desk, the setting for so many of our shared hours. With a small smile, he dipped his pen and wrote boldly across the bottom of the photograph: "To Delmer Daves—The world steps aside to let any man pass if he knows where he is going. David Starr Jordan."

Silently he handed me the picture, let me digest the inscription for a moment, then offered me his hand and said: "Goodbye, Delmer, and good luck."

I never saw him again. But I shall be grateful to him—and to those other blessed mentors—all of my life. That is why I advise young men and women today who are fortunate enough to attend Stanford, including my own son, that much of Stanford's greatness lies outside the classrooms; it lies in the hearts and minds of those great men and women who will guide their destinies, in faculty offices and homes and laboratories, and under the long arcades of the Quad. And it lies with those who have gone before.

# Letter from Ceylon

## FRANCES WILLIS, A.B. '20, Ph.D. '23

*Frances Willis, United States Ambassador to Ceylon, has been a senior career officer in the United States foreign service for many years. She has served in posts all over the world, and has been Ambassador to Switzerland and Norway. One of the first three women to qualify as a foreign service officer, she is the only one of the three who still remains in the State Department.*

*The Willis family is related to the late Bailey Willis, noted Stanford geologist, and has long been connected with Stanford.*

Stanford meant so much to me in so many ways that it is difficult to reconstruct in isolation specific instances of what was important.

Certainly no course had a more lasting effect on me than Victor J. West's "Poli Sci I." It was a lecture course, but in the midst of a lecture he would fire a question at a student who was not allowed to "get by" with a slipshod answer. Mr. West would pursue the subject, and his supplementary questions showed up the weakness of the original answer, or led the student on to more profound probing—yes, even in Poli Sci I. It was in that course that I became aware that a student was expected to think for himself. The demonstration of ability to memorize and retain facts was not enough. From then until this day "figuring things out for myself" has proved to be one of the most stimulating things in life.

Another thing about my days, and years, at Stanford that I treasure was the keen intellectual competition. I hesitate to use the word competition because it may be misunderstood, but I can find no other word. It was good to be in a world where many had as good or better minds than your own. You had to do your best to keep up with them, and more and more you came to appreciate a fine piece of work. I can remember vividly the impression it made on me when Professor

132

Adams would read to the whole class samples of what he regarded as the best answers to questions on the last written test. I also remember my admiration for some of the briefs that were presented in Professor Cathcart's course in constitutional law.

The things that make a lasting impression and that I enjoyed at Stanford were not all intellectual. A canoe on Lagunita could be wonderful fun, particularly if the right man was wielding the paddle. There never were better chocolate malted milks (or "rocky roads") than those made at "Sticky" Wilson's. I still have a weakness for them and lamented the passage of Sticky's until Blum's came on the scene. And best of all, there was always something interesting to do at Stanford and people you wanted to do it with.

*Where formerly our armed forces were our first line of defense, today our diplomatic representatives at home and abroad may well be regarded as the sole agency for the maintenance of peace and the preservation of humanity. Stanford finds itself well represented in these "ministers of peace."*

GRAHAM H. STUART, Professor of Political Science

# The Roaring Twenties on the Stanford Farm

## THEODORE C. ACHILLES, A.B. '26

*Theodore Achilles has been a career Foreign Service offi-
cer since 1931. He has served as Counselor of the State
Department, Ambassador to Peru, Minister in Paris, and in
lesser capacities in London, Brussels, Rome, and Havana.
He has also been a member of the American delegations to
a score or more international conferences. Among the nego-
tiations in which he has played a part were those leading to
the North Atlantic Treaty and the "Reverse Lend-Lease"
agreements of World War II. Currently he is director of the
State Department's Operations Center.*

Looking back to my years at Stanford, the first impression is of
a gloriously misspent youth and happily missed opportunities.

Those were the Prohibition days of bootleg joints and the "Friday
fizz frisk," when on a spring afternoon a joyous group would head
for a shady tree in the great open spaces with 50 pounds of ice in a
washtub. We would add a gallon of homemade gin, the juice of
many lemons, a little sugar, and a few quarts of soda, and then settle
all manner of human and intellectual problems to our own satisfaction.

There was little serious study, as far as most of us were concerned,
and the wind of freedom blew so freely through the curriculum that
courses were chosen more for reputed ease than for content. More
or less concurrently, I was taking an amorphous collection of courses
in Chinese History, Accountancy of Investment, Insects and Disease,
Esthetics, and Greek.

I learned something about China and have a general idea what
amortization means. I remember that malarial mosquitoes stand on
their heads and that the best ratios of width to length are 2 to 5 or

134

3 to 5. I remember that Aristotle's dictum "Art imitates nature" means that art evokes the same emotions as nature. I remember most of the Greek alphabet, in Greek letters, but one of my fraternity brothers was less fortunate. Thanks to an excellent "trot" he did well all through the course but at the final exam (oral) he forgot his book and had to borrow the professor's. To the latter's horror, Llew stared in utter blankness at several paragraphs of Xenophon he was asked to translate, failed to conjugate a single tense of a single verb or, finally, even to repeat the alphabet. The poor man got a B while the rest of the class got A's.

Yet somehow we learned, largely by osmosis and in spite of ourselves. The very heterogeneity of our courses was broadening. Some of us who didn't study much spent many evening hours talking or reading about anything under the sun, and some of the talk and some of the reading was well worth-while.

I was a philosophy major and, while I managed to get reasonably good marks (and it wasn't like the Greek Department, either), I never did understand much of what philosophy I heard or read, and I remember practically none. Yet I do remember someone's definition of philosophy as "an unusually persistent attempt to think clearly" and have been persisting in that attempt ever since.

To return full-circle, Harold Chapman Brown's senior courses were seminars, without papers or exams. They met one night a week at his house over a jug of his wine, and six or eight of us argued for hours over all manner of problems. In the process we learned subconsciously to seek the essence of things, their meaning and their relationships in over-all perspective. Who could ask for more?

# Six Professors

## FRANK PRIOR, A.B. '19

*Frank Prior started as a roustabout in Salt Creek Field, Wyoming, in 1919. He is now chairman of the board of the Standard Oil Company of Indiana, director of four banks, of the American Petroleum Institute, and the Transportation Association of America. He is a member of the American Institute of Mining and Metallurgical Engineers and of the American Institute of Electrical Engineers. He is married and the father of two sons, one of whom, Frank O. Prior, Jr., was a member of the Class of '47. His hobbies, he writes, are dry-fly fishing and hunting.*

One of the first things I remember as a freshman was meeting two long, skinny Californians—Harley Earl and Red Greve. Harley Earl and I are now practically next door neighbors on the Atlantic Ocean at Palm Beach, Florida . . . two native sons who have gone east. Another thing that impressed me was the tradition—the then old tradition—of saying hello to any persons you saw on the campus, whether you knew them or not.

Of professors I have several recollections. On the character side was Professor Manning, tall, lean, long coat, standing with his back to the class and writing complicated mathematical equations on the blackboard with *both* hands. On the distasteful side was Professor Lesley, whom I had to consult once a week as a freshman enrolled in Mechanical Engineering. He asked me to keep track of my time to test my efficiency. He regarded sleeping as not working and therefore reducing efficiency. This was too much for me, so I never consulted him further—and, naturally, never passed his course.

But my major impressions, the ones that have remained fresh and influential in my mind through the years, have to do with four others whom Stanford gave me a chance to know—Professor Durand, Professor Ryan, and Professors Charles David Marx and Guido Marx.

Professor Durand I remember for his air of austerity, my feeling of the deepness of his knowledge, and because I had met him at his home and enjoyed his understanding and friendliness. I continued to meet him for many, many years after Stanford at various and unusual places—such, for example, as Winnemucca, Nevada, both of us sitting on a baggage truck and waiting for the track to be cleared of a wreck to allow us to go on our way.

Professor Ryan I remember for his friendliness, his great enthusiasm, and his faculty for making tough subjects understandable. He encouraged me to take some special work that helped me while in the U.S. Army Signal Corps.

I did not take any courses from Charles David Marx but came to know him when he was acting president of the University and I was in trouble with the regime that he headed, particularly with Professor Lesley, who had formed an unfavorable opinion of me when I was a freshman and had never permitted himself to alter it. Professor Marx was understanding and interested in my problems and went so far as to offer to go into the situation himself—an offer I appreciated but declined because I had decided to go into the army.

My impressions of Professor Guido Marx are hard to explain. He was a wonderful teacher who kept his students interested, no matter what course he was teaching, but also he was a man you felt close to, one you could go to whatever the reason.

All of these four men taught a long time at Stanford. There must be alumni the country over who knew them as I did and who remember them as I do—the very core of the University, a large part of the reason for Stanford's being a university at all.

# Stanford and the Hyatt Family

## PHYLLIS HYATT, A.B. '24

*Phyllis Hyatt (Mrs. Robert Ashton Gardiner), the eighth
of Edward Hyatt's children to attend Stanford, is the author
of* The Hyatt Legacy, *a biography of her parents and, indeed, in part a biography, too, of the flock of Hyatt children
on whom, in the face of all difficulties, the parents bestowed
the one gift they thought to be worth having—that of a liberal education. As Mrs. Gardiner points out in a letter to the
editor, the Hyatts are by no means through with Stanford.
Grandchildren, entering or preparing to enter, are numerous,
though not all of them bear the Hyatt surname.*

The association of the Hyatt family with Stanford is a prolonged
one. It began in 1891, the year that David Starr Jordan arrived in
California to establish the daringly conceived university in the Far
West. It was one of Dr. Jordan's duties to go forth and personally
explain the new institution, its plans and prospects, and on his schedule of speaking engagements was the city of Riverside.

Forty miles away—a hard day's travel by horse and buggy—lay
San Jacinto, where Edward Hyatt was principal of the four-teacher
school. To Edward Hyatt the founding of a new university was a
thrilling adventure, a making of dream-stuff into reality. Not for any
price would he miss the chance to hear the famous scientist and prospective university president. Seeing him in person, he might per-
suade him to grant admission to Stanford to Mr. Hyatt's grammar
school graduates, those whom he and his wife Margaret had tutored
to prepare them for college work.

Dr. Jordan had heard of "The San Jacinto Plan," and he was ready
to welcome to Stanford all students whom Mr. Hyatt recommended.
In that first year went engineer Charles H. Stoddard, and soon after
Frank Fowler, football star Ferd Snyder, and others who helped to
build Stanford's earliest years.

138

By 1900 the oldest Hyatt daughter, Inez, was registered at the University. She was followed by Shirley, '06; Marguerite, '08; Edward, Jr., '12; Victor, '17; Antonia, '18; Persis, '21; Phyllis, '24. The line did not end in '24, it no more than paused, for throughout the Forties eleven of Edward and Margaret Hyatt's grandchildren were on the University rolls.

Out of the many who came, many would be better fitted than I to write their reminiscences of the University, for I was of the minority group of Stanfordites who just barely managed to grasp the bottom rung of the success ladder. I did not, alas, understand that I was at Stanford for any purpose other than fun (in this I did very well). But I did at least recognize and appreciate the precision and accuracy of intellect of certain teachers and fellow students with whom I brushed elbows in Professor Mitchell's and Professor Brown's laboratories. It was Stanford, too, that gave me a glimpse of the wonder of the Greeks, and it was a class of Miss Mirrielees' that taught me to observe the malleability of words.

Then, too, there was Memorial Church which did not require me to conform to any doctrine, but which gave me an experience of beauty. I still remember Mr. Allen's choir direction and Sunday afternoon organ recitals with pleasure, although it is nearly forty years since I heard them.

*To those parents who turned defeat into victory by instituting in 1891 a great university in the name of their son, we are all their sons and daughters—individual volunteers to extend this great idea.*

GORDON HAMPTON, '35

# Failing with Praise

## HARRY F. HARLOW, A.B. '27, Ph.D. '30

*As an undergraduate Harry Harlow assisted Professor W. H. Miles, who was then studying factors influencing maze learning in rats. His graduate training was directed by the late Professor C. P. Stone.*

*On leaving Stanford he joined the psychology department of the University of Wisconsin. In 1949–50 and in 1954–55 he was chairman of the department. He resigned the chairmanship in 1955 to accept appointment to the George Cary Comstock Research Professorship. He is also founder and director of the University of Wisconsin Primate Laboratory and director of the University of Wisconsin Regional Primate Center. In 1956 he was awarded the Howard Crosby Warren Medal by the Society of Experimental Psychologists, and in 1960 the Distinguished Scientist Award by the American Psychological Association.*

*He has published widely in scientific journals and has served as editor of the* Journal of Comparative and Physiological Psychology *(1950–1962).*

I entered Stanford without the enthusiastic endorsement of the administration. My older brother had been accepted into law school, and my family started inquiring, a month before the new semester began, about my admission. The answer was a qualified no. Admission was closed, but I could come and compete by examination for 30 spaces that were always open.

When I entered the test room and looked around me, I decided that the competition was not going to be rugged. Obviously Stanford needed two tackles, two guards, and one center. They were admitted and so was I. Pop Warner was on his way to become a tradition.

My first day at Stanford I obtained a map and was pleasantly surprised on that dusty September afternoon to discover that Stanford had a lake. But in spite of my best exploratory efforts, it eluded me, and finally in desperation I asked what appeared to be a more sophisticated student, "Can you tell me where Lake Lagunita is?" "Yes," he said, "you're standing in the dead center." No center could have been more dead.

The courses I enjoyed most during my tour of duty were given by Dr. Martin on the history of South America. He lectured with brilliance and also with gaiety, wit, and charm. The first semester I made a B, but the second semester was an educational experience. The day before the midsemester examinations, an older man suggested to me that we get together and study for the test. The concept of deliberately studying for an examination had never before crossed my mind. That semester I made a straight A average; how I had achieved a B in the previous semester I shall never know.

Miss Mirrielees, for whom I have the warmest memories, turned me into a psychologist. I was an English major but was having some trouble with English 2B—exposition. It was agreed that a final book report would determine a B or a C grade. I slaved and was delighted to have the report praised, read before the class, and returned marked A. My final grade in the course was C+. I became a psychologist.

My last undergraduate day at Stanford brings especially clear memories. I graduated. It hadn't been easy. My grades in my junior year had been acceptable, and for the senior year the psychology department selected me as a candidate for their independent study program. Unfortunately, my independent study program was more independent than theirs, and Dr. Terman tenderly told me in June that I would not graduate—and I didn't graduate until the end of the summer session. But on that last, late day of the summer session I received my degree *cum laude*—doubtless one of the few men to fail in his senior year with praise.

After Commencement I found that I was so devoted to Stanford that I wanted to stay on as a graduate student. But just as my undergraduate stay turned out to be longer than expected, my graduate stay came close to being shorter. After a year and a half, Professors Terman, Miles, and Stone gathered together and, as I was later told, they came regretfully to the conclusion that I was so timid that I would never be able to speak effectively in public. Their solution was to recommend that I take a job teaching psychology and philosophy in a California junior college. Fortunately, their plans failed: the California junior colleges had standards I could not meet, and I was thus condemned to continue to a doctoral degree. I carefully withheld this part of my graduate school history until years later, when I had completed some hundred public speeches and a tour of duty as a National Sigma Xi Lecturer.

Memories are always tied to times. In 1924 one went from Palo Alto to the University on the now long-defunct "Toonerville trolley." It wasn't as dull a ride as one might think because the boys on the third floor of Encina Hall could throw an orange through a window with deadly accuracy. When I left in 1930 I went in a Model T Ford down the comparative safety of El Camino Real.

The in-between was a period when every male wore corduroy pants and a Stanford belt and everyone was your friend until you learned that "hello" was a Stanford tradition, not a word from *Webster's Unabridged Dictionary*.

The era of 500 coeds was almost at an end, but the limited 500 were still there. They swam in the pool beside the women's gymnasium in bathing suits—at least that was the official position—protected by a high wooden fence. A hardy breed of woodpeckers was constantly drilling holes in this fence, but the sanctity of the coeds' bathing suits was protected by full-time employees who continuously tacked tin squares over the apertures.

Things were not the same in the men's swimming pool, which was just across the road from the varsity tennis courts. There was a wooden fence, but the top of the high diving platform was above it. While the outcome of the Cal-Stanford tennis match was in doubt, a Japanese student climbed to the top of the platform and dived off with a regularity that was not monotonous—he was stark naked. As I remember, Stanford won when Holman beat Chandler in three sets.

In 1930 I went to the University of Wisconsin, but memories of Stanford have never wholly faded. Sometimes they fade in the day but seldom at night. In my dreams I am summoned before Professors Terman, Miles, and Stone and told that I can never hope to teach in a major university because I would never be able to lecture to large groups. They then suggest I find a job in a junior college. I waken while being rejected by the junior colleges and find solace in recalling that the University of Wisconsin has expressed its confidence in me by appointing me, five years ago, to a research professorship with the request that I continue to lecture to undergraduates.

It has been my pleasure, through the years, to revisit Stanford from time to time. One recent summer I served as visiting professor and found to my delight that the campus had not changed too much— I could still find the Mausoleum, the Post Office, and Lake Lagunita. My colleagues of the Twenties who had remained at the University were more mature, the old buildings were a little older, and the students seemed younger than their parallels of my day.

There were physical changes. Sequoia Hall was gone in deference to the atomic age, and the rose-surrounded tennis courts had disappeared. The Medical School had moved from San Francisco, and I had uneasy moments until I found that the cactus gardens still remained. On the road leading from Stanford to what had once been Mayfield, there had mushroomed housing for married students with symbolic white plastic domes to relieve their tattle-tale gray. Married undergraduate students? I believe two did get married in the Twenties.

*I do not know exactly what may be the objects of speculation, inquiry, investigation, scientific pursuit, artistic creation, or logical analysis which shall interest the future students of the university, the foundations of which I have ventured to lay.*

LELAND STANFORD
Address to the Trustees

# Stanford's Third President

## NORTHCUTT ELY, A.B. '24, J.D. '26

*Northcutt Ely is a senior partner of Ely, Duncan and Bennett, a Washington, D.C., law firm. At Stanford he was editor of* Chaparral, *and a member of Men's Council. He also wrote Ram's Head shows, and since his graduation has written several Bohemian Club Low Jinks.*

*In 1929–33 he was assistant to Secretary of the Interior Ray Lyman Wilbur. He is chief counsel for California in the Supreme Court case of* Arizona v. California *and the author of books on water resources and on mining and petroleum law.*

*His two sons, Northcutt, Jr., and Craig, both attended Stanford.*

The Stanford with which I became acquainted in 1920 was only 29 years old, and I was even younger. It is a school's perpetual youth that accounts for the nostalgia of alumni; the beloved of our youth has stayed young, while we have not.

Even a very young student in a very young university could sense that he was in the presence of something extraordinary. It was not just the Stanford spirit, which is an excellent thing, a sort of distillation of the romanticism of college life that has largely evaporated elsewhere. It was not just the unique environment of elbow room. Underneath was the spirit of a "university of high degree," a demand for excellence. And after a while, we discovered, still deeper, the steel core of this structure: the personality and character of Dr. Ray Lyman Wilbur, which shaped that of Stanford for a third of a century.

We speculated about him a good deal. Some alumni disliked him; we discovered that we liked him very much, for the very reasons that they did not: he was organized, a granitic character on which a

144

boy could depend. One of the kids remarked that Wilbur had an abstract quality of mind, call it mental discipline, or whatever, that would have made him a success in any walk of life. It did, as a matter of fact: pioneer, surgeon, professor, dean of the Medical School, University president, writer, Cabinet officer, president of the American Medical Association.

We discovered that this tall figure, aloof but courteous, looking more like Lincoln than Lincoln did himself, with piercing eyes and steady surgeon's hands, possessed a singular gift. It was the gift of catalysis, of making a boy or a man see in himself possibilities of performance that he did not know were there, and enabling him to rise to equal what Wilbur expected of him. It wasn't done by exhortation or emotion, or really by direct help or advice. He just quietly gave you tasks which seemed beyond your strength, gave you the assurance that you could do them because he knew that you could, and you accepted his appraisal because you believed he knew more about your powers than you did. The next thing you knew, a job was done, and you were on another impossible assignment for him. There never was any praise; just a laconic "Good job." This was part of the equation: your good performance was taken for granted, and needed no remark. Youngsters were learning that this austere character had a sense of humor better than theirs, he got things done, he enabled you to get things done yourself and feel proud, and he was as appreciative of excellence on the athletic field as we were. The Stanford teams began to win national recognition. One by one, national championships in track, swimming, football, and tennis were being brought home to hang on the walls, which by this time were beginning to grow a little ivy.

If he had to "drop someone off the edge of the campus," the farewell interview (I am told) was memorable. But he didn't hold it against the malefactor, any more than he disliked a bad appendix he might excise. As a matter of fact, he regarded many of these nonconformists as interesting and maybe superior specimens. He said if too much hell was being raised, it was a sign that the boys had too much leisure, and the curriculum needed tightening. Some of the faculty regarded this as putting the burr under the wrong saddle.

It illustrated, however, his principle that correction of abuses is bad administration; find the cause, don't just dress the sore.

His background as a doctor showed through all the time. He liked to say that life and time were man's only real assets. I never saw him waste either of them. But fishing and fellowship and reading were a good accounting for the life and time given a man, as were the hours of uninterrupted work and hard decisions. If Stanford in his time produced any "hackers," they were boys who hadn't got very well acquainted with Wilbur. He told an alumnus who wanted to get rid of him that he wouldn't succeed: "You're working only part time at firing me; I'm just as smart as you are, and I'm working full time at not getting fired."

Wilbur liked to tell about a mother who sent her son to Stanford to "have his sights raised." He had contempt for only one human animal: the bluffer, the liar. He reserved his highest respect for the fine professor, the fine surgeon, for that very reason: a man in either of those spots could not lie or bluff. If he tried it, bright students would expose the one, the issues of life and death would destroy the other. When confronted by a troublesome situation, he went to the heart of it, confronted his critic or opponent, never appeasing or by-passing. He said you had to go where the microbes were, and that was to the sickbed.

The antithesis of the bureaucrat, he was never willing to assume that a boy was wrong, his professor right, in case of trouble between them. That stemmed from his own experience as a Stanford freshman. He completed a whole semester's experiments in one of the scientific courses in two or three weeks, and was confronted by a lightweight instructor who refused to believe that this was possible. The reaction was impressive.

He had great respect for the young fellow with initiative. He said every generation had to discover for itself that the stove was hot. When he was a Stanford student, he had put in one summer in Arizona collecting specimens for a biology course. When someone suggested he should collect some baby skunks, housed under a porch, he regarded this as a challenge to his resourcefulness, and successfully gathered them in a sack. But the mother came home, so he brought her along, too, by the tail, as he had been told to do by a cowboy who said he was an expert. This was a mistake. Wilbur's horse got a whiff of the operation, broke away from the hitching post, and left him to walk into town, a social outcast. Dr. Wilbur's long face and big nose gave him a natural advantage in depicting a horse's indignation on smelling a skunk.

He used to say that when you believed you were 80 per cent right you ought to act; if you waited until you were sure you were 100 per cent right, you would be dead. He was a great man to "drive pegs" and move ahead. If he had a choice between shaping Stanford's budget so as to use its meager funds to keep one program healthy and vigorous, or support a half a dozen anemic ones, he could be ruthless in concentrating the available funds in one successful channel, and scrapping the others.

When Dr. Wilbur was Secretary of the Interior I served under him for four years. I began to realize the significance of some of the little vignettes I had seen of him at Stanford. When trouble arose with a Senate investigating committee, which was pursuing a subordinate of his, he appeared personally. Wilbur brought along a whole room full of files and demanded an immediate investigation of all of them. "Your quarrel is with me, not my subordinates, Senator." The Senator wasn't used to anything like this and dropped the whole proceeding like a hot potato. Wilbur had gone "where the germs are," and stayed until the patient was well.

He never laughed at anyone's expense unless the other fellow was in a position to talk back. But if you were fair game, watch out! At the Bohemian Grove, when a famous novelist asked the inventor of Harvard's "electric brain," the first big electronic computer, whether he could build one to write a novel, Wilbur said, with surprise, "From reading your stuff I thought you already had one; better ask him whether he can build one to read your books. That's what you really need."

When he was Secretary he performed an emergency appendectomy in a national park infirmary, off in the wilderness, the first time he had operated in 20 years. Asked if he felt nervous, he said as soon as he had that scalpel in his hand he remembered his Medical School professor, who said, "Just cut down through all those Latin names until you come to the gut." That typified his administrative methods, too.

He respected survival values—a redwood that had outlasted the centuries, a wild animal that successfully endured the desert, an athlete who gave everything he had and didn't quit, a scholar who gave that last five per cent of excellence—these coins all had the same ring to him. It was that final five per cent of performance that counted.

If joy is defined as pleasure in the success of others, Wilbur was a joyous man. He was happiest when his students, his faculty, his subordinates in the government earned recognition. He was quick to give it. He didn't aggrandize or expropriate their success for himself. If a man or boy didn't measure up, he was quietly switched to another track. Big decisions were made with minimum heartache or emotion. He conceded everyone his human dignity, which is the secret of the successful negotiator. When he complimented a boatman on making a good landing in a cross-wind, it wasn't patronizing; it was recognition of an expert by a man who was an expert in his own field, and both sensed it.

In short, if Stanford at 70 is a sturdy and growing youth, it is largely because nearly half of this youth was spent in the competent hands of Ray Lyman Wilbur. No person, no institution, could remain so long under that guidance without carrying his stamp from that time on. The high look about Stanford is the high look that distinguished Ray Lyman Wilbur: he raised our sights.

*. . . I can but think of the boyhood friendship of fifty years ago on this campus of Ray Wilbur and Herbert Hoover. . . . Who knows how much of the great progress of this University, the great stamp it has made upon the people of the world, comes from that boyhood friendship?*

LELAND CUTLER, '06

# Athletics at Stanford, 1918–1930

Before the first World War Stanford had made and deserved a tremendous reputation for fighting spirit.

After the War Stanford made a fine national reputation for developing great athletic teams.

Alumni Le Cutler, Dick Barrett, and Dr. Tom Williams planned the change to American football, and got the okay from Dr. Wilbur. They announced the great surprise in the spring of 1919, but Walt Ames, student manager, had been 'way ahead of them. Walt had known about it in 1918, and when he was allowed to pick a coach to start basketball, baseball, and track, he selected the best young football coach in the country, Bob Evans.

The alumni did not like him, thought he was a busher. He broke old tradition, such as refusing to name his first string Thursday afternoon. What a season of harassment for the brilliant young coach! The old alums had decided to get rid of him before the season started.

Bob tried to hire Boles Rosenthal, a young physician and All-American center from Minnesota, for $500 as his one assistant, and was turned down flat by the B.A.C.

So Boles became the line coach at Cal, and at the Big Game that year who should turn out to be the umpire but Boles! When, with 30 seconds remaining in the game, Stanford's Herc Bihlman blasting Cal tacklers right and left to score the winning touchdown on the tackle 'round play, who would it be but Boles who called Stanford for holding!

Referee Kienholtz looked at Boles in amazement and asked, "You call Stanford for holding on that play?"

"Yes," answered Boles.

"Well," said Kienholtz, shaking his head, "all I can do is call California offside. There is time for one more play."

So Bob was fired and there were troublesome times. Walt Powell did well next year with a new system, but the Cal Wonder Team was under full steam for the Big Game and rolled over Stanford 38–0.

In '21 it was another coach, Gene Van Ghent, and his season was worse. So during the winter, Le Cutler took off for Pittsburgh and persuaded Pop Warner to come out to Stanford. Pop had two years left on his contract, so he sent Andy Kerr out to start the Warner system, and in 1924 Glenn Scobey Warner took charge in person.

Wondrous things soon began to happen as Pop made Ernie Nevers into the nation's greatest fullback, the key to his system of reverses, fake reverses, and hand-offs to either halfback in the new double wing system.

But before the Big Game, Ernie broke his ankle. Pop put a thin, wiry halfback in his place, Peabody Cleveland, and trained him for the key job. But on the eve of the Big Game, Stanford athletic director Dr. Barrows, through a misinterpretation of the rule, declared Cleveland ineligible, and nothing could shake him.

So Cliff Hey, poorly prepared, took over the fullback spot for what turned out to be the greatest football game ever played on the Coast.

Stanford led at halftime, 6 to 0, by virtue of two goals kicked by Murray Cuddeback. But, in the second half, the Wonder Team, unbeaten in five years, started to roll. With four minutes to go Cal scored its third touchdown, the score was 20 to 6 for a routine win, and Andy Smith took out his first string backfield, and of course in those days they could not return to the game.

That's when the Warner ingenuity took over. He took Ed Walker from his end position and put him at fullback. Everybody in the stadium knew that the one thing Walker couldn't do was pass. Pop had tried to make a fullback out of him but had to give up. So, obviously, Ed was back there to hit the line, and the defenses moved up to stop.

Then came the pass that shocked the daylights out of everyone in the packed Cal stadium—everyone except Pop. A long pass from Walker, the guy who couldn't throw, to Cuddeback. Quickly they went back into formation. The lucky guy could never do it again in a million years, but of course he'd be trying it. Ed dropped back to pass, then passed off to Cuddeback, the defenses came up again to stop the run, and Cuddy threw another long one to Ted Shipkey over the goal line.

I've seen a lot of packed stadiums gone crazy, but nothing to equal this one. If the Christians had started tearing the lions apart and eating them, it could not have been a greater shock. People were moaning, banging themselves on the head, covering their eyes. Marjorie Curry Williams turned around on her knees, bent her head down to the seat, covered her ears with her thumbs and her eyes with her hands and shrieked, "Don't tell me. I can't stand it!"

Cuddy calmly kicked the goal; Stanford took the ball away, ran a couple of plays, and then the ungainly Ed Walker threw another miracle pass, over the goal line and into the sure hands of Cuddeback, who proceeded to kick the goal that tied the great Wonder Team, 20 to 20. No one who sat through that emotional experience can ever forget it.

And after the game Pop Warner drawled, "It'll be a long time before Cal wins another Big Game."

It was. Seven years later, in 1931, Cal nosed out Stanford 6 to 0.

Big Game Week in 1925 was a magic time. The very air was charged with electricity as Ernie Nevers, Dick Hyland, and Don Hill prepped for their first win over Cal in the modern American football era by running over UCLA 82 to 0. There was no mistake. Nevers was at his greatest as Stanford triumphed 27 to 14, and the reign of the Wonder Teams was over at last.

In 1926 USC, under Coach Howard Jones and powerful financial aid from the movie moguls, took an early lead of 12 to 0 over Stanford in a packed Coliseum. It looked like a rout, but George Bogue scored on the bootlegger play for one touchdown, and Hyland took Biff Hoffman's pass, 60 yards in the air, on the dead run for another. In the meantime Stanford was playing the finest defense I've ever seen, especially Dick Hyland, who ranged the entire backfield, knocking down passes and making tackles for no gain from the safety position.

In 1928, the golden Warner era climaxed with a victory over Army in Yankee Stadium. Army was great that year, and Red Cagle was the game's greatest player. Stanford was a 3-to-1 underdog, and rated no chance of winning by the Eastern critics. Before that day was over all New York, and the East, acclaimed Pop Warner as the wizard of football.

Cagle was on the verge of breaking all the way throughout the game, but he never quite did. Bob Sims and Mush Muller chased him across the field and back again, and always just caught him.

The big battle was in the line, and Army was famed for its right-hand "blocks" to the jaw. Which was all right with Bull Driscoll, whose retaliating right hands, as he whooped it up in glee, tamed a lot of West Pointers that day.

Stanford beat the East's best by the incredible score of 26 to 0, and the double wing system, like the T Formation under Clark Shaughnessy 12 years later, became the national rage in offensive football.

It would be hard to convince anyone of how much more the old school teams meant to the student bodies than they have for the past couple of decades. Perhaps this incident from the Antwerp Olympics will give some sort of measure. There were seven Stanford athletes on the track team, three from Cal. One day in the old broken-window schoolhouse, someone started the discussion, which is the most important, the Big Meet or the Olympics? A vote was taken, and resulted in a sweep, 10 to 0, for the Big Meet.

Stanford's representatives were hurdlers Feg Murray and Johnny Norton, shotputters Reg Caughey and Herc Bihlman, sprinter Morris Kirksey, javeline thrower Flint Hanner, and myself.

The Cal reps were Brick Muller, Johnny Merchant, and Pesky Sprott. The Olympics were the honor, the trip, the goal we had all dreamed of. But the Cal-Stanford competition was what we wished to win more than anything else. Today that seems incredible, but the Stanford-California competition, still strong, *was* incredible in those days.

Three- and four-sport athletes were common. Two from Oregon were amongst the finest I've ever known—Bob Pelouze and Ken Lilly, both of the class of 1920. Bob was an end and Ken was a halfback after their first year of rugby. Both were on the first conference championship basketball team, produced by Bob Evans in the winter of '20. Both turned up whenever possible for track meets, Bob a quarter-miler and Ken a sprinter, though you'd never believe it to look at him. In the '19 USC meet he led the great Charley Paddock all the way, and was inched out only at the finish; no one ever impressed the famous Paddock with his athletic ability as Ken did.

Returning from the Olympics in '20, Charley and I went out to the Polo Grounds to see the Giants. From high in the bleachers I saw the familiar form of Lilly just as he stepped into the dugout after fielding practice, and said, "Hey, there's Ken Lilly."

Charley turned and said, "Now you've gone too far. I admit Lilly is the greatest athlete of all time. He can do everything. But he can't just move off the Stanford campus onto the Giants' ball club."

But it was Ken, and later he went in as pinch hitter and lined a double to the fence. Ripley had been on the Olympic trip with us, and all Charley could say was, "This I can't believe, but I'm going to send it to 'Believe It Or Not'." However, Ken wrecked his knee sliding into second base, and it never healed. He used the $5,000 bonus from John McGraw to finish law school, but he would have become one of the great center fielders of all time.

Pelouze finished up his Stanford career as the number one pitcher for the baseball team, also coached by Bob Evans, which won the PCC championship. This was truly amazing, for in intramural games we used to hit Bob all over the lot, yet in the championship games he was unbeatable.

Bob gave a lift to every team he was ever on, just full of bounce and the joy of living, and when I think of Bob I automatically think of my introduction to American football. It was in the St. Mary's game in 1919, and Bob Evans told us to try an onside kick return of the first kick-off, with Pelouze onside.

We won the toss and notified the officials. I caught the kick-off on the five, started to run, then uncorked a long spiral and sat back watching Bob run, and how that guy did fly! On the second bounce the ball was just going over the goal line when Bob dived high in the air to take it and land over the line for a touchdown.

Freddie Adams was a rugby star before the War, a great end after the War, one of the finest basketball players we ever had, and put the shot in his spare time. And big Swede Righter, also rugby and American football, and next to Hank Luisetti still my idea of the greatest of all our basketball players.

In those days training rules were a matter of honor, and from the day the coach posted the sign, always headed by "1. No Drinking. 2. No Smoking. 3. No Chasing," the athlete was in training. They couldn't dance and they couldn't swim. Yet I never heard anyone complain, and I never knew of the modern habit of sneaking off Saturday nights "for a few beers."

There are many things about the 1919 season better forgotten. Bob Evans was really fired before the season ever started, but it didn't become known until ten days afterward, by which time most of the players were convinced that we had the genius of all coaches.

But a couple of things should go down in history. The alumni, remembering that Cal, in 1915, had been walloped 72–0 in their first game with Washington, decided not to schedule a Big Game that year, and did schedule Oregon in its place.

Half way through the season they discovered with a shock that student manager Walt Ames had quietly canceled the Oregon game and scheduled California in its place. Ah, those were the days of true individual initiative, and Walt was one of the giants.

And then there was the big student meeting of protest when the firing of Bob Evans became known. A few days before, the athletic director had called me in and told me gravely that he had something on Evans so serious that it would ruin his life if he were forced to divulge it at the meeting.

My God, a murderer? A rapist? I decided to relay the report to Bob, which I did. He exploded, "You tell that s.o.b. if he doesn't I'll squeeze it out of him if I have to kill him."

The meeting went on for hours in the old Stanford Inn, the student body serenading outside. We were getting no place with the alumni and faculty, and finally the A.D. arose and started gravely, "This I hate to say about any man, but I feel that it is my duty now."

Here it comes, I thought, and braced. For fifteen minutes the A.D. built up his tale of woe over the troubles of the past season. I think we were all ready to pop out of our skins. Finally he started to come to the point—"and this ingrate, this viper whom we have nourished to our breast and put in charge of our young manhood, called our president, the president of this great University, Dr. Ray Lyman Wilbur, a son of a bitch."

A murmur of horror swept the room, all except one great sacrilegious guffaw that rang out above everything else. I realized it came from my relieved throat.

Dr. A. T. Murray, father of Lin, Feg, and Bay, turned to me and demanded in unbelieving tones, "Robert, do you mean to say you can still support such a man as this?"

"Dr. Murray," I replied, "I believe you are the only person in the room I haven't heard speak of Dr. Wilbur in such terms at some time or another. The name has become in effect almost a term of endearment."

But this heinous charge broke up the meeting. I left, quite certain none of them would ever speak to me again.

So it came as a complete surprise when the Board named me as track coach a year later. It could only have come from the tremendous impression my brother Rick had made as coach in 1917, the year before the War.

But the Board was up against an emergency. The wonderful Harry Maloney had returned from France, where he had been head track and field coach of the Inter-Allied Games, personally appointed by General Pershing. After being tied down by track in 1920, Harry suddenly decided he had too many other interests in the department, soccer, boxing, fencing, wrestling, and his marvelous boys' Saturday classes. So they stopped the gap for a year by naming me.

In that 1921 season the Cal track team followed the football Wonder Team to a national championship, being the first coast team ever to win the ICAAAA in Boston, and it looked like a long, tough job ever winning from the Bears again.

We tied them in the dual meet, but at a sacrifice never to be forgotten. The half point that made it 65½–65½ was made by Mint Howell in the high jump, and Mint should never have been out of bed that day.

He lived in San Jose and commuted, but for ten days before the Big Meet he'd been home with the flu, sending word on Friday he was okay and would be on the train. He was, but he kept hidden out all the way to Berkeley. I never saw him until he was stripped in the dressing room, and he looked ghastly.

I said, "You can't jump today. Get your clothes on."

But Mint's deep set eyes glared at me as he blazed. "You know more than the doctor? He said I was okay." And he went out to jump.

They started at five feet and raised three inches at a time. Mint could scarcely get his feet off the ground, and he missed twice on every height, then forced himself over on his last trial by sheer will power, finally clearing the 6 feet that gave him the half point. Such guts I never have seen exceeded.

But from flu Mint sank into tuberculosis. He fought it for three years, and at times seemed to have it licked, but in 1925 it killed him.

In '24 Stanford finally broke the Cal run, and off we went to Boston. With all events over, it appeared that we had the ICAAAA won, but the hammer throw was going on at an outside field, and by the time those results came in Yale was the winner, we were back in third.

So in '25 the Board of Athletic Control decided not to send a team. Dr. Tom Williams was the chairman, and he gave me the bad news on a Sunday morning when the athletic department was gathered at Sam MacDonald's place for a barbecue. Tom thought it was a great joke on me. I told him if we didn't go USC would win. He thought that was even funnier, and said "We're going to send you up to Seattle for the Pacific Coast Conference meet. Maybe we can win that one."

By then the NCAA was becoming a very important national championship. The Board decided that Tiny Hartranft should be sent to Chicago as our representative because of his great three years in the shot and discus. Then they added Swede Leistner, the hurdler, Ted Miller, quarter-miler, and Bill Richardson, half-miler. We won the PCC meet big in Seattle and Tommy Work set a new conference record in the high jump, so they wired him onto the NCAA team.

I tried to get Biff Hoffman included, but graduate manager Paul Davis didn't think Biff had a chance to place in either the shot or discus.

Paul said, "Now, you have money for five men and yourself. If you really want Biff along why don't you sacrifice a bit and stretch it out between you?"

I guess we still owe Northern Pacific Railroad one full fare, but Biff made the trip. The morning we were to land in Chicago we held a little discussion on where we could afford to stay, when Bill Richardson got a bright idea. "There's a friend of mine from Culver whose dad is manager of a hotel in town, and he's working for his dad this summer. John Dewey. Let me give him a call as soon as we get in."

Bill was on the phone for about two minutes and came out with a big grin. "It's all fixed," he said, "come on." "Where are we going?" I asked. "To the Edgewater Beach," answered Bill. "What are the rates?" I wanted to know. "Three and a half a day," said Bill. "For room?" "No, for room and meals."

We were there for nine days, and every day they broke the all-time heat record. We'd go over to Stagg Field on the south side for workouts, and back to the cool Edgewater Beach. All the other schools were calling Stanford the millionaire university. At breakfast I'd see the weightmen stuffing away 5 or 6 dollars worth of food. I guess the word got back to the Farm, because coming back from Stagg Field after a workout, we ran into Paul Davis on Michigan Boulevard. He'd just gotten off the train, obviously to investigate. I took him to the Blackstone for dinner, waiting for the cross examination to start, but it just happened that we were seated at the table next to Mr. and Mrs. Herbert Hoover, and in his excitement Paul forgot about his quest.

Michigan was the strong team, a cinch to win, but our boys all came through that day, with Biff Hoffman winning the discus, Tiny Hartranft winning the shot and taking second in the discus, Swede Leistner winning the high hurdles in world record time, Ted Miller second in the 440, Bill Richardson, despite an attack of sinus, third in the 880, and Tommy Work fourth in the high jump.

In the meantime Michigan had some disappointments, and though nobody had paid any attention to our little band through the running, it was enough to win our first NCAA championship.

What a wonderful gang of athletes we had in those days of no proselyting, no athletic scholarships, and 15 Bs to get in. But there were no distracting influences to compete on the same level, or anywhere near it, with athletics.

We won the ICAAAA three years in a row, '27, '28, and '29, with marvelous competitors such as high jumper Bob King who won his event in the Amsterdam Olympics on a mud take-off; hurdler Ross

Nichols, quarter-miler Bud Spencer, the great weight team of Eric Krenz and Harlow Rothert, and that finest competitor of them all, Ward Edmonds, pole vaulter.

In '29 Ward started high hurdling and won the Cal meet when Nichols hit a hurdle. In the USC meet we needed a big place in the low hurdles. Ward had never run a flight of them, even in practice. He cleared 13-6 in the pole vault to ensure no worse than a second place, then had to run all the way up the straightaway as fast as he could to get to the start in time for the low hurdles. The Trojans had two great ones, both named Paine but not brothers (one had a "y" instead of an "i" in his name); both won national championships.

They didn't bother Ward. He came out of the chute four yards in the lead with a big grin all over his face, bucking a 12-mile wind, and he held it to the tape to win the meet.

We won the double in 1928, the ICAAAA in the mud at Harvard and the NCAA at Soldiers' Field in Chicago. That was the year Bud Spencer first broke Ted Meredith's 4.7 400-meter record, and Bud is one of the great Stanford comeback stories.

As captain of the winning freshman team, the first in the history of the two schools, Bud had won both hurdles and anchored the winning relay team against the Cal Frosh. He was coming home as a rushee of a fraternity group, when the car in which he was riding skidded in the gravel, turned over, and the corner post pinned Bud down, cutting straight across both eyes, clear down into his brain. After midnight that night Dr. Tom Williams and Dr. Kirk emerged from the old hospital, tears streaming down their faces. They had saved Bud's life, and, finding one optic nerve unsevered, had saved the sight of one eye. But Bud had asked not to have an anesthetic. He wanted to "see what was going on," and after six hours of grueling surgery, he had called each doctor by name, shook hands, and thanked them for all they had done for him. That was what got the doctors.

After a year Bud returned to the hurdles, but his judgment of distance was bad. He changed to the 440, and turned into the first of the truly great Stanford quarter-milers, his long, powerful stride carrying him in for a 47 flat 400 meters in the local Olympic tryouts. He didn't know it was fast and loafed in the last fifty yards, urging Johnny Morrison in for the second place.

# FIVE

Whether Herbert Hoover took office as President of the United States, President Wilbur obtained leave of absence to serve in his old friend's Cabinet. Absent or present, however, he continued to be the guiding force in the University throughout the twenty-seven years of his term.

Within that term, the United States passed through World War I; through the balloon-like inflation that accompanied and followed it; through the depression; and into World War II. If, as the accompanying reminiscences seem to show, these national misfortunes failed at the time to imprint themselves heavily on undergraduate minds, their imprint was deep enough on the minds of those in administration.

With prices rising steadily before and during the Twenties, private colleges the country over were feeling the strain and calling on their alumni for help. Stanford's alumni were still too few, too lately graduated, and therefore too poor to be of notable assistance. The Trustees, doing what they could, set fees in Law, in Medicine, then, reluctantly, a tuition fee of $40 a term for all undergraduates—this last reviving Senator Stanford's early pronouncement, later withdrawn, "Certainly there will be a charge for tuition. I do not believe anyone should have something for nothing."

Curiously, the imposition of the fee goes unmentioned in the reminiscences of alumni who were undergraduates at the time. Perhaps it does because $40, compared with charges later paid for sons and daughters, becomes all but invisible. Or perhaps, as Rosemary Drachman Taylor points out, the remembered pleasantness of undergraduate years pushes their occasional hardships out of mind. Whichever the reason, the fact is there—in a series of reminiscences, nobody remembered to complain.

All fees added together were still, however, inadequate. Only one expedient was left—a public solicitation. Other colleges were carrying on drives for money. Why not Stanford? Through its research and still more through its training programs for the professions, Stanford was serving the whole nation. The Board of Trustees and the president were at one in feeling it worth-while to find whether such service would be paid for.

The drive planned was not over-ambitious. Three million was its goal—one million for faculty salaries, one million for buildings, the third as the beginning of an endowment for the Medical School. Dr. Wilbur had, of course, taken an active part in the planning. He was equally active in the campaign, with no hesitation over soliciting. The University needed support; any individual, in his often-expressed opinion, should be proud that he was offered the chance to help.

However worthy the cause and however vigorously pursued, the drive, nonetheless, was partly a failure. Only one of its three millions was raised in full. It did, however, dispel whatever remained of the once general belief that Stanford University was the Stanfords' school and theirs only. Also, for good or bad, it set a precedent: For the first time, fund-raising was recognized as a prime presidential responsibility, one to which his time and strength were rightly given. One other thing it accomplished, too. In the West, as had been much earlier true in the East, some of those who were personally unconnected with Stanford yet came to feel that the University had a claim on them. "You daren't die within five hundred miles of Cambridge," a Massachusetts man worded the claim, using an older institution as his example, "it isn't decent to die as near as that and not leave something for Harvard in your will." Harvard had had, of course, a several hundred years' advantage in the instructing of its public, but Stanford had made a beginning and was edging inch by inch toward that same solution of some of its money needs.

Inside the University, both before and after the drive, alterations and additions went on. Alterations had to be only such as could be made with little cost. Additions, if they were to be accepted, must bring with them the means for their installation.

One of the alterations was the grouping—"the regrouping" President Wilbur called it, of the nonprofessional departments into schools, each school presided over by a dean who stood as buffer between professor and president. . . . Another was the addition of an aptitude test to the requirements for freshman admission from the secondary schools. The terms of admission had long lain heavily on professional minds. Were those admitted actually the best? Or were they only the more docile and well-mannered? Or had they profited from attending a school where A's were more numerous than elsewhere and whoever wanted recommendations was sure to get them? With the limiting of the number of freshmen to be taken in yearly, the questions doubled their importance. The aptitude test, adopted in 1924 and made compulsory for all freshmen, set faculty minds at rest for the moment—though only for the moment.

One of the additions made was that of the Food Research Institute, financed from outside the University and established for study of the production and distribution of food. Another was the Graduate School of Business, except for one at Harvard the only such school in the United States. It was underwritten for five years by individuals and corporations on the Pacific Coast, and by the end of the five years was amply able to make its own way to further financing.

With these two to bolster what was already there, it is understandable that Dr. Wilbur could refer in his memoirs to the depression when it arrived in 1929 as a "not too 'ill wind' after all." He would, though, have found few teachers or students to second him, for to both it had been an ill wind indeed, cutting salaries, reducing enrollments, taking its heaviest toll in the professional schools, and blowing in distracting gusts long after '29 was past.

*He—President Wilbur—was the leader, often in the background, rarely credited fully, sometimes not appreciated, but always forging ahead.*

J. PEARCE MITCHELL, Registrar, 1925–45

# A Friendly Place

GEORGE GRIBBIN, A.B. '29

*George Gribbin came to Young and Rubicam, Inc., as a
copy writer in 1935. He was made copy supervisor in 1942,
left to enter the Army as a private the following year, and
returned a captain in 1945. In 1951 he was promoted to vice-
president and head of radio-TV commercials. By 1954 he
was copy director and in charge of both print and radio-TV
copy. In 1956, two years before he was to become the agency's fourth president, he was appointed a senior vice-president.*

*Mr. Gribbin is a member of the Advisory Board of Manu-
facturers Trust Company, New York; a member of the Public
Relations Advisory Committee for the United Hospital of
New York; Chairman of the Public Information Committee
of the 1961 campaign drive for the American Red Cross in
Greater New York.*

*He lives in Greenwich, Conn., and is the father of six
children.*

Before coming to Stanford in 1927, as a junior, I had been at the
University of Wisconsin. At Wisconsin one did no more than say
hello—after a decent interval of, say, one or two months of polite
silence—to the person seated next to him in class. No easy, extended
conversations. And you never took the liberty of speaking on campus to a student to whom you had not been formally introduced.

Registration day at Stanford I walked over to the spot near the
railroad tracks where the old trolley picked you up. Before the trolley
arrived that day, a student in what would now be called a convertible
but in those days was known as a roadster stopped and asked several
of us standing there if we would like a ride to the Quad.

Surprised, I climbed in with the others, and said to myself, "What
a friendly place!"

After registering, I was walking along the arcade when a young man in moleskins, obviously a sophisticate, stopped me and with hand extended and a warm smile said, "My name is David Hulme, what is yours?"

I was so amazed at the nonformality and the wonderful friendliness that—for a few seconds—I could not even remember my own name. Those few seconds were long embarrassed minutes of time, but eventually a piece of knowledge that I had carried for some nineteen years came to my rescue and I, too, smiled broadly and said, "Mine is George Gribbin. Good to know you."

And it *was* good to know him and to begin to know Stanford.

*Stanford University is a democratic institution, and it proposes to remain so. It aims to continue, as in the past, on the principle set down by Senator Stanford in his last letter to President Jordan:*
"I want the standard of social life to be
not according to wealth, but to depend upon
manhood and womanhood."
*Stanford University Bulletin,* Series 8, No. 79.

# A Sense of Serious Purpose

## MONROE E. SPAGHT, A.B. '29, Ph.D. '33

*Monroe Spaght, leaving Stanford, joined Shell Oil Company as a research chemist. He was later in refinery operations, then vice-president and president of Shell Development Company and executive vice-president of Shell Oil Company. In 1961 he became president of Shell Oil.*

*He is a member of the Board of Trustees of Stanford University and president of the Shell Companies Foundation, Incorporated; also, a director of Stanford Research Institute and of the Institute of International Education.*

In my years at Stanford there were problems in gaining an education that seem less commonplace today. A college education was often accomplished with real sacrifices by parents as well as students. A mother's insistence that a good education be obtained could be the motivation, while the financial problem would be real and constant. This was my circumstance, nor was I alone. Life at Stanford, for all its color and fun, had a constant undertone of seriousness.

Not unrelated is my recollection of Edward Curtis Franklin, Professor of Chemistry, easily one of the greatest teachers it has been my privilege to know. He taught Organic Chemistry and had that genius of displaying the order and the beauty of his subject. Yet my most vivid memory of that fine man was his intolerance of the person who neglected to study. His concern was not only that the individual was missing his opportunity to gain knowledge, but equally that he was being unfair to whoever was making a sacrifice to put him there.

Also in my list of greatest teachers was Charles Moser in Engineering. His classes in Hydraulics and Strength of Materials attracted students from every discipline. I remember some of the same traits about him as about Franklin. He convinced us that his subjects were clean and simple, and the answers to problems obvious. But

166

again, the most vivid recollection is his underlying sense of serious purpose. I recall his charge to us as he announced an examination for the next meeting.

"You may bring with you anything you can get through the door; books, slide rules, calculating machines. I shall insist on but one thing. You shall not consult your neighbor. Someday you will have similar problems to solve, and your neighbor won't be there to help."

In Moser's eyes our study was for a purpose, to gain the knowledge to do useful "chores" (as he called them) later in life.

It was this sense of serious purpose, almost of urgency, that most impressed me in those Stanford years. My personal circumstances undoubtedly colored my view, yet I think it was more than that. Stanford was blessed with great minds and gifted teachers. In concert with the times, they molded a generation of serious people.

If I could do it all over again, I would want it to be that way. One hopes we may be worthy of the faith of our mothers and the contributions of those fine people. To be so involves, I suggest, not only good and useful performance in our time, but in turn working dedication to serious and continuing education for generations to come. I hope that Stanford can always instill that charge in its sons and daughters.

*When we consider the endless variety of the wants and desires of civilized society, we must fully appreciate the value of labor-aiding machinery, and the necessity for having this of the best character. Too much attention, therefore, cannot be given to technical and mechanical instruction. . . .*

LELAND STANFORD
Address to the Trustees

# No Longer a Minority

KENNETH COOPERRIDER, A.B. '31

*Kenneth Cooperrider grew up in Arcata (Humboldt County), California, and attended school there, including two years at Humboldt State College. He taught in various California high schools, then served in the United States Navy as a communications officer during World War II. Following this he was Associate Editor of* Fortnight Magazine. *He has been with* Sunset Magazine *since 1949, and is currently its managing editor. He is married, lives in Menlo Park, and is the father of two sons, one of whom, Neil Cooperrider, is now a Stanford student.*

Those of us who came from the isolated parts of the West had a special reason for appreciating "Die Luft der Freiheit weht" at Stanford. Intellectual freedom of this sort was a new experience for us. Instead of being in a minority that valued learning and culture, we were suddenly surrounded by hundreds of our contemporaries who took these things for granted.

Another impression of Stanford in "those days"—what a tremendous collection of talent in music, literature, journalism, science, politics, every field. And all this among people no older than their early 20's. This is undoubtedly quite as true today, but in my day it was an important part of the impression the University made on the newcomer.

*As a place . . . where certain standards can be insisted upon, where one can work as part of the long tradition of civilization and learning, the university is probably the most congenial and productive atmosphere.*

RICHARD SCOWCROFT, Professor of English

# "Whatever in Myself I Find . . ."

## Lawrence A. Kimpton, A.B. '31, A.M. '32

*Lawrence Kimpton, a member of the Stanford Board of Trustees, was Dean of Students and Professor of Philosophy at Stanford from 1947 to 1950. Prior to 1947 he was both chief administrative officer for the University of Chicago's atomic bomb project and the holder of a series of administrative posts there. On leaving Stanford he returned to the University of Chicago, first as vice-president in charge of development, then as chancellor and professor of philosophy, and finally as president, a post he resigned in 1960 to become general manager of planning for the Standard Oil Company of Indiana.*

My first memory of Stanford is that of standing at the gate to Palm Drive on my arrival and wondering if I could ever succeed in this big, wonderful University. I remember the confusion of Encina Hall as we registered for our rooms. In this confusion I ended up next to a chap named Dick Dole, and I was overwhelmed as a naïve youngster from Kansas City to discover that he was from the remote Hawaiian Islands and a member of the famous Dole pineapple family.

My first year at Stanford was both awesome and wonderful. I remember the terror I felt in shaking the hand of the great Ray Lyman Wilbur at the presidential reception in the gruesome marble morgue in which he lived, but I clearly recall how beautiful the girls were at the dance that followed the reception. In the brave new freedom we felt, I and my roommates at Encina stayed up until 4:00 a.m. every night for the first two weeks, until we finally got tired.

I had been a mediocre high school student, completely unchallenged by my secondary school environment. I believe I first became aware of the world of the mind in my freshman course in Citizenship, as it was called in those days. I had a young instructor whom I regarded as the most learned man of our time, and he shocked me into an awareness of the importance of rigorous thinking. It was not until I took Professor Hulme's course in my sophomore year—the name of which I forget—that I became aware of the wonders of the humanities. Hulme was a picturesque and postured fellow, and as I see him now, no great shakes as a scholar; but he had precisely that enthusiasm for culture and that touch of ham that "sends" the undergraduate, and leads him on to a wider and sterner discipline. And it was finally in my senior year that I came to know Henry W. Stuart, the head of the Department of Philosophy. He gave a seminar 'way over my head in Kant's *Critique of Pure Reason,* but I grasped enough of it to awe me with the power and sweep of Kant's philosophy and the magnificence of Stuart's teaching. I still think of Stuart as one of the finest minds I have ever known, and I ended by writing my Doctor's thesis on Kant.

But blending with and quite as important as all these things to me during that period was the charm of the campus and the beauty of California; the soft green hills in the springtime, Lagunita in the moonlight, the mosaic over the Church, the smell of coffee and sweet rolls as I took a late, quick breakfast in the basement of Encina, the spine-tingling thrill of beating UCLA once at football, the wonders of "The City" at night, and the warmth and intimacy of college friendships.

These are just some of the things that I remember of my undergraduate days at Stanford. They are all made tender by nostalgia, of course, and the difficulties and the worries about exams and money and girls and grades are all erased. I can truthfully say, however, that Stanford was a turning point in my life, and whatever in myself I find today of quality and goodness, I attribute in large part to my alma mater.

# Debater to Diplomat

## ROBERT McCLINTOCK, A.B. '31

*Robert McClintock, now United States Ambassador to
Argentina, has served in many diplomatic and consular posts.
In 1959 he was the recipient of the Superior Service Award
of the Department of State. He also lectures and writes on
subjects dealing with diplomacy.*

S O MANY MEMORIES of Stanford are in my mind that they could not
be contained in 3,000 words; even less boiled down to fifty. I
shall, however, endeavor to give three highlights of my Stanford
experience.

The thing which impressed me most when I arrived at Stanford
and which has served as a guide in subsequent life was the very motto
of the University: "Die Luft der Freiheit weht." It was the fact that
the wind of freedom actually did blow at Stanford which made the
educational experience there different and more inspiring than might
have been the case in a more regimented institution. Furthermore,
in my subsequent career in the Foreign Service I have found myself
always striving to achieve situations in diplomacy "where the wind
of freedom blows." Given the trend of the world during the past generation, with its second universal war and the encroachment of total-
itarian imperialism, the struggle to maintain conditions where the
wind of freedom could continue to blow has, in my case at least, been
a lifelong one.

The second reminiscence relates to David Starr Jordan. It was
my privilege as a freshman at Stanford to attend the Thursday evening meetings at Dr. Jordan's house. On these occasions he would
reminisce over the amazing variety of experiences which he had accumulated in a long life; and students who were privileged to hear
the Chancellor Emeritus never forgot his fund of knowledge, his wisdom, and his wit. At times, the "Dippy" would publish aphorisms
from Dr. Jordan, such as: "The bird in hand is not worth ten in the

171

bush. You cannot afford to sell your future at so heavy a discount."
"Boys who are *sent* to college often do not amount to much. From
the boys who *go* to college come the leaders of the future." "You
spend your entire life in your own company. An educated man is
better company than an uneducated one."

The third reminiscence deals with my experience of Stanford debating over a period of more than four years. Thanks to the efforts
of Professor Gordon Emerson and his then assistant (now Professor)
Leland Chapin, Stanford had developed the most urbane and at the
same time competently researched style of extemporaneous debating
of any university in the United States. Unlike as in many other
schools, no first-class Stanford debater ever read or memorized a
speech. I chanced to be selected as Captain of the All-America Debating Team which went to England in 1930, made up of three men—
one from the University of California, one from U.S.C., and one from
Stanford. To have won thirteen out of fifteen debates in Great Britain
by audience decision showed how the Stanford tactics of debate,
similar as they were to those in the House of Commons and in the
Unions of Oxford and Cambridge, had proved their worth. I can
only add that the habits of thought, of mental discipline, and of the
ability to speak easily and surely on one's feet have been the single
greatest asset, in a professional sense, which I took with me from
Stanford.

# A Legend Smashed

## Winstead Sheffield (Doodles) Weaver, A.B. '37

*Doodles Weaver is known to several generations of Stanford students as a sort of Till Eulenspiegel, an almost legendary individual responsible for fantastic pranks during his undergraduate days. The legend is not supported by his career on either side of his years at Stanford. At his preparatory school he was an honor student, a letterman in four sports. In his later activities he has been successful in many movies and on television and is the author of science-fictions and of comedies.*

*For amusement he fishes for sharks, maintains his two classic automobiles, composes music and words. He lives in Beverly Hills, is married and the father of two children.*

ONE SPECIFIC OCCURRENCE overshadows all my memories of five years' attendance at the University, far superseding any legendary gyrations and antics attributed to me (most of them vilifyingly false); that was the day of my graduation in June, 1937. Because of three divagations from the normal routine of studency—a leave of absence, a spring employment as athletic director of a boys' camp in Vermont, and an altercation with the offices of the administration—my stay at Stanford enjoined an extra year (not much time, actually). Because of my overt activities as performer, musician, comedian, play-actor, fraternity president, rally committeeman, columnist for the *Daily*, contributor to the *Chaparral*, yell leader, party organizer, traveler, delver into literature, psychology, and philosophy, plus cavorting as letterman in three sports (football, when I was on the Indian squad that won two games in Hawaii in '36, basketball, and soccer)—because of these diverse activities and an attitude of pleasant optimism which I have never lost, my tangible status with the interior mechanics of the University powers was somewhat ephemeral, and twice Dr. Ray Lyman Wilbur had questioned me at length

173

concerning my objectives. Nonetheless, in spite of arched eyebrows, I was graduated with high grade points, and herein lies my tale—a small but intense tableau: When I stepped to President Wilbur to receive my diploma (*not* wearing roller skates as has been rumored), that fine gentleman halted the line of robed seniors for the only time that afternoon, and as he shook my hand he spoke some highly complimentary words and presented me with an autographed copy of his book, *Stanford Horizons.*

One might wonder at the importance of this reminiscence—therefore, let me elaborate: the words I write, the occasion, that event of years ago are simply a part of a pin prick into the diaphanous bubble of baloney built around Doodles Weaver. The decades, the bull sessions, and the fables all have combined to distort my Stanford days into an incredible daze. No one likes lies—especially the one who bears the brunt of the fallacies. Contrary to popular belief, my undergraduate existence was not a series of idiotic pranks, wildman gyrations, and uninhibited calisthenics of a gleeful thoughtless buffoon whose main motive seemed to be the invention of sordid practical jokes, but that of a near-normal energetic young man who used the Stanford stage as a good foundation for a career that has been highly rewarding.

I hope your disappointment is not overwhelming if my essay has served only to smash the Weaver legends into flinders.

*I approve of lighting the front of the Church. When students are driving up the avenue at night, if the light does not turn their thoughts to higher things, at least it gives them a mark to steer for.*
ROBERT M. MINTO, Chaplain of the University

# "...documents for breakfast..."

## VICTORIA SCHUCK, A.B. '30, A.M. '31, Ph.D. '37

*Victoria Schuck has been professor of Political Science and Co-director of the Amherst-Mount Holyoke Colleges Political Studies Center since 1940. She is also a trustee of the University of Massachusetts, a member of the Massachusetts Building Authority, Chairman of the South Hadley Planning Board, and Consultant to the* Encyclopaedia Britannica.

*Recently she finished a term as Secretary of the American Political Science Association and two terms as a public member of the Massachusetts Commission on Interstate Cooperation.*

*She has been consultant to the Temporary Commission on the State Constitution in New York, president of the New England Political Science Association, and president of the Massachusetts Division of the American Association of University Women.*

*During the War she was with the Office of Price Administration in charge of planning for Local Boards. In 1945 she was a member of the Secretariat of the United Nations Conference in San Francisco which wrote the United Nations Charter.*

*She is the author of numerous articles in professional and popular journals.*

YOU ASKED FOR reminiscences of Stanford? As I begin to write, all sorts of disparate memories come to mind—a freshman's glimpse of the beauty of Palm Drive and the façade of the Church silhouetted against a globe of orange sinking beyond the hills, the days in Roble and the later years on the Row, the flipping of cards in the Stadium to outline the Axe in color for Cal fans at the Big Game and the open house and dash to the Mark in the City afterward, the coloring of Easter eggs for the Chi O Easter hunt for the children at the Convalescent Home and their eager faces, the gatherings of small clumps of us in the Cellar after a political theory class to ponder further upon the philosophy of Aristotle or Locke, and so on and on.

But most of all for me, Stanford means the intellectual vigor, the good teaching and related research, and the professional and personal values of individual members of the faculty. Professor Graham Stuart, Professor Edith Mirrielees, Dean Mary Yost I came to know as friends—and there were many others.

But the influence of three men into whose classes I drifted almost by chance has been dominant through the years. First, Professor Edgar E. Robinson, a penetrating historian. His course in American history entitled the Westward Movement and fondly referred to by his students as "Westward Ho!" introduced me to the meaning of the peopling of this continent. His lectures—models for any future college teacher—presented perceptive interpretations and were nothing short of thrilling. Although his advanced courses were primarily for history majors, he did allow me to enter his pro-seminar and then his seminar. In these advanced courses he turned his students into historical sleuths and taught us the ways of historical writing and analysis. Who even now could forget how we tracked down through conflicting accounts in newspapers, biographies, diaries, histories, the actual incidents surrounding the discovery of gold in California.

If Professor Robinson led us into the path of scholars, it was Professor Thomas S. Barclay who left us with the mark of empiricism. He vividly disentangled the theories and practices of political parties and of interest groups and their relation to the issues before Congress. His scholarly intrepidity tore into many sacredly held political myths. He introduced us to the mysteries of the *Congressional Record* and the proceedings of national party conventions while we wrote papers on the "sons of the wild Jackass," as the unorthodox midwest Republicans in Congress were labeled at that time. His first-hand accounts of Democratic conventions, related with wry humor, made potential delegates out of all of us. To this day I have not ceased racing to the quadrennial Republican and Democratic conventions to report their proceedings for newspapers and to collect new illustrations for the classroom. Once introduced to this course I knew I could never leave the field of politics.

And if Professor Barclay taught us the need for empirical research, it was Professor Edwin A. Cottrell, tall, bespectacled, reserved New Englander (in appearance like a quiet de Gaulle), who took us beyond pure research to show its use in the world off campus. Adviser to governors and managers, researcher for state commissions and charter groups, he brought his students into these research projects with him. From the gloomy document room in the library (lighted up, by the way, with the humor of the librarian, Miss Minna Stillman) where we learned to live off documents for breakfast, he directed us into the process of converting our learning into action. Yet there was something incongruous about this, for one would rarely suspect Mr. Cottrell of being an activist. Withal he impressed upon one the need for imagination and creativeness in thinking about political behavior and governmental institutions. How encouraging Mr. Cottrell was to a woman who dared venture into the field of politics and public administration!

These men welcomed me and others into the warmth of their homes. Often we sat in their gardens and enjoyed the kind of close association not ordinarily thought a part of the ethos of a large university. Their example led many an undergraduate into graduate work and ultimately into teaching.

These are among my most vivid reminiscences.

*I would like to believe that you will take with you, as a heritage, something of the spirit of the old Stanford, as well as the benefits of the new.*
    Thomas S. Barclay, Professor of Political Science

# Prelude for Public Service

## NAJEEB E. HALABY, A.B. '37

*Jeeb Halaby is the head of the Federal Aviation Agency. Prior to this appointment he was a Pacific Coast business executive and secretary-treasurer of Aerospace Corporation, which advises the Air Force on technical problems. He has also held technical posts in both the State and Defense Departments in Washington.*

*During World War II he was a test pilot for Lockheed Aircraft Corporation and for the Navy. He still holds a commercial pilot rating. In 1945 he flew the first transcontinental jet flight.*

*He was born in Texas, the son of a Syrian immigrant, and describes himself as "half Syrian, half Scotch-Irish, and all Texan."*

THE PERIOD of my undergraduate stay at Stanford—1933 to 1937—was one of depression and exhilaration. We arrived at the Farm, were herded into Encina, and crammed indiscriminately three in a room, to start the great adventure of college. There was only a little selection and no psychological evaluation. America was in depression, and Stanford accepted most of those who applied—thank God!

Finding, after the first ten days of facing 260-pound Jack Walton, that I was too light for football, I turned to the rather dreary alternative of soccer and the goal of a Circle "S." As the winter moved into spring I, like many other 17-year-old freshmen, discovered—GIRLS! This Eden-discovery was and continues to be one of man's highest achievements.

The great things of Stanford—the freedom to think and talk and roam, the joyous life that Miss Mirrielees put into literature, the dignity and high dutifulness of President Wilbur, the glorious freshness of the golf course in springtime with the dapper Coach Twiggs presiding, and the sharing of all the new ideas with the friendly faculty and a student body, some eager, many indifferent—all of these things stand out almost 25 years later.

Of all the memories, however, some of the best revolve around that great teacher—Tom Barclay. Without ever straying over the line of teacher-student propriety, he effortlessly gained the confidence, the respect, and the affection of his students. He did what every great teacher must—he taught us to yearn to learn and to act in the service of the public. He made politics the most exciting pursuit, he made public service a high calling, and he did all this in one of the most challenging periods in the history of American politics, the coming of the New Deal.

*You of today and countless others of earlier days have learned here to respect facts, to honor loyalty and honesty, to think straight, and to realize your obligations to your community and to your country.*

THOMAS S. BARCLAY, Professor of Political Science

# Memories: Vintage '36

## ALAN CRANSTON, A.B. '36

*Alan Cranston is State Controller of California. As an undergraduate he was one of Dink Templeton's quarter-milers. His father, William Cranston, was graduated from Stanford in '01.*

*Prior to his election as Controller he was in the real estate, investment, and property management business in Palo Alto; was a foreign correspondent in Europe and Africa; an executive in the federal government in World War II, until he enlisted in the army; a leader in mobilizing support for the United Nations, and president of the California Democratic Council in the early '50's.*

*He is married and the father of two sons.*

THE FARM was all farm then—the red roofs nestling in the hills, the hills yellow in summer and fall, green in winter and spring, splashed year 'round with the darkness of the many, many trees. There was no shopping center then, no industrial park, no subdivisions, no veterans' hospitals. The community clustered from the Quad and Encina out through the fraternities, sororities, and aging homes of professors and old-timers, tapering off out where the Frenchman dug his cave and built his bridge across his long-gone lake.

The men of '36 came to the campuses in cords, the women in bright blouses and skirts and low shoes. . . . Most were afoot, or pedaled bikes around—few cars on campus then. The Depression was on in full force. . . . Herbert Hoover, '95, sat grimly in the White House, challenged by Franklin Roosevelt from far-away New York.

One Adolf Hitler was on his way to power in Germany. His name was known only to a handful of us, but he would shape our lives and shake our world.

Depression . . . WPA . . . New Deal . . . Hitler . . . Mussolini . . .

180

Stalin . . . Ethiopia . . . League of Nations . . . Merriam . . . Upton Sinclair . . . Lincoln Steffens . . . the Waterfront Strike. . . . These and countless other names, places, concepts, events, eruptions, made their way into many a classroom debate and many a night-long bull session in Encina and Roble, Toyon and Lagunita, and out along the Row. . . . There were professors and instructors, and many a '36er, too, who insisted these topics be explored, criticized, taken apart, put together, turned upside down. These were the ones, in class and out, on campus and off, who made hitherto nonthinkers think, who seized upon the English major, the would-be lawyer, doctor, scientist, the would-be master of money and banking, and carried him on to the significance of affairs beyond his chosen specialty. They hammered and hammered on the anvil of our time, striking sparks—sparks destined through us to have their influence in a world of upheaval. . . .

It was pleasanter, and simpler far, to count and recount the exploits of our incredible Vow Boys—Bobby Grayson, Bones Hamilton, Monk Moscrip, Owl Eyes Alustiza, and the rest, slashing and slouching around the stadium, clowning and cavorting around the campus, always demolishing USC, Cal, and virtually all comers—and collapsing every New Year's Day in the Rose Bowl.

A mere youngster a class or so behind, Hank Luisetti came along to transform Stanford basketball into something Stanford basketball had never been before; and after winter came spring and Dink Templeton track miracles, a handful of stars conquering all save invincible USC . . . with skinny Chuck Nimmo scratching his legs 'round and 'round the track to victory after victory in the mile, tiny Sammy Klopstock leaping over the highest hurdles to wins Saturday after Saturday, Levy and King heaving discuses at each other in their ferocious competition. . . .

There were the dashes in the dusk on the brand new, amazing, four-lane Bayshore to San Francisco—to dance at the Palace, the Mark, the St. Frantic to "Smoke Gets in Your Eyes" and to "Body and Soul." . . . Prohibition came to its happy ending while Ray Lyman Wilbur dourly warned that gasoline and alcohol did not mix.

There were the afternoon adventures and the week-end wanderings through the foothills, sometimes past the Frenchman's Tower (with a pause to carve initials and hearts in the red bricks) and on up the Page Mill and over the Skyline, and sometimes up the Alpine twisters and across the mountains to the beaches and cliffs of Pescadero, Half Moon Bay, Año Nuevo . . . the lazy days of spring, the tranquil time of summer, when the drums and bugles of Hitler, Mussolini, and the Japanese War Lords seemed so far, so very far away.

There were all the hopes and plans, the dreams and visions of the future. . . . There were those who prepared by study—full attention in class, copious notes, full-time residence in the library, oceans of midnight oil—and straight A's. . . . Those who prepared by laughing and living—and straight D's. . . . And a few who led the full life: A's in studying, A's in laughing, A's in living.

Among us were the impatient ones who hoped that June, 1936, would hurry along, would soon arrive so we'd be out in the world. . . . And the ones, wiser perhaps, who somehow knew we were out in the world already—and that the world would never, never be better, never, never again be quite like this. . . .

"Oh, that thou couldst know thy joy, ere it passeth, barefoot boy" —so few, so very few, knew in those days that this was addressed to us, too, not just to the kids in kindergarten, not only to the lads and lasses back in grammar school.

*Education is the prime and most abiding asset of any society. It is susceptible of manipulation, as in the police state. But when uninhibited by the state, when guided by a sense of responsibility to society, it is capable not only of overcoming pestilence and poverty but also enhancing that freedom which places and preserves the individual in the center of things.*

J. E. WALLACE STERLING

# Athletics at Stanford, 1930–1945

Stanford's athletic fame continued to grow through the '30s with Coach Tiny Thornhill's famed Vow Boy teams and, of course, the team that revolutionized football from one end of the land to the other, the great Clark Shaughnessy's 1940 Wow Boys team with the new T formation.

At the 1961 Big Game the third Vow Boy, Bob Reynolds, was honored by his election to the national Hall of Fame. At the big tackle's side were teammates Bobby Grayson and guard Bill Corbus, Ernie Nevers from the mid-Twenties, and Frankie Albert from the Wow Boys.

Three Hall of Famers from the same team is the most, yet when the ceremony was over, Grayson told me, "Frankie Alustiza and Monk Moscrip were the ones who made the team go. They should be on there." Yes, and so should Bones Hamilton!

The Vow Boys came along just at the time when Pop Warner resigned because high grades and tuition made it impossible, in his judgment, to get the material. But the freshmen had made the vow never to be beaten by USC, and they never were.

Their first meeting was in 1933 at the Coliseum. The Stanford team wasn't given an outside chance against the powerhouse Trojans, the greatest team ever turned out by Howard Jones.

The night before the game the green team was marooned in the mudflats outside Watsonville when the Lark became stuck, and Southern Pacific trouble crews battled through the night to get them on their way. And finally did about 8:00 in the morning.

From there they had the clear signal, Casey Jones at the throttle and here I come. The game was postponed a half hour. The Stanford team was bundled into fast cars and rushed into uniforms at the Coliseum. SC's scooter, Cotton Warburton, scored on 'em the first time he had the ball, and it looked like a rout.

But that was the last time that day. From there on the Vow Boys outfought and outplayed them up and down the line. Grayson just plain ran right through the All-American tackle, Aaron Rosenberg, to score, and Corbus kicked the goal to make it Stanford 7, USC 7. Bill Corbus booted two field goals, and when that day was done the miracle of the Vow Boys' three-year career was on its way with a vengeance. Nowhere in the annals of football will you find anything to equal the exploits of this small, green, carefree bunch of Vow Boys.

We think of them now as a group of All-Americans from prep school who just happened to come to Stanford. This isn't at all true, as was shown by the fact that they were lucky to get a 7 to 7 tie with an ordinary Cal frosh team, Bones Hamilton getting the score on a long run.

Hundreds of moments of glory still flash through my mind from Stanford athletics: Ernie Nevers hitting a three-run homer against Cal in '25, the ball sailing far over the 450-foot fence in the center field corner. Bill Richardson turning the tables on Cal's Elmer Boyden to win the '25 Big Meet, starting 10 yards behind in his relay lap and winning by ten, the first time he had ever beaten Boyden. Sophomore Bob King kidding with Feg Murray while winning the ICAAAA high jump and setting a new record in 1927. Bob was not a record man but a competitor, and one of two men I coached who went through an entire season and won his event in all competition, local, sectional, ICAAAA, NCAA, AAU, Olympic trials, and the Olympics themselves. The other was Ray Malott, in 1938, who traveled Europe for two months after the season was over and never was beaten in the entire season.

No one could forget the magic of Clarence Pinkston's final two-and-a-half from the high tower at the '20 Olympics; he seemed to hang in the air at will, as the entire crowd went wild. Three times in a row Coach Ernie Brandsten turned out the Olympic diving champions, Pinky at Antwerp, Al White at Paris, and Pete Desjardins at Amsterdam, as the world's coaches attempted to learn his techniques.

Nothing could beat the exquisite thrill of the moment when left-handed Bill Miller cleared 14-1⅞ with inches to spare to beat the Japanese star, Nishida, and win the pole vault in the L.A. Olympics. Bill was a San Diego boy, and another, Bud Deacon, won the NCAA meet with an equally unforgettable vault, also in the Coliseum.

That was in 1934. We had sent a seven-man team to the ICAAAA meet in Philadelphia, and eastern scribes had called it a vengeance trip to get even for Columbia's 7–0 win over Stanford in the Rose Bowl. What baloney, but nevertheless we were on the spot. It came up mud and rain at Franklin Field, but how our men came through! Johnny Lyman won the shot and took third in the discus. Slinger Dunn won the discus and took third in the shot. Alan Blackman won the 440 and finished third in the 220. Sammy Klopstock failed to qualify in the high hurdles, his regular event, but got mad at slipping in the mud and won the lows! Johnny Mottram was unused to mud but got third in the javelin, and Bud Deacon placed in the pole vault.

It won the meet, but the eastern writers laughed it off. Wait until they run up against USC and Louisiana State in the NCAA, they said.

But with all events in except the pole vault, it was a three-way fight. Deacon had one last try at 14 feet. If he cleared it we won the championship. If he missed we dropped down to third. Then all of a sudden Bud got the balks. He'd start, run half way down, and then stop. This went on and on. He must have balked 15 times. I thought he'd never get the vault off. But finally he went through. A beautiful vault. Bud cleared by a good six inches. But then, instead of floating on over, he jerked violently out of his semi-jackknife position and hit the bar. It bounced once, then settled, and Stanford had won the double national championship, the ICAAAA and the NCAA, for the second and last time.

Ben Eastman was the greatest of all Stanford runners. Tall, blond, and bashful, Ben smashed the world records in the 400 meters, 440 yards, 800 meters, 880 yards, the 600 yards, and the 1000 yards in the early 1932 season. And when Ben broke a record he broke it by plenty. Serious sinus infection slowed Ben down in the late season championships, and it was only the understanding treatment of Dr. Fritz Roth that allowed him to make the Olympic team, or take the second to Bill Carr, which was remarkable after the eight days in bed before the actual Olympics. In his senior year Ben suffered a pulled muscle, but he came back two years later to set an 880 record, though he never ran the 440 again.

Ben's methods completely revolutionized the training of middle distance men. In his 46.4 record run, Ben had run the first 220 in 21.3, where the rule was 23 to 24 and be sure to save a finish. And in the 880 Ben always ran the first lap in 53 to 54, whereas even the champions before that aimed for 58.

The Bill Carr–Eastman races found Carr, a sprinter with a terrific finish, winning all three times, as Ben set the pace and Bill out-sprinted him. I never did believe that Bill could have done it except for the sinus infection Ben wished to keep anyone from knowing about.

But it looked like a great senior year between them. Ben trained for that sprint finish and got it, but already Bill had been injured in an automobile accident in the east and never ran again. Then Ben pulled a muscle, thus ruining his season.

Yet I'll never forget Big Ben, after a two-month lay-off, his leg still sore, insisting on running the final of the ICAAAA in Boston, and fighting as he never fought before to get his fifth place. What a wonderful athlete, and what a wonderful sportsman!

Most outstandingly different quarter-miler was Truck Dellinger, who looked and ran like he belonged at tackle, but when Truck ran there was no doubt he was using everything he had to get there as quickly as he could. He ran second lap on our '36 relay team, and it was a good one. Alan Cranston, tall, long-limbed, and only a year away from greatness, made the change to Dellinger a real contrast. Then back to Malott in his first year, who was running the 880 for strength and did become one of the world's greatest 440 men. And finishing with the old Iron Man, Jack Weiershauser, sprinter, hurdler, quarter-miler. Not the fastest of our relay teams but certainly one of the most distinctive.

# SIX

"CHANGE THE METHOD OF TRANSPORTATION and you change all," one of the wisest of Stanford's teachers used to point out to his classes, emphasizing the inclusiveness of the "all" by examples covering the centuries from invention of the wheel to invention of the airplane. At Stanford, the prime invention preceding the airplane made entrance only slowly. Mrs. Stanford would have no automobiles on Stanford ground, and even after her death the prohibition held good for a time—though with a growing list of exceptions.

Frank Taylor, noting in his reminiscences how he used his Model T to promote the sales of kitchenware, was evidently one of the exceptions. He did not, though, remain an exception for long. By the middle-Twenties automobiles abounded; by the Forties the student who came to college without a car was likely to feel as handicapped, especially in his social activities, as if he had come without shoes. And as this next-to-newest method of transportation gained its place, all was, indeed, changed.

There were disadvantages in the course of changing. Parking lots pushed beauty off the campus. Noise and fumes filled nights as well as days. Scores of drivers, not all of them students, dealt negligently with road signs and stop signs, and accidents quadrupled by the year. But whatever the drawbacks and however much complained of, nobody would have surrendered the new freedom where one hour took the place of three or four and experience and enjoyment expanded in proportion.

The Thirties had begun badly for the University, as they had for all the nation. As they progressed, however, they brought some lasting benefits to balance the depression's losses. One of these was the forming in 1934 of an organization which named itself Stanford Associates. It was headed by Harry B. Reynolds, '96, and it had as one of its main objects that of securing money, present or prospective, in amounts sufficient to put Stanford finances on a solid base.

The earliest Associates, self-chosen, assured the continuance of

189

the group by electing others. Their plans were made systematically, the effort being divided under two heads: first, the solicitation of immediate gifts; second, the urging of inclusion in wills of bequests to Stanford. Their practice was as systematic as their planning. What they accomplished was by man-to-man asking, whether the individual asked was invited to join the organization or only to contribute to its aims. Both plan and method showed themselves so effective that before the Wilbur term had ended, the amount gained, in money or in bequests, had reached a sum equal to the original endowment.

A second aid, one perhaps as important though in a different form, came from a group of senior women. In 1930 several who wished to prolong their association with the University decided on holding a one-day conference on the campus in the spring following their graduation, with chosen professors invited to give them fifty-minute lectures as though they were again in classes. The first conference proved so successful that it was repeated the next spring and again the next—adult education crowded into a one-day term. Conference numbers increased steadily. Finally the Alumni Association took it over as part of the annual program, spreading it to places other than Stanford as alumni in one or another city asked for it. In 1962 sixteen conferences were held, two on the extreme Eastern coast, the attendance at them aggregating more than five thousand.

The conferences bring no money to the University; they take the time, freely given, of many professors; but through them Stanford men and women remain students still, gaining, as year follows year, a clearer and more adult view of what a university's reason for being really is in a troubled and swift changing world.

President Wilbur reached retirement age in 1940. Like his predecessor, however, he stayed on. In June of 1941 the University was to celebrate its fiftieth anniversary; at the same time the Hoover Library, newly finished, was to be dedicated—its distinctive height, as against the low built Quad, forming, in Dr. Wilbur's words, "a great shaft of light into the blue for a long look at history." To the Trustees it seemed right that the man who had been at Stanford's head for more than half of the University's life should preside at both ceremonies.

When the ceremonies were over he was again asked to continue in the presidency. World War II was entering its third year, able men were absorbed in War work, and the Board had found no one whom they wanted as his successor. Again, he consented, though this time asking for relief so soon as it could be found. He was placed in the chancellorship in January, 1942, though his successor did not actually assume the presidency until later.

The successor on whom the Board had finally settled was Donald Bertrand Tresidder, one of their own number. He was a Stanford alumnus, a graduate of the Stanford Medical School, a man experienced in the management of large business affairs. He had been for some years a Trustee and was at the time president of the Board. Both positions he resigned when his colleagues broached to him the question of his taking the University presidency.

Dr. Tresidder entered on his new office in September, 1943. His term was ended by his death in January, 1948. In four years and an added month or two, there is no more than time to find out what a university is, let alone forming and putting into effect a policy. Much may be begun, but little can be carried far enough to show its worth or to reveal its need of changes. The editors are especially fortunate, therefore, to have from Irma Cunha, '44, a reminiscence emphasizing one of the outstanding features of President Tresidder's relation to the University—his friendly consideration for undergraduates and his continued efforts for their welfare.

*It is unfortunate that the public has bestowed its admiration of atomic science mostly upon the merely destructive side of its activity. Its true value, in the past and in the future, lies in its intrinsic beauty and in those other of its applications which will benefit mankind and advance our civilization, helping it to gain its freedom from fear.*

FELIX BLOCH, Professor of Physics

# "A Letter I Still Possess"

## ALLEN DRURY, A.B. '40

*Allen Drury is the author of* Advise and Consent, *which won the Pulitzer Prize for fiction in 1960. Previous to this he covered Washington politics for 18 years for United Press, Pathfinder,* The Washington Evening Star, *and* The New York Times. *He received the Sigma Delta Chi Award for Editorial Writing in 1941. His second novel,* A Shade of Difference, *a sequel to* Advise and Consent, *was scheduled for publication in 1962.*

STANFORD MEMORIES, and which ones remain? . . . I think it is not the days along the Quad, the warm, hazy autumns, the long, slow, heartbreaking springs, like none other anywhere, of the Santa Clara Valley, nor all the lovely days of youth that never return.

These will remain as long as thought remains. Yet underneath there rested, in my time, a firmer foundation, and this, I think, is of all my Stanford memories the most treasured, and the best.

It was summed up and symbolized in a sentence I shall not forget, in a letter I still possess.

The writer was a tall, shy, awkward, most plain, most strangely uncommon-looking man, with deep-set eyes and heavy jowls and a big, bony figure that stalked the campus in dark blue suits with high, old-fashioned collars. His name was Ray Lyman Wilbur, former Secretary of the Interior in the Hoover Cabinet, and he was president of Stanford University in the days when I was a student.

He was, of course, no flaming liberal, as the term "liberal" is glibly misused in this present era. Yet even had he been the most dashing and flamboyant of radicals, it is likely that he could not have pleased all of the students all of the time, for I suspect that no university president ever does. Particularly did he not please those of us who had access to newsprint.

Looking back upon the free-swinging savageries of one's youth in the pages of *The Stanford Daily*, it is possible now to be startled and sometimes appalled by the venomous vigor with which "Dr. Wilbur and the Administration" were attacked. Scarcely a week went by, it seems now, that I was not landing a few haymakers on these vulnerable targets in "Bull Sessions" or the editorial columns.

Once in a great while there would be a patient protest, a mild rejoinder, but never was there any attempt at suppression, any threat to interfere with one's right to speak. Trust was placed in time and developing maturity to show one that there really were occasions when the facts did not justify the intemperate treatment they sometimes received in the rich, purple prose of one's carefree youth.

There came the day, after I had graduated and gone on into my profession and begun to acquire some of the moderation that had been so patiently hoped for by my elders, when it was announced that Dr. Wilbur would retire.

I sat down and did what sense and sensibility, as well as sentiment, now required: I wrote him a letter expressing my gratitude, as one member of the Stanford Family, for the job he had done as president, and I thanked him particularly for all the personal kindnesses and tolerance he had shown to me back in the days when, as I admitted, I was sometimes much harsher than I should have been about his administration. I told him I had always felt that no matter how unfair I might be, or how vigorously I might express it, my right to say it would always be respected; and I told him how greatly I valued that, as I looked back upon the four years of our sometimes uneasy friendship and association.

He replied with a most kind and gracious letter, and in it there was the sentence that will always be Stanford to me.

"*We can stand a good deal of knocking about,*" he said, "*as long as people are thinking.*"

Days along the Quad, the beautiful autumns, the lovely springs, the golden days? Well, yes; they remain, and can never be forgotten.

But in that sentence there rings the spirit of the Stanford I knew and shall always treasure above all else.

The winds of freedom really *did* blow, in my day.

May Stanford always be so fortunate, and may her children always be so blessed.

# "Not by One Road Alone"

## Sherman M. Mellinkoff, A.B. '41, M.D. '44

*Sherman Mellinkoff took his medical training first at Stanford University Medical School, then at University of Pennsylvania Hospital and Johns Hopkins Hospital. He is associate professor of Medicine, in charge of gastroenterology at the University of California Medical School in Los Angeles and an Associate Editor of the* American Journal of Digestive Diseases. *His research interests include studies of the inborn error of metabolism, familial Mediterranean fever. His many publications include editorship of the textbook,* The Differential Diagnosis of Abdominal Pain. *He is married and the father of three children.*

I CANNOT SPEAK for others, but from my own introspection I feel that all men derive their aims in life, their guiding (or even goading) convictions from a sense of kinship with someone, an identification with some lineal heritage that runs from an uncertain past into a brighter but unpredictable future. Such an emotional source of ideas and judgment is a vital force—to some degree a potential good or perhaps a potential evil. The sense of belonging, whether to a person or a group, imparts to the mind a sort of passion. And passion is essential to effort and even to thought; it determines which ideas a mind will accept and which it will cultivate, and often, indeed, what things in the world the eyes can see and the ears can hear.

I came to Stanford with the unjustified confidence of the late 'teens, unaware that the source of what energies I possessed was a fierce pride in my family and my ancestors. Whatever I felt capable of learning was linked by energizing roots to a heritage I believed it was my unspoken duty to sustain. When I left Stanford, those roots had branched and divided, all without my conscious knowledge or consent. I left Stanford feeling a kinship not to the few only but

195

to many, and a large number of the bonds then formed I have never lost.

This process of acquiring new relatives in the family of man was not accomplished by studying Shakespeare or the History of Western Civilization or Atomic Physics or Comparative Biology, exciting as these and other subjects were. And yet, it seems as I look back that academic courses were an important element in the transformation. New identifications grew slowly but strongly from the simple fact that others with whom I was in daily communication were exploring the same realm of ideas that I had been allowed by Stanford to enter. A man who speaks one's own language cannot long remain a stranger, and those whose aspirations, whether for themselves, for all mankind, for science or for some art, have led them into common studies soon begin to feel a family-like relationship. Xenophobia, with the anxiety which is its inseparable companion, is cut down by every added friend. It is only late along the way that we come to recognize how isolated a man can be in his own country, in his own town, even sometimes in his own family.

It is, then, chiefly for many friends that I remember Stanford with gratitude. In an atmosphere where "the winds of freedom blow," I was privileged to discover so many relatives that I know now how accurately life was described by the old Roman, Quintus Aurelius Symmachus, "Not by one road alone is it possible to come at so great a mystery."

# I Remember E. Whitney Martin

## AL ZELVER, A.B. '41, A.M. '49

*Al Zelver has worked as a reporter on the* San Francisco Chronicle *and as Building Editor for* Sunset Magazine. *During World War II he served for three years in the military intelligence service as a Japanese language officer. Now a city planning consultant, he is presently working on a series of economic studies for urban renewal agencies. He lives in Menlo Park, California; is married to the former Patricia Farrell, A.B. '46, A.M. '49, and has two sons.*

Summer quarter, 1937, I signed up for "Bird Lore and Classical Mythology" Tuesdays and Thursdays at 11. Two units. The professor was E. Whitney Martin, a tall, heavy, shaggy man in double-breasted dark-blue suit coat, grey flannels, and white shoes.

It was Professor Martin's last quarter (my first) before he was to become emeritus. "Bird Lore and Classical Mythology," he told us the first day, was a little indulgence on his part, a last gesture at teaching, combining the two great loves of his life, collecting bird skins and the study of myths. Tuesdays, he would talk about one; Thursdays, the other.

Occasionally, however, the mention of a bird would pop up in one of the Tuesday myth lectures.

"An eagle fed upon the liver of Prometheus . . ."

"A dove flew through the Clashing Rocks to guide the Argonauts . . ."

"Zeus visited Leda disguised as a swan . . ."

"Swan? Did I say 'Swan'?" Professor Martin asked rhetorically. "There, you see? Bird, birds, birds. They run all through these grand old tales. Yes, yes . . . bird lore and classical mythology. . . ."

Thursdays, Professor Martin simply brought stuffed birds (called "skins") from his personal collection. The skins were mounted on long sticks, making the birds look like feathered lollipops. Professor

197

Martin stood before us, stroking the little creatures, ruffling their tails, identifying marks and coloring, and telling us how they lived.

"Not a very good skin, this one," he said one morning. "Anyone tell me what's the matter?"

"It's dead," called Jack Lipman from the back of the room.

"I don't like that, Mr. Lipman. Mr. Lipman, you come up here and sit in the front of the class."

Near the end of the quarter we were assigned projects. (I don't recall a final.) My project was pasting together an album of bird pictures cut from children's books bought at the 10-cent store. Then Professor Martin gave us all (even Jack Lipman) either A's or B's, and quietly retired.

I would see the professor on campus during the following years, carrying books to and from the library, always in his same basic outfit, except for seasonal variations. Fall quarter, the white shoes changed to black, and winter quarter the grey flannels changed back to dark-blue suit pants to match the coat. Spring quarter, the grey flannels reappeared, and by June the black shoes were again exchanged for white.

I don't remember, now, exactly how many seasons I watched Professor Martin's changing wardrobe pace the passing years, until, finally, one day I was deeply saddened to read in the *Daily* that he had died.

What did I learn at Stanford (besides bird lore and classical mythology)? There is no single, simple path in the pursuit of knowledge, but the E. Whitney Martins at a great university go on teaching and stimulating their students, each in his own wonderfully alive and personal way.

# Stanford Pageant

FRANK CHURCH, A.B. '47, LL.B. '50

*Frank Church, United States Senator from Idaho, was elected to the Senate in 1956, when he was only 32 years old. Before this he served in the United States Army during World War II and engaged in private law practice in Boise. He was the keynoter in the Democratic National Convention in 1960.*

*When not in Washington, he and his wife and two sons make their home in Boise.*

M Y MEMORIES OF STANFORD form a pageant too long to relate in a paragraph. I should need many pages to recount the happy moments that flash back to me—the pleasant walks beneath the sandstone arches; the clustered conversations on the Inner Quad; the rebellious rendezvous at "L'Omelette" to sing, "Tuesday night is here at last, another busy week has passed!"; the extracurricular fun, the frenzy over football in the autumn; the quest for culture in "the City" during the wet winter months; and the pilgrimages to the beach when spring turned to summer.

But my recollections of Stanford focus mainly on particular people. I still savor Tom Barclay's salty irreverence—"Warren G. Harding proved that any American boy can be President!" I wonder yet how Professor Bailey managed to make a dry subject like "The Diplomatic History of the United States" as exciting as a good adventure novel. And who among the legion of law students that has groped its way through the mysteries of John Hurlbut's course in "Evidence" can forget how he matched a dexterity of mind with movement, lunging, swooping, and all but pirouetting behind his lectern?

Most of all—for personal reasons—I remember Dr. David Wood,

199

the great pathologist at the Stanford Medical School, whose tests disproved a diagnosis that I had been afflicted with an incurable cancer.

Stanford tendered me learning, and gave me back my life again. What more can any man ask of his university?

*We must constantly bear in mind that policies are made for nations, not nations for policies, and that it would be stupid to cling to outmoded ideas simply because some great name is attached to them.*

THOMAS A. BAILEY, Professor of History

# "We Do It for Ourselves"

## MAXWELL ARNOLD, A.B. '48

*Maxwell Arnold was a Stanford freshman in 1936, dropped out, and returned after World War II to graduate in 1948. While he was a member of the Writing Center, one of his short stories won a Stanford Humanities prize. He has published stories in* Harper's *and* The Sewanee Review, *and his work appears in* Stanford Short Stories *of 1948 and 1950. Since graduating he has continued to write, while working in the hotel business, public relations, and advertising. In the national election of 1960 he was in charge of advertising for the agency handling the Democratic presidential campaign. He lives in Palo Alto, is married, and is the father of three children.*

WHEN I WAS A MEMBER of the Writing Center the question most often asked me by campus visitors was, "Can you tell us how to get to the Hoover home?" If anyone had ever asked me how to get to the Writing Center, I wouldn't have known how to answer that, either.

The Writing Center, unlike the one-time Hoover home, is not even in a particular place. It is merely a certain number of teachers and writers who all work, talk, and traffic with each other in classrooms, homes, apartments, dormitories, restaurants, and backyards all over Palo Alto. The first year I was there I did all my writing in the billiard room at Toyon Hall, where I and my brother, also in the Writing Center, often wrote all night, playing pool-table baseball whenever one of us got stuck on a transition.

A center like this was not what I had expected when I returned to finish Stanford after the War. I think I thought it was going to be in a plaza, or under a dome, or up a tower or something. I remember figuring I would report there at once, unpack the stories I had written during the War, and get right to work with Wallace Stegner.

Instead, I found I would be taking a program fairly routine for an English major, including one writing course near the bottom of what the Center called its ladder system. (It *was* like a tower, after all.) Later on I could try to get into Mr. Stegner's class.

That became the thing that had to be done—to succeed with Wallace Stegner, a writer whose work I thought was great before I had ever heard of the Writing Center. (At that time I thought it was almost as good as my own.) Eventually a list of writers selected for Mr. Stegner's advanced class was to be posted on the bulletin board in the English Department. The day the list was due my brother and I were driving back from a Christmas vacation in Los Angeles. We drove straight to the English Department, late at night. The list was there. We had to light matches to read it, and it was a very difficult moment. Each of us felt his writing life depended on it. Neither wanted to be on the list without the other, but like all good jealous writers neither wanted the other to be on it alone. Anyway, we were on it together, and I have never felt better than I did that night.

I have had no difficulty recalling that night in 1946, but I have had to think hard to remember many other things about the Writing Center. In fact, when I sat down to write this, my immediate recollection of the Center was the same as I originally imagined it. I seemed to remember a group of writers isolated somewhere in their own special plaza, under their own special dome. But now I remember many things, many people, and many feelings, and I remember what they all meant to someone who wanted more than anything else to succeed as a writer of consequence.

That of course was what almost every one of us wanted to become—a writer good enough to have some impact on life and literature. A few of us were soon found out to be more interested in commercial success, but these were an unmolested minority.

What the Writing Center did for all of us, whether we wanted to write classics or commercials, was make us feel professional. We all learned how to be better writers in time, but from the beginning the important thing was the feeling we were given of being professional writers. We were treated that way. We were made to work that way. We were judged that way. And we had a ball, besides. We got to talk to visiting editors and publishers. We got to talk to famous writers, poets, and playwrights, and we ate and drank with them all. We had some good times with some writers, and some good fights with others. One of them insulted the hell out of us.

The shock came at a rather select faculty party for one of my literary and intellectual heroes, Arthur Koestler. Mr. Koestler arrived late and dramatically. His entrance was dark and commanding. He proceeded to talk about everything from yogis to commissars, smoking up a storm of cigarettes, hypnotizing us with his voice, sounding, as many English-speaking Hungarians do, like Bela Lugosi. And then, when the talk settled down to writing, he told us his opinion of the Writing Center, or any writing center. "The idea," he said, "fills me with horror."

In a way, Koestler was right about writing centers. Ring Lardner once said, "You can't make a writer out of a born druggist." Koestler thought the Stanford Writing Center was a place (or perhaps Plaza) that taught folks how to write. What he later said he did not understand was that we had all been writers before we ever came to the writing Center. There were no born druggists among us. And all we hoped for from the Center, and all we were told to expect, was the opportunity to write and be read and be judged, something that even then was becoming otherwise almost impossible in the highly organized society of the postwar years.

It was this professional opportunity to write and be read that made the Writing Center valuable to us. It was also a professional opportunity to get published, for the first time for most of us. Stories were taken by magazines like *Harper's, The Atlantic,* and *The Sewanee Review.* Poems were printed and plays produced. Novels were encouraged and accepted in early form. Fellowships, prizes, and grants from other universities and institutions were awarded. And all of this has been going on ever since.

Each year the best of the Center's short stories have been collected by the Stanford University Press, and I have just been rereading the ones written during my time. Some of them still look very good to me, and some look not so good. But they are all evocative of the personalities of their authors, and this is proof to me that a writing center need not cause, as some critics suppose, a leveling effect on the individual. Every one of the stories I have re-read is completely different, every one is by a writer who has something completely different to give of himself, and every one has brought the writer back to life for me.

I wonder what has happened to them all. So far as I know, most have disappeared. But I do know that one of us has become famous; that two or three others have had outstanding critical successes; and that a few more continue to be published here and there and now and then. As for the rest of us, some have gone into teaching (without writing); some have gone into business, politics, publishing, and for all I know law and medicine; and some of us have seen our writing talent drift or be forced into advertising, public relations, the slicks, and show business.

As for me, I am not the one who has become famous. I have an advertising job in San Francisco, and I live with my wife and children in Palo Alto. I like living near Stanford, and I like being near that nonexistent tower, the Writing Center. I have never gone back to sit in, although I have been invited. But I have a feeling that if I remain living near the Writing Center, I'll always believe I'm really a writer. And like many of us who have not made it as writers, I consider that I have not made it *yet*. I think we feel that if we were good enough to make it with the Writing Center, we still have a chance.

There must be several like me, writing at night, on week ends, when we get the chance and have the will. It isn't easy, but I know why we do it. We do it for ourselves. We do it for what Salinger calls the Fat Lady. And we do it for the Writing Center.

# The Fabulous Fagan

HARRY MUHEIM, A.B. '41, A.M. '48

*After his graduation from Stanford Harry Muheim spent four years in the United States Navy, learning and speaking Japanese. He then returned to Stanford for his Master's degree. He began to write prose at the Writing Center after the war, and now is a writer of documentary motion pictures. With his wife and two children, he makes his home in Washington, D.C.*

In the winter of 1940, a grim winter in many parts of the world but not particularly uncomfortable in the lounge at Dinah's, some thoughtful people on the campus organized a variety show. The aim of this show was to collect money for the Finnish Relief Fund. The big, erratic production was put together in less than a week, and as the Thursday performance grew near, excitement about it spread across the campus. The *Daily* had taken a characteristically negative view of the whole enterprise. Consequently, the house was completely sold out by Tuesday evening.

On Wednesday the cast was announced. It was to be headed by Dr. Wilbur, who seldom appeared in variety shows, and the cast list also showed that Professor Elmer D. Fagan of the Economics Department would give a lecture. Charlie Bulotti had routined the show so that the final number was the one by Elmer Fagan. His performance remains in my memory as the most delightful lecture I have ever heard.

Elmer came out, just slightly embarrassed, squinted over his glasses at the vast audience, shoved his left shoulder forward a little bit, the way he does, and said simply, "Evening." Then he turned and set about getting his blackboard adjusted just right. This took maybe five or six minutes. Finally he embarked on his lecture in that slightly apologetic fashion of his. It seemed to be a straight lecture about the impact of relief funds on the world economy and it was liberally salted with such legitimate-sounding phrases as Average Total Unit Cost, Price Fluctuation, and Marginal Revenue. He made references to the prices of oranges in Florida as opposed to the prices of oranges in California and compared the output of American and European "widgets"—that mythical, ubiquitous commodity Fagan uses to keep the student mind open to new ideas in place of old product images. As he explained just where the Finnish Relief money would come from and where it would go, he tattooed the blackboard with a stump of chalk. Then gradually — but only gradually — the whole thing degenerated into a completely cockeyed presentation. Only when the board was completely cluttered with numbers and lines and symbols did his thesis begin to emerge. Elmer was contending that the relief money would be distributed so widely that even the boys at the Fire House would get a cut.

As he approached the climax of this fantastic lecture he ran out of space on the front of the board and shot around behind it to continue lecturing and writing out of sight. Great puffs of chalk dust billowed up over the top as the tempo of his talk increased; finally the eraser shot up over the board and landed down at the footlights. Elmer emerged, came downstage to retrieve the eraser, then looked at the audience and said, "Well, I guess that's it, eh?" It was indeed. The applause roared for a long time, for we all knew that we had seen a true comic gem and that there was a touch of Chaplin in this econ prof.

As I walked back up the Row that night, I saw a new dimension in Elmer Fagan. Here was a man who could take his own wonderfully effective teaching and put it into a comic context with no help from anyone. It was the first time I had ever seen anybody satirize himself. And as I have gone through the years, I have found very few people who are big enough, or wise enough, or talented enough to do this.

# Katherine Anne Porter:
# A Stanford Memory

## N. V. M. Gonzalez, '51

*N. V. M. Gonzalez is a native of* The Philippines. *He came to the United States under a Rockefeller Foundation grant to study writing, and part of this time was spent in the Creative Writing Department at Stanford.*

*He has published two collections of short stories,* Seven Hills Away *and* Children of the Ash-Covered Loam and Other Stories, *and three novels,* The Winds of April, A Season of Grace, *and* The Bamboo Dancers. *He won the Philippine Republic Award of Merit for Literature in 1954 and the Pro-Patria Award, a decoration from the President of the Philippine Republic, in 1961. For* The Bamboo Dancers *he won the Republic Cultural Heritage Award in 1960.*

*He is at present assistant professor of English at the University of The Philippines, lives at Diliman, Quezon City; is married and the father of four children.*

"We don't really trust ourselves to feel at all. I believe in shades. I once followed a ghost down the hall. Words that contradict themselves: Free Love. Capitalist Democracy. Light Housekeeping.

AMONG THE THINGS that come readily to mind when I think of Stanford are phrases such as these by Katherine Anne Porter. She happened to be on the program as visiting lecturer at the Writing Center at the time I was there.

I had taken pains to jot down her many aphorisms on life and letters, thinking that some day I would need them for a profile or sketch. Time has turned to buff the once white sheets I had written my notes on; more years will scarcely leave them less yellow. Fortunately, the occasion has now come to use them—if not in the man-

ner a Proust might "use" a cup of tea, then certainly by way of cele-
brating a school and an apprenticeship that has become more valuable with the years.

The magazines report that Miss Porter's first novel, *Ship of Fools*,
has just been issued. This must have been the book we knew she had
been working on. It was then called *No Safe Harbor*, a phrase so
nostalgic to me that it made me homesick for The Philippines.

I do not recall her having read to us any portion of it. We listened
instead to her readings from Henry James—from *A Small Boy and
Others*, in particular. Her favorites among James' books were *The
Wings of the Dove* and *The Golden Bowl*. She was a confirmed
Jamesian: you couldn't go wrong on James, she said.

Our own enthusiasm for Roger Martin duGard and Jean Giono,
I realized with dismay, did not impress her; but then hardly was she
impressed by anything. She was, it seemed, beyond being ever fazed
or shocked. I remember jotting down an understatement of hers on
this subject: "After two revolutions in Mexico, seven years with the
U.S. Foreign Service, two world wars, and seven months as Fellow
of the Library of the Congress, nothing can surprise me now."

As a student I had found it difficult to differentiate her preferences from her opinions. Even now I see in my notes a hint of this
difficulty. I have indeed documented more her enthusiasms than her
judgments. There is, for example, her remark on her reading *Dub-
liners* for the first time: "It was like a revelation. It was like finding
Shakespeare's sonnets when I was thirteen. It was like reading Sterne
for the first time."

Of Joyce's *Portrait,* she said: "A sublime job. Couldn't have been
done better." And of *Finnegans Wake*: "You can have *Finnegans
Wake*. Life is too short for me."

Could it be that in class discussion she felt required to infect us
with her preferences rather than have us bear with her opinions?
Ten years of teaching has taught me that infection is sometimes about
the best thing that can happen in a classroom and, although for my
part I have missed infecting others with the Jamesian virus, I have
perhaps succeeded a little in the case of the Joycean one. In connection with the KAP virus, I am afraid I have been also somewhat

successful—afraid because I know how quickly that takes, and for a long time the student is helpless to strike out healthily on his own.

"You go back and learn," she used to say, although in what context I do not now recall. Yet it is not too difficult today to reconstruct the situations that evoked such remarks as: "The French should be warned of the naiveté of the American." It was the year everybody talked about the Kinsey Report. On the novella, she once said: "I have been fighting with Whit Burnett on that *boneless* word." And, it now reads like an afterthought, but she must have said it on some later occasion, in any case: "I don't love everybody. You have to have enemies."

Her one enemy, we knew, was the writer whom you couldn't trust. Anton Chekhov she would trust—completely. And Hollywood trusted her, we heard, with the scenario for "La Cigale," only to abandon the idea of filming it. A good deal of money the scenario made, she told us; but she had only some furniture left—and it somewhere in storage—to show for it.

I recall our apprehension when for a week or so she failed to meet her classes. Believing ourselves to be her friends rather than her enemies, a classmate, Jim, and I sought her out; it was said she lived all by herself in a cottage up on the road beyond the campus.

Jim and I walked the whole way and found the cottage without difficulty. A flight of steps the top rung of which was on the same level as the curb took us some fifteen feet below to a *patio*. From there Jim called.

Strangely enough, I do not remember exactly whether we found her at home or not. I have a vague picture of Jim entering the house and coming out as quickly as he had gone in—to tell me that she was not there; but I cannot trust my memory. I know, though, that her voice seemed to be following me—"Don't say vicious when you mean depraved; don't say pious when you mean religious"—as Jim and I walked home disappointed, puzzled, even mystified.

# Stanford's Fourth President

## Irma J. Cunha, A.B. '44, A.M. '46

*Irma Cunha started her career as a newspaper reporter for the* Honolulu Star-Bulletin. *From 1948 to 1950 she worked for the Yosemite Park and Curry Company in various positions, her favorite being over-all manager and liaison with the hotel division, work which gave her the opportunity to ride horseback from one High Sierra camp to another.*

*From 1950 to 1953 she worked for the Shell Oil Company, traveling the country as a lecturer in public relations. She is presently a partner in Executive Program, a management and personnel consultant firm, and a partner in three personnel agencies—Empire, Best, and Bay, all in San Francisco.*

Some of us are lucky enough to meet a person whose warmth, courage, and love of life stay with us and strengthen us for a lifetime. Doctor Don Tresidder, known to many of us during his presidency as "Uncle Don," provided me and others with this strength.

Not only did he contribute substantially to our development as human beings, but he also had a great deal to do with our continued love for two places—Yosemite and Stanford.

It is not possible to ski at Badger Pass, walk through the lobby of the Ahwahnee, or look at Half Dome (on top of which he once sat with his feet dangling over the edge!) without realizing how much this one man was responsible for the deep and lasting attachment to the Valley which so many of us feel.

At Stanford my first meeting with him was in his office. I had come to call on him with a supreme confidence befitting the editor of the *Daily*. I told him I planned editorially to criticize his administration. Recalling our conversation now, I realize how kind he was

210

to an arrogant and know-it-all girl who took a half hour of his time just to listen to the sound of her own voice.

He and his charming and talented wife, "Aunt Mary," came to the rescue of many of us on many more than just a few occasions when we were suffering from the hardships of acquiring an advanced education. The experience that stands out in my mind is one that came when I was sitting dejected at lunch at Hurlburt House. I was a graduate student living in the cook's shack in the alley. Housing was at a premium on the campus and I had just got notice to vacate immediately. I had had no luck in finding a place to live—and finals were starting in a week.

Out of the blue came a phone call. It was President Tresidder: "Mrs. T and I have been thinking for some time that we would like to have graduate students live in our home. Would you have any interest in being the pioneer in this? If so, I'll pick you up on my way home tonight, so you can see if you would like it." I did like it and I did move in, and as a result of the many hours and days I was fortunate enough to spend with them, I have been aware of facets of life which I'm sure I never would have recognized without their opening of certain doors.

Several other students followed me in the big house on the hill. To all of us, "Aunt Mary" and "Uncle Don" gave gifts of knowledge which no course of study possibly could have provided.

So far, I have written of my personal gains, of what "Uncle Don," all unconsciously, did for me. Someone within his administration will have to spell out what he did for the University. Only a very small piece of that came within undergraduate view. From his predecessor he had inherited the sorority problem, the "to be or not to be" of sororities on campus. Decision lay in the hands of the Board of Trustees, but Dr. Tresidder's tact and fair-mindedness went a long way in making the final decision accepted, however regretfully, by all but a very small minority. His plans for an all-University center—only now in course of construction—even the newest undergraduate knew about. So did they of his student-accompanied horseback rides. The rest—the regrouping of departments, the emphasis he placed on the arts, the search for and often the success in finding scholars who were an important addition to the faculty—these things lay mostly outside undergraduate knowledge. Nonetheless, they probably added to what his warm personality had begun—the sense each of us had of *belonging*, and of our actions, like our personal welfare, being important to Stanford.

*Knowledge is re-creating the world—for good or ill; change is the most certain thing in an uncertain future; and education is the price of survival.*

JOHN W. GARDNER, '33

# Athletics at Stanford, 1945–1960

Greatest of all Stanford trackmen were Gay Bryan and Bob Mathias, both coached by Jack Weiershauser. Gay was a five-event man, the broad jump at 25-3 his best. In the Big Meet of '49 Gay won the 100, 220, high hurdles, high jump, and had a cinch win in the broad jump with a mark of 24-10, when a Cal unknown uncorked a 25-footer, holding him to just 23 points!

Mathias was the double Olympic decathlon champion, winning the title in London as a high school boy under the most severe difficulties. Four years later at Helsinki Bob was the finished article, the champion of champions. Late the night of the second day a wonderful feeling came over the stadium as you realized all those people were staying out in the rain and dark because Bob Mathias was THEIR champion, and the fans of all nations had taken him to their hearts. That night Bob Mathias was the finest ambassador of good will this nation has ever had, as well as the greatest athlete in the world.

There has always been something about the Stanford Farm that made for greatness in athletics. College professionalism as encouraged by the NCAA rules has taken some of that away. The tendency to catalogue youngsters before they get out of high school, either a basketball man or not, has killed off many a great athletic career.

Ben Eastman had a 440 record of 52.8 from high school. Nowadays a boy would hide out with such a mark.

As tuitions were raised higher and higher, Stanford athletics sacrificed more and more. Now the trend is for genius students, but there still is the basic desire amongst the administration, from Dr. Sterling through the Board of Trustees and Dr. Rix Snyder, to keep Stanford a university for virile, dynamic, active students with the energy to temper off grinding studies with wholesome athletics. There are directors and coaches who are not only willing but are actually wagering their lives they can bring back anything lost from Stanford athletics, and here's hoping they never give up the fight.

# SEVEN

I F A MEMBER of Stanford's earliest faculty were to arrive on today's campus, he would find himself as much bemused as would a soldier from the Continental Army or a courtier from the Court of Elizabeth I. The cause for wonder might be different, but any of the three, looking around him, would be inclined to believe in the existence and potency of Aladdin's lamp.

Even to a graduate of no more than fifteen or twenty years ago and so one unawed by speeding vehicles or invaded air, there is still something close to the marvelous in Stanford's alteration. Seeking reasons for the change, the returned alumnus would find two that stood above the rest. One of the two would be, of course, Stanford's new president, J. E. Wallace Sterling, now (1962) in his thirteenth year in office; the other, the Government of the United States.

Dr. Sterling came to the presidency already knowing Stanford well. He had been an instructor in history here, a research worker in the Hoover Library. Leaving Stanford, he held a professorship at the California Institute of Technology, then a directorship in the Huntington Library at Pasadena. He was, that is, acquainted with academic life at its various levels and in several places. This alone would have been helpful, but besides this (as witness Fuji Imamura's reminiscence) he possessed a gift for spreading good will around him; also, for giving to his colleagues a sense of his willingness to accept and advocate useful suggestion from any University source. Probably he would have been a successful president in any era; he chanced to enter on his office in an era when government stood in especial need of the aids a university could offer.

Two wars and the cold war that followed them had taught officialdom to turn to those centers where ideas and the apparatus for developing them were both to be found. Stanford was but one among many which drew enormous federal grants for the carrying out of projects enormously expensive. The pouring in of government funds quickened the pace even in divisions of learning where federal money never went. The quickened pace quickened public interest, and gifts increased which could be used for purposes unconnected, so far as any action could be, with war or fear of war. That Far West "seminary" of the Nineties, a university long ago, stood easily now among the three or four great centers of learning in the nation.

Both composition and tone of the student body had changed with growth. Of the more than nine thousand registered in 1962, 3,721 were in graduate standing. They came from all over the world, picked men admitted to the professional schools because of high college records. Undergraduates, 5,523 of them, had altered, too, in attitude and in performance. Two publications, the so-called Bawlout and *The Stanford Daily*, mark the degree of transformation.

The Bawlout is almost as thick with figures as formerly, but the purpose of it has changed. An entry today gives the student's name, his address, his class year, his major subject. Whether in units or honor points he stands higher or lower than his mates is now the student's concern and only his. Competition still exists, perhaps is keener than before, but it is no longer competition between student and student; it is between the student and his subjects of study.

Usually he wins. Through careful selection, bulwarked by tests and interviews, the Committee on Admissions has reduced the number of those who, once accepted, prove unable to carry the work expected of them to less than five per cent—a reduction of waste in the University and of disillusionment in the home.

*The Stanford Daily*, in constant publication since the University opened its doors, reflects with considerable accuracy the interests of its readers. Those interests call now for a *Daily* in which a third of the space and often more devotes itself to world or national news. Campus boundaries are not the boundaries of present-day undergraduate thought. The reminiscences in this section, five of them written by students whose A.B.'s are still to come, make clear beyond need of comment why they are not.

# "Farther and Further and Father"

## Fuji Imamura, A.B. '50

*Fuji Imamura (Mrs. Fuji Ozake) returned to Japan after completing her work at Stanford. There she has been engaged in teaching and in social service. Her home is in Anhikana on the island of Hokkaido.*

W HAT IS YOUR impression of America?"
This was the question which I had to answer the most. Knowing that what I know about the United States is only the finger-tip of this large country, yet I could express my impression of the States as a foreigner without much difficulty and hesitation. But could I answer for the question "How was the Stanford?" so easily? No. Then why not? I did not only see but experienced Stanford. Stanford is built in me.

Staying up till late to prepare for the exams and papers with roommates from Colorado, California, Missouri, Washington, etc.; and going for a cone of Edy's ice cream or for a bite of Kirk's hamburger and a drink of Rudy's cheer-up and bubble-up beer with a bunch of boys and girls; yelling for the Cardinals at the rooting section with red feathers and pompons, I was more a Stanfordian than a foreign student.

To tell the impression when one is not the constituent element of an institution (or component part) is rather easy. On the other hand, to speak about the 70 years old university, especially when one is sentimentally involved, it is not so easy as one gives answer like, "Oh, it is a quite big country," or "I am surprised at the number of cars and wonderful highway system," and so forth. Perhaps this little Japanese girl is still in love with Leland Stanford, Jr. So many events are in my reminiscence.

Among all, the series of events of our graduation week such as

217

Commencement, Baccalaureate Service, Class Day Exercise, etc., would be the highlight.

In black cap and gown, I was the mixture of the satisfaction from my achieving the goal and the excitement of our big days and the sadness of my leaving the school.

Many congratulatory addresses were presented by distinguished persons at every occasion. I am quite ashamed to tell that some of the speeches whirled up into California's metallic blue sky and disappeared from my remembrance, and some faded away as time passed.

Among these, one thing that has been very vividly remembered is President's hand. It was one of those very fine days in June when a reception was held at the home of Dr. and Mrs. Sterling. A Scotch musician was going up and down playing his jolly pipe music, and beautifully dressed-up graduates and their families were standing in line to be greeted by Dr. and Mrs. Sterling. I had been thinking of my parents in the country cross the ocean till my turn came. I tell you that I never shaked with any hands which were so large and thick and warm as our President's. Being wrapped up with his shovel-like hand, I could feel his understanding of human nature, wide mind and warm heart, and his strictness residing with kindness. I spent a very pleasant afternoon at his garden.

As to the academic phase: "I remember one course which was the hardest for me. That is English 102, "Introduction to English Language." It was explained that ". . . the course was designed to give the student a knowledge of fundamental matters about the English language, to familiarize him with terminology, classification of language; to enable him to form standards of judgment about good English."

Well, naturally, I thought that this was the course for me. After attending the class several times, I found myself left in the middle of the Pacific Ocean.

"He stole my thunder."

"Having a crepe on your nose."

"Barnum was right."

Etc., etc.

Professor M. often used these examples to explain the idiomatic usage of English. As it is clear, example is given to clarify the matter and make it easy to understand. But as to the examples which were used in the course, they needed another explanation. Examples were the toughest to understand. Once he began to explain the difference between *farther* and *further* and *father*. I could know the difference in the meaning and the usage but never the pronunciation. Doctor's *farther* was also *further* for my ears.

You shall never know how much I had been discouraged and disappointed as to my untrained ears till I found out that he had a terrible Southern Carolina accent and till I devised a means to console myself saying "Well, he is not an authority of pronunciation but an authority of Chaucer and Shakespeare."

The course was really something for me, but Professor M. was very nice and understanding and I think that is the reason why I decided to commit a double suicide with English 102 and was pulled up from the mess of Etymology, Semantics, Phonetics, Grammar, and Middle Age English, and finally passed all right.

This is a part of my reminiscences.

*It is no longer One World but One Room.*

THOMAS A. BAILEY, Professor of History

# Helpless Against the University

## BRUCE MITCHELL, A.B. '62

*Bruce Mitchell entered Stanford as a freshman in the fall of 1956. At the end of the fall quarter in 1958 he left school to join the army. During this time he married a Stanford graduate, Carol McKanna. He returned to Stanford in January, 1961, as an American Literature major. In the summer of 1961 he became involved in the "Student Projects Group" mentioned in his reminiscence. In addition, he is employed by the Art and Architecture Department as a teaching assistant to help continue academically the same type of work the volunteer Student Projects Group began. He is now in his senior year.*

Frost Amphitheater became my sanctuary during my first two years at the University. Seated high on its green turf banks, I escaped the barrenness of Wilbur Hall, rationalized the disappointment of a poor exam or theme grade, wrote poetry for the girl I loved, and mentally waged my own personal battle against Stanford.

Perhaps it is the nature of every undergraduate to fight the university he attends. Maybe it's a personal quirk, a natural perversity—maybe just adolescence. In my case, it might have been the abrupt transplantation from a provincial Midwestern village to the bustling worldliness of a university community. Whatever the cause, years passed before Stanford and I reached a compromise.

The final crisis came during the first quarter of my junior year. What seemed then a serious, almost catastrophic situation is now much softened by the humor of hindsight. I had launched a full-scale offensive against Stanford's policy of requiring two years of physical education. At my adviser's insistence I continued to sign up for gym classes, but never attended them. Consequently, I failed two consecutive quarters of weightlifting, a course in which attendance counts 90% of the final grade.

In November, I received a letter, brief but devastating, from the registrar:

*Your failure to complete the physical education units required by the General Studies Program makes it necessary to withdraw your registration privileges for next quarter and all subsequent quarters at Stanford University. This decision may be appealed only by petition.*

Despite my initial anger, I knew that much of my resistance to the physical education program was pure laziness. Expecting the worst, I composed an apologetic petition and submitted it to the registrar. To my surprise, the petition was granted and registration privileges reinstated on the condition that I complete my physical education requirements by the end of the year. On hearing the news, my adviser congratulated me but suggested I steer clear of weightlifting. "As a major, that is," he added with a wry grin.

But the elation over my successful petition faded quickly and as I made the long train trip home that Christmas, I was troubled. I had wasted the first two years at Stanford and it looked as though the second two would be no better. I was beating my head against a sandstone wall. There were no major achievements I could point to, no contributions to any phase of University activity, and no circle of close and challenging companions. Stanford remained for me a coldly impersonal environment. I joined the army the day after Christmas.

Two years later, the girl for whom I had written such bad poetry was my wife, the army had changed my draft classification from 1-A to 4-A, and I was preparing to enter Stanford for the second time. It was just before winter quarter and almost everyone was home for the Christmas holidays. One evening I drove to the campus. A winter mist was falling and the street lamps looked fuzzy in the moist air. My footsteps echoed through the long rows of brown-beamed stone arcades as I retraced the familiar paths of my first days at Stanford. I climbed to the ridge of Frost Amphitheater and looked down into its vast green emptiness. The memories had softened, the bitterness subsided, and the frustrations, only two years past, seemed buried beneath decades. For the first time, I was ready to meet Stanford on equal terms.

"I've called every damn surplus store in the Bay Area," moaned Styp, "and only three of them have Navy signal flags. Mitch, we must have been out of our minds."

"We were!"

Styp and I had decided more than once during the summer that, back in May, we had both been temporarily unhinged. Perhaps it was just spring fever. There's something about the fragrance of a warm May afternoon . . . anyway, once we took the first step, there was no turning back. At the end of two hectic weeks of persuading, arguing, pleading, and hoping, we had sold Stanford University a service program that was proving immensely difficult to fulfill.

"Give us three months," we bubbled confidently, "and we'll show you that Stanford's students are her most valuable asset." I had been back at school less than two quarters, and Stanford was involved in one of the most important fund-raising drives of her history. Our plan was to tell the public about Stanford from an undergraduate's point of view. We were to work primarily in the visual display medium but were to perform many secondary functions. Projects of a specialized nature, such as constructing models of future buildings on campus and designing a series of information stations for visitors, were placed in our hands. "Our" refers to a group of four students: John Stypula, James Bischoff, Alan Jones, and myself.

The summer was now half over and we were well along on our third display. The deadline was a week away and we had hit a serious snag. A structure had been built to house the display; it was a series of wooden frame triangles, each about sixteen feet high. The triangles were hinged together at the top, forming an archway large enough for a man to walk under. Our problem was finding a lightweight material to stretch over the triangles as a sun screen. Our first inclination was to use Navy signal flags since they had worked out well in an earlier display. But this time we needed thirty-two flags instead of only ten.

"Well, come on, Styp, let's try those surplus stores. Maybe they have just what we're looking for." We drove to Oakland and spent the morning going from one store to another; none had the flags we needed. That afternoon we went to the Twelfth Naval District Headquarters on Treasure Island. "Can't help you, boys," said the Communications Officer, "but perhaps Seaman Fobes can be of assistance." We were directed to Fobes' office and, after being introduced, were asked to explain our problem. He was optimistic at first and confident he could find just the flags we wanted. Five hours later when we had tried the Naval Supply Center in Oakland, the Naval Reserve Armory, the Twelfth District's purchasing department, the Civilian Affairs Liaison Office, and Treasure Island's own supply room, all without success, Fobes muttered wearily, "Dammit, I'll go around to every ship in dry dock here and ask to borrow flags from their own lockers." . . . That didn't work either.

When we got back to Stanford, Alan was bent over the sink in the architecture studio, dipping great strips of canvas into a bleaching solution. He was surrounded by bottles and cartons of commercial bleach and a huge unrolled sheet of canvas. "Five hundred yards," he lamented, "five hundred free yards of canvas and we can't use one inch of it because of that horrible green color!"

"Where's Jim?" I asked.

"Downstairs, seeing if he can paint the stuff."

Neither the paint nor the bleach made the canvas usable. Styp went to Treasure Island again the next day to have another go at getting flags. He came back early. "You know those ten flags we used in the last show . . . there are forty in existence. They were used on the largest carriers, and the Navy hasn't manufactured any more of them since the War."

Without another word, we climbed in the car, drove to J. C. Penney's, bought one hundred yards of the cheapest unbleached muslin available, cut and pinned it into triangular flags, and had our wives sew them.

The "Flag Episode" was only one of many similar incidents that summer. One day Styp asked, "Why are we knocking ourselves out? I mean, what do we owe the University?" I couldn't answer the question until we had completed our last summer show. It covered the first sixteen years at Stanford and in researching the period, we were repeatedly delighted by accounts of the early days. The school was so small then that it was easy to translate it into human terms. David Starr Jordan, the first president, was simply the man you could go to with your problems any time of the day—whether you were a freshman or a full professor. He was the robust athlete who covered first base in the faculty-senior baseball game and once split his vest down the back by swinging too hard at an inside strike. Jane Lathrop Stanford was the woman who fought unwaveringly to keep Stanford open through the years of legal and financial crisis after her husband's death. The faculty were the hardy men who each day tramped two hot, dusty miles from Menlo Park to campus and who unanimously agreed, for six consecutive years, to accept a twelve per cent cut in salary so the University could stay open.

It was then that the hectic events of the last three months assumed a kind of order in my mind. Suddenly they seemed so appropriate, so logical a part of my experience at Stanford and of the Stanford tradition as a whole. For the four of us that worked during the summer, the University had opened itself up. The formerly distant "administration" was now the friendly smile and sympathetic ear of Don Carlson or Bob Hind. The Art and Architecture Department was Ed Farmer and those colleagues of his who had first approved our program and stuck by us through the summer. And so it was with all departments of the University with which we had worked. They lost their identity as departments and became a group of individuals, each performing a different task but all working for a common purpose. And any individual was limited, was helpless against the University, only to the extent he limited himself. He would be heard only if he spoke and win only if he competed. A humble lesson, and one that is often told, but Stanford, with infinite patience, had had to prove it to me.

# Kartozian–for Everything

## WILLIAM KARTOZIAN, A.B. '60

*William Kartozian, head yell leader in his senior year, four-year holder of a California State Scholarship, and student representative on the annual Alumni Conference program for 1960, gives the following account of himself since leaving Stanford:*

*"I reluctantly left California to come East to Boston, where I am now in my second year in the Harvard Law School; unhappily I must report that there is no crying need for ex-yell leaders here. . . . I intend to return to San Francisco and begin the practice of law as soon after graduation as possible, and I harbor an ultimate goal and desire to someday enter politics."*

One of the unique features of Stanford is the feeling of belonging that permeates campus life, a feeling extended from the lowliest freshman to the mightiest senior. This atmosphere of belonging does not lead to conformity. It leads, rather, to the development of each student's individuality. It makes no real difference whether a person lives in a fraternity or a dormitory or off campus; he goes to Stanford, and his opportunities to maximize this fact are as good as anyone else's.

As a result, nearly every student develops a desire to contribute something to University life—to become somebody on the scene. I was a little different; I wanted to become everybody. It must be admitted that this desire was prompted by forces beyond my control. Stanford, however, provided me the opportunity.

It started, as so many things at college do, during a "bull session" in a fraternity living room. We were berating student government and bemoaning the fact that there was no centralized power which undergraduates could command. I offhandedly threw out the remark

225

that if the government of the Associated Students were run like a dictatorship, we could really get results.

"That's it," cried Bill Pereira, a remarkably talented young man. "If I manage your campaign, will you run for every office and become 'El Benefactor'?"

"Sure," I laughed, and with that bade the group good evening and went to bed.

The next morning I walked down to classes as usual; I was dumbfounded to see a 150-foot sign draped across Cubberley Auditorium, proclaiming KARTOZIAN FOR EVERYTHING. (I may as well point out here that I believe none of this would have happened had my name been Smith.) This sign caused me some embarrassment, but nothing compared to what I felt when I walked past the main library and saw hanging from it the keynote of the campaign to come, "KARTOZIAN IS MORE THAN A MAN: HE IS AN IDEAL." This was too much. I turned tail and ran back to the shelter of the house. But there I decided that if we let this thing die now, I would certainly be left holding a very empty bag. I had to go through with it. The fellows in the house were more than willing, and a work force was quickly organized for the first attempted imposition on student government of a dictatorship.

My great knowledge of everything had to be imparted to the student body before they could accept me as their unquestioned leader. So I expressed my views on a number of items of interest to various segments of the University. Outside the Law School, a poster was put up—KARTOZIAN SAYS, "CHESSMAN IS INNOCENT"; near the Political Science Department, KARTOZIAN SAYS, "RED CHINA DOES NOT EXIST"; by the Psychology Department, KARTOZIAN SAYS, "I WILL NOT STOOP TO THE UNDER-HANDED, MUD-SLINGING TACTICS OF MY OPPONENTS AND THEIR COMMIE PALS."

Like any good politician, I also made my share of promises: "Kartozian promises to pin every girl who votes for him"; "Kartozian promises 21-year-old girls for fraternity house mothers"; "Kartozian says off-campus living is great; if elected, I promise to move Stanford off campus"; "Kartozian promises bigger and better cactus gardens."

The time came for my first speech. One of the fellows in the house had a siren on his car, and we planned to arrive at Roble Hall with a great deal of hoopla. But something struck me as wrong; a person couldn't go around saying the things I was and at the same time look like a normal human being. So my "public image" was created; first an overcoat which I had always liked but which everybody else laughed at; then a straw hat; then, not to be outdone by Carmine DiSapio, a pair of dark glasses, and finally a cigar.

As the days passed, the campaign grew more intensive. The entrance into every race by a mysterious, overcoated figure caused more than the usual excitement about the elections. It was thought by some that such a creature as Kartozian did not exist; but their doubts diminished after a series of torchlight parades, and a series of speeches which in style did justice to Mussolini and in substance to Doodles Weaver. Now, more than doubt, there was curiosity as to what kind of person would run for everything. I very simply explained in my speeches that I had always wanted just to be everybody. Once, walking on the Quad, I overheard two girls talking in front of me. One turned to the other and said, "That Kartozian, you know, he's so ugly, he's good looking." I knew when I bought that overcoat that it would serve me well.

The day of the primary elections arrived. We were confident that the campaign had gone well, but we were worried about one thing; because of our late entrance into the races, I was forced to run as a write-in candidate. There were certain subversive elements on the campus who were opposed to our attempted coup, and we feared they might go to any means, and that included having ballots invalidated because of improper spelling. So, a group of fellows were stationed at the balloting places while the polls were open, whose job it was to go around to every voter and ask, "Say, how *do* you spell Kartozian?"

That night I was called before a meeting of the student legislature. Unprecedented developments had taken place. The election returns were late because of an extraordinarily high voting percentage and a large number of write-in votes. I had been voted into the finals for some seven or eight offices, including president and secretary of the Women's Recreation Association, Women's Council, Stern Hall representative, off-campus representative, Men's Council, and yell leader. The student body president informed me of the facts, and I graciously replied that I was sorry we had not made a clean sweep, but that I would continue to seek election to all these offices. With that remark, the Legislature seemed to panic, and there was a hurried consulting of the school constitution.

After a lengthy discussion and a series of votes, the Legislature decided, in spite of my heated objections, to allow me to run only for the office of yell leader. And thus it was; yell leader I became.

Despite the seeming success of my campaign I was disturbed— terrified might be a better word; when the whole affair started, I was willing to settle for any of the offices—any, that is, except yell leader. How could a person who had never been able to turn even a somersault be yell leader? I decided that, rather than try to learn to somersault, I would carry forward the figure created in the campaign. At the opening of the next football season, therefore, the alumni were surprised to find that the usual agile young man in white sweater and Bermuda shorts had given way to a cigar-smoking figure who would think of exerting himself to no greater extent than lifting a finger when a yell was to be led.

Being yell leader was both a challenging and rewarding position. It meant getting to meet and know people, including a weekly meeting with the Dean (who, incidentally, was quite tolerant with his No. 1 problem boy), and working with the "Red Hot Professor," Dr. James T. Watkins IV, whose inspired and inspirational cheer leading led us to a glorious victory on one Saturday afternoon.

It also meant being able to refute the statement that "apathy was king" on the Stanford campus. True, the so-called Golden Age of Yell Leading as exemplified by the Rah-Rah boys was gone, perhaps never to return. But, the Stanford Spirit was still there; it was a more sophisticated spirit coming from a more sophisticated student, and I felt it was necessary to develop new means of bringing out this spirit (especially since our football teams had not been doing especially well for several seasons).

Anybody who witnessed the Big Game of the 1959 season could

not deny the presence of this spirit. Even in the aftermath of a heartbreakingly close defeat, the Stanford rooting section cheered long, cheered louder, and more graciously saluted their team and school than did the victors. To this day, I believe that the students would have stood for a half hour longer, expressing their appreciation to the team, and, of course, to Stanford itself. For me it was my final task as yell leader; I'll never forget that day and that game and the enthusiasm that 8,000 students showed for their school.

It is difficult to say exactly what Stanford means to its students and alumni; it is buildings, professors, a football game, the Row, the City, Rossotti's. But, you can't really describe what Stanford is; you can describe it only in its relation to people. Stanford's meaning is what it does for its people. After all, look what it did for me.

*Strictly interpreted, no historical period has a life of its own apart from the past of which it is the projection and the future to which it leads. Yet in a sense each day has its own biography. It is born, reaches high noon, lives on into its turbulent or passive afternoon, and dies into night.*

JOHN W. DODDS, Professor of English

# No Time for Ivy

## SCOTT THOMPSON, A.B. '62

*Scott Thompson is now a junior at Stanford. In his fresh-
man year he was reviewer and president of the Political
Union. He was also freshman representative to the Legislature, vice-president of the Institute of International Relations, and on the Dean's List. Among his plans for the future,
he includes Law School and politics.*

I didn't want to go to Stanford. In fact, I did everything conceivably possible to avoid it just before entering: I applied to take
part in exchange programs in English schools, and was rejected; I
tried to contrive a way to extend a summer of hitchhiking in Europe
into an eternity, and ran out of money.

It started in the winter quarter of my senior year at Andover—all
anyone thought about was college. As it happened, I was virtually
broke, and it cost only five dollars to apply to Stanford and ten dollars to apply to Harvard. The clincher, however, was that Stanford
didn't require College Board achievement tests; as my exams were
over on a Wednesday, by applying to Stanford alone, I could go home
Wednesday night. But with Harvard, which required the tests, I
would have had to remain shoveling snow till after the Saturday
afternoon Boards.

By Commencement it was all too, too late to change my mind—
as far as the colleges were concerned. And, as the ivy was still cling-
ing to me, I was, quite frankly, disdainful of going to school in buildings of bare, brown sandstone, at a place so bucolically referred to as
"The Farm." That was in 1959. It is two years later—and I still don't
know what happened to me.

Perhaps it was . . . in the Poli Sci building on a cold January
day, 1960. Our freshman house had decided to try something new:
a weekly "liberal arts fireside," for which we would attempt to get
some of the Stanford "greats" to take part—co-educational discussions

followed by an open house. We first went to Professor John Mother-
shead, whose encouragement and promise to participate got us off to
a good start. By a constant bothering of the president's secretary,
we even succeeded in getting Dr. and Mrs. Sterling to spend an evening at our house. We then felt accomplished and proud enough in
our proselytizing to dare to ask that current myth, James Thomas
Watkins IV, to speak. So there was I, invading the citadel of Political Science, standing behind 37 other students, waiting to see him.

After a two-hour and thirty-eight minute wait, I was asked in.
The fact that nineteen more students were outside wanting in, and,
furthermore, that I was in the presence of The Man Himself, who
was clearly looking way, way down at me in a way that only a professor can look at a freshman, did not encourage me to stay very long.
So my usually fuzzy rapid clip was speeded into a totally incompre-
hensible embarrassed speech, in which I attempted to embody my
entire philosophy of life—and thus why Cedro House should have the
best participants in its fireside series—all in about forty-five seconds.

On completion he said to me in a tone clearly indicating that I was
wasting his time, "All we need is a tape deck to play it back at one-
tenth the speed . . . But if I did hear something about my giving a
speech, the answer is NO (as he opened his datebook, showing "New
York," "LA," "Salt Lake City," etc. written all over it). "Besides," he
continued, "why should I do it for you?—you're probably a Republican and a ——— engineer." With the type of modesty only a scared
freshman can have, I managed to blurt out in retort that not only was
I in the HUMANITIES Honors Program, but was chairman of the
DEMOCRATIC caucus of the Political Union. But to no avail.

Perhaps it was . . . early on the morning of April Fool's Day,
1960. Around four o'clock in the morning, the president and rush
chairman of the Inter-Fraternity Council found me just returning to
my room from a night of running through and around all the freshman dorms—to demand to know if a certain group of freshmen, who
had bound themselves together to pledge a certain fraternity that
had gone downhill, had broken any rules. Their main intent, though,
was to see if we had been brainwashed, no less, by a certain professor
. . . But I am ahead of my story.

For that episode in the Poli Sci building was hardly the last I was to see of The Professor. Just three weeks after that incident, the vice-president of the student body asked me to take part in a panel for a conference at Rickey's Inn. The moderator: James T. Watkins IV. Afterward, The Professor, seeking to prevent my exposure to the evils of society after the panel (I was three years short of the legal drinking age), took me to his home for refreshments. Such treatment was slightly in contrast to that of three weeks before. Our conversation went from Why I Thought Women Should Not Go to Stanford (how much one learns in a short time) to Why He Thought He Alone Understood Stanford Students. Finally, he asked me what I wanted to do about the forthcoming living choices afforded all freshmen. When I replied that I wanted to help get a group of top freshmen started to pledge a house that was in real trouble and help make it into what a fraternity really could be, he ran into his kitchen, came out with an elegant looking bottle and said "We'll toast to it—I've been saying that's what should happen all along."

Two months, two days, fifteen midnight meetings at his home, three hundred twenty-five cups of cocoa, and fifty-three Watkins puns later, the plot was on the eve of its execution: March 31. Twenty-three freshmen had virtually sworn in blood to be faithful to the end, and there were a dozen more who had just been brought in and were still doubtful.

Back in mid-February the Dean of Men had been informed of the "April Fool's Club." He was highly doubtful of the possibility of keeping that large a group together. He concluded by saying that if it did succeed, it would have been the best-kept secret in the history of Stanford; and it couldn't succeed unless kept a secret.

Knowing this, we used only code names, with nothing ever on paper. In fact, I even used my job as co-chairman of the freshman Convalescent Home Drive to make nearly all the early joiners in the plot dorm chairmen for the drive—so they could tell their roommates they were going to "Con Home" meetings. It was a wonder some roommates weren't suspicious of so many midnight "Con Home" meetings in Palo Alto.

There we were, in the middle of rush week. We knew that if the secret got out that a huge group was going to pledge the house with the lowest-rated chances of success in rushing, our members, once found out, would be sucked off one by one into the other houses in which they'd originally shown interest.

That evening, March 31, I had been at the open house of the fraternity which at least half of our group would have alternatively liked to pledge. I noticed I was getting an unusual amount of attention—a quite cold attention. A large group gathered 'round, and the house president commented, almost in the middle of some polite conversation, "You know, Scott, freshmen have tried before to get together and group-pledge houses, and it's never worked." Three hours later I left, despairing of any success. For the secret was out and spreading up and down the Row. I rushed up to the house we intended to pledge. About a dozen members were up there, inspecting it. One of them saw the look on my face and told me not to worry: every one of them had had the same treatment—and once they had all gotten together, had regained the original strength.

All we had to worry about were the many others back in Wilbur Hall who didn't feel so confident. For some fraternities were sparking rumors all through the dorms that our group had already broken up, leaving no chance of success. And so, some were beginning to be tempted not to pledge the first night, to wait till the second night, to see if it would succeed. Obviously, it could not succeed if even one member were to do so, and a lack of communication between the much spread-out group could finish the killing. So we decided to reassure every doubtful member. Four hours later, 4:00 a.m., all I could wish, as far as the Inter-Fraternity officers were concerned, was that our group had been ADEQUATELY brainwashed by The Professor—enough to last another 16 hours.

Somehow, miraculously, spectacularly, we came through. That "April Fool's Party" was even anticlimactic: the moment we'd been waiting for for two months had arrived, and it was exactly as we'd expected. We were nearly dead—but pledged, all of us. And The Professor was there, armed with Shakespeare and champagne. I shall never forget the St. Crispin's day's speech read to us at that April Fool's party, 1960 . . .

"We few, we happy few, we band of brothers . . ."

Perhaps it was . . . the day of that first major Political Union program, on February 12, 1960. We had been working for some time to get a very big name from Washington to speak at Stanford—to try to stir a little politics into the air and draw attention to the long dormant Political Union. Late in January we got word from a San Francisco advance man that one of our many invitations was to be accepted. Stanford would be the only Bay Area appearance of our guest. We compromised nothing in preparation — and just prayed that enough people would appear at Mem Aud so we wouldn't have to be apologetic to our guest for the lack of interest shown. We even arranged to borrow President Sterling's brand-new official car. I doubt that any of us had ever dressed more carefully than that morning, before going up to the Hilton Inn at the airport.

And, when we got there, we were allowed to look into a real smoke-filled-room political discussion. Our pulses had tripled by then. With hardly a minute to spare, we got our guest and his aide into the car, and the cavalcade headed down the Peninsula. I had already wrecked my fingernails worrying—afraid lest everyone at Stanford forget the speech. And then, the mortifying thing happened that could only have happened at such a time: while going through Palo Alto, the guest decided he needed some Alka-Seltzer; while he was opening his car door to go into a nearby drugstore, another car came too close and damaged the door. The short, cigar-smoking aide jumped out and handed the stunned young driver of the other car an impressive bill and we drove off, having suffered only a damaged door. Our guest was not even fazed by it. What a sigh of relief! But what a real relief, as we rounded the bend to Mem Aud, to see a vast mass of 4,000 students trying to gain entry to the auditorium, obviously more than just curious to see what the man looked like who was destined, in less than a year, to be President of the United States.

I say now without hesitation that the luckiest break of my life was that I was broke that cold winter quarter of my senior year of prep school. Being a student is a wonderful thing—but being a student at a place with growing pains—one that allows us to seek a better school without the encumberment of three centuries of ivy between us and the goal—is even better. It makes me think of The Professor, who once said, "Stanford is absolutely perfect—with lots of room for improvement."

*Stanford undergraduates today are more concerned about public affairs than any other student generation I have known.*

J. E. WALLACE STERLING

# Stanford to Me

LINDA LEE HAWES, A.B. '62

*Linda Hawes (Mrs. James A. Clever) has won a series of honors, both curricular and extracurricular, during her undergraduate years. She was on the Dean's List in her sophomore year, won the Dinkelspiel Award, was sponsor president for Roble Hall. She is now a graduate student in the graduate School of Medicine. Her husband, James Alexander Clever, is a Stanford graduate, Class of '58.*

Four years ago I was a freshman at Stanford. I think back and my impressions are kaleidoscopic: pre-reg week, the hurried meals, the tours. I was a stranger in a strange land, and home was a continent away. When Dr. Sterling spoke at Freshman Convocation in Memorial Church, his wit, his wisdom, and his sincerity in the proffer of friendship created a new pattern of belonging. The deans were helpful, persistent—"Think this through"—and the faculty reached out in encouragement. As my association grew closer with those who made up the University, from the staff to the students, so also places became familiar and loved. I knew the Quad: in the morning with its cool promise for the day; at noon—shaded arcades offering sanctuary; at twilight, the walls warm from the setting sun. I went through the seasons with Lake Lag: summer dry, autumn desolate—and living again with winter flood and spring rain.

I remember studying late at Roble and on the Row. Inside, the study lamp's yellow circled light; outside, the soft sounds of night—the leaves rustling, whispering. I was staggered by Western Civ and the Upheaval . . . a world I hardly recognized.

The kaleidoscope turns. I see Tresidder Union Committee, a beginning. And sponsoring and crew auxiliary and AWS. Student-Faculty Committee, the Black and White Ball, and San Francisco, San Francisco. Pre-reg Committee and BEAT CAL!

There has not been time yet for my memories to mellow. Along with the inspiration of learning, and people, and places, there was confusion and hurt . . . it has always been so. Nearly three thousand years ago Homer told of Ulysses, the Wanderer. From the beginning of history poets and philosophers have been concerned with man's journey through life, his travels in time, in space. As an undergraduate, I found that at Stanford there was solicitude for the wanderer. There was a real attempt to give direction to the journey of the student, and a never-ceasing struggle to help him to aim high and to travel with his courage.

We found at Stanford how much we did not know—how much we could never know. And we learned, too, that our horizons can be pushed still farther, even toward infinity.

*We are caught up in a burst of scientific discovery in which new knowledge about matter and the physical universe has outrun new knowledge about man himself . . . Somehow, at Stanford, we must test our ability to relate more intrinsically these two manifestations of knowledge and experience.*

J. E. WALLACE STERLING

# Stanford–in–Deutschland: Zweite Gruppe

## BROOKSLEY ELIZABETH BORN, A.B. '61

*Brooksley Born attended Stanford-in-Germany in 1958, a member of the Second Group. In 1960–61 she was editor of* The Bridge, *a quarterly publication of the Stanford Institute of International Relations. She is now a first-year student in the Stanford School of Law.*

Somewhere above the mountain of warm feathers a harsh brass bell joined the clanking of struggling radiators, increasing my realization of cold ears and feet numbed by inexpert handling of the covering feather bed. Whines of German-like nonsense words, muffled by the mattress, rose from the bunk below, and the bed rocked against the wall as my roommate's feet hit the bare floor. I poked my head from beneath the feather bed—waking in a new country!—and let my eyes fill with the suffused light which seemed to sanctify the room with whiteness, turning the wardrobe at the foot of the bed into a grotto and the long narrow table at the window covered with shining, worn cloth into an altar.

"Zimmerkameradin, snow!" One hand linked to the iron grille at the head of the bed, I swung my body to the floor. My roommate was already struggling into sweaters and woolen slacks. I unlatched the window and leaned far out, looking across the encrusted lawn on which German chickens picked their way with dignity and scolding, shaking the coldness from each foot as they picked it up from the ground; looking over the snow-capped barn to the fields of dormant, twisted grape vines stretched black against the ground and toward the forest, quiet now with even the cuckoos gone and the stream silenced by snow. I looked, too, down the line of trees to the valley three miles below where the villagers were opening their shops or boarding the train for Stuttgart. The bell rang again—breakfast.

The boys began to pour out of Kleines Haus beyond the barn,

238

wrapping scarves around their necks and scraping snow from the grass for the first snowball fight at the Burg, and their laughter gradually began to well up from the dining rooms below, where eggs and Broetchen and tea were being served by red-cheeked German girls, striving to disguise their amusement at the American accents.

As I sat trying to learn how to break the hard-crusted Broetchen and to remember how to say "Please pass the jam" in German, I realized that this was a southern German house built for the slight and sleepy-eyed. The tanned, big-framed Californians overpowered the room with intensity and enthusiasm, made the tables sag and the light fixtures ring, even though we all were comparatively hushed with the wonder of a new country, new companions, and a new kind of winter. As breakfast finished we rose, standing tall above dark little Herr Gruenewald, the owner of the Burg, to whom we all bowed and said "Guten Morgen" before racing out through the narrow French doors to build snowmen, hike through the vineyards and orchards and forest, and descend to the village at the bottom of the icy hill, where we could talk to babies, blacksmiths, and the Buergermeister, explore the Fifteenth century church and the new apartment buildings, and eat Kuchen, drink the local wine, and buy postcards to send to Palo Alto.

A spring rain was falling in Berlin that afternoon as we four sat under a peppermint-striped canopy at the Zoo eating hot Wurst and drinking Berliner Weisse, listening to a German um-pah band, and talking of the refugee camp we had visited that morning and of summer plans to return to Berlin to work at the camp. Today was to be a big day in East Berlin; public officials were speaking in the squares, workers' and students' rallies were to be held under red flags and signs denouncing NATO, festivals and parades were to fill the sector —and we were to see it all.

As we walked out of the Zoo and turned toward the Brandenburger Tor, we sighted two fellow Burgers, carrying with determination toward East Berlin a banner on which they had painted Stanford's motto, "Die Luft der Freiheit weht"—"The wind of freedom blows." They were followed by an equally determined Herr Doktor Boerner, the Burg's German director, who, having implored them in vain to give up their plan to display the sign at a workers' rally, finally halted them with a direct order to cease and desist.

"Remember who you are and what you represent! You cannot allow yourselves to let the other students down, or Stanford, or your country, by being rash. It takes work and understanding to teach people, not an exhibition." The director's formal words, carefully translated by his tongue from the German in which he felt more at ease, followed us through the Brandenburger Tor and into the chaos of a rally. The speaker's sentences were cliches, forgotten before they were spoken because they did not need to be heard to be known to the people standing around us, people with roaring mouths and dead eyes, holding their signs as though they said "Eat at Joe's" rather than "Peace through Communism" or "Down with the American warmongers." At the edge of the rally there was a Communist youth group carnival, and the shout of a boy running a shooting gallery, "Hey, you Americans, come and show us your skill!" took us from the repetitions of the speaker and across the cobblestoned square. One of the boys began rhythmically putting down his Mark, picking up the gun, shooting all the ducks down, putting down his Mark, and people from the fringes of the rally gathered and praised his ability, grouping about us to watch until the clouded sky was checked with their white and red signs. The rhythm continued at an increased pace, and the crowd's praise grew, perhaps in wonder at the number of Marks spent rather than at the ducks shot down, until suddenly the boy who was running the gallery and who since the crowd had begun to gather had been agitated and flushed with embarrassment or excitement or anger, said, "Now, you have had your turn. There are many people waiting here to shoot. If I were not the manager, I would show you how I can shoot. But you must leave now."

Later that afternoon it stopped raining, and we took an S-Bahn to Pankow, a quiet suburb of East Berlin right on the border of the East Zone where the festivities of the middle of town had not penetrated. We bought chocolate ice cream for two soccer-playing little boys and sat with their mother on a bench in the playground, watching the sun dry the puddles and listening to her chatter about the problems of shopping in a government-owned grocery store and of getting shoes to fit the boys' "big, healthy feet." When we got back onto the S-Bahn for West Berlin she said, "God bless you."

The last night on the Burg was summer, with the cuckoo calling from the forest for hours after supper and the smell of the rhubarb field hanging in the air. The sounds of dancing and the Beutelsbach brass band filtered through the hedges to Grosses Haus as I clattered down the stairs to our last Fest, to an evening of saying farewell to our German friends, drinking our last beer, singing "Einmal am Rhein" twenty-eight times, watching the lights in the valley flash out in the warm moonlight, and dancing until morning.

Herr Zimmerman, our German instructor, was standing at the bottom of the stairs waiting for me, his tired face made young by a look of pride and by smiling blue eyes. To me, he is the embodiment of Germany, he who held fast, refusing to order his students to salute Hitler during the NAZI regime despite threats of losing a job that was his life; he who approaches the stature of Schiller and Wagner and Mann in his understanding of them and of the panorama of German culture; he who made us cry and exult by his sensitivity of perception and his force of personality in the classroom and then played soccer with us after class.

"Brooks, I have been waiting for you. I have wonderful news," he said, saluting me on both cheeks. "We have done it! I have now read your final paper, and you did learn German." Laughing and crying at the struggles I had had with the language, at the classes cut because of the overwhelming knowledge of my own ignorance, at what we had done together, we went out into the night to the party.

*It is altogether fitting that Stanford was the first to blow* Die Luft der Freiheit weht *back to its source with the establishment of Stanford-in-Germany.*

GUNTHER W. NAGEL, Clinical Professor of Surgery, Emeritus

# Stanford–in–Florence

DIANE VIVELL, A.B. '63

*Diane Vivell, who writes of Stanford-in-Florence, has now returned to Stanford-in-California. Her major is history; her expectation is to study law after she has finished her undergraduate work. Her home is in San Francisco.*

I am home again and have a chance to think over my past six months at Stanford's Florence campus. Two thoughts seem important. I know, for one, that, meaningful as the experience seemed while I was in Italy, many of the effects of my stay are only now becoming apparent. Secondly, many things which I learned there would appear to have little direct relationship to Italy. Yet, I believe it was only in such a place, living with 79 other Stanford students, away from home and all that has molded us into the particular individuals that we are, that some of these lessons could have been learned. Right from the beginning I had expected the first thing to be true. All during our stay in Florence visiting students from the first group, guest speakers, administrators, and our own half-formed understandings told us that only after we could get home, compare, see again the familiar things against the fresh memory of Europe, could we really formulate some lasting impressions and modify our previous thinking. It was like writing my first term paper when I gathered many isolated facts on 4″ x 6″ cards, but did not know what I had until I sat down and organized them with an hypothesis of some sort in mind. It was from the reliving of the United States in small ways such as exclaiming over the sign "Harry's Hash House" or saying *grazie* by mistake and realizing that for Italy the Renaissance is still today, while in the United States progress is our most important product and concern, that I learned most and continue to learn from the six months in Italy.

But these, as I said, I expected to learn. My second thought deals with the bonus, the surprise, sometimes I think the most important part of those six months: what I learned about myself, about those other American students, about our University and what we call the "pursuit of knowledge."

I learned that I was not the independent, easily adaptable girl I had believed myself to be. My family has never traveled and so at first I was exhausted. I remember spending my afternoons on the first field trip taking naps! In addition, I remember that I was really afraid of the Italians at first. That seems so funny now that I know them better, but it was an adjustment, and in these and many other ways I was forced to reappraise my image of myself.

Then, too, I saw how different it was living with the other students so closely. At Stanford in Palo Alto if one chooses he can have very little to do with bothersome members of his dormitory or residence. In a foreign country we all had to learn to eat, sleep, travel, study, entertain, and share new things *together*. This interdependence was hard to accept at times, but more often it was so rich and warm that most of us will never forget the friends we made while in Florence.

I learned what it is to study something and then go out and live it or see it or notice its results. I think all of us were excited by the vitality of our studies. I believe we will take some of this excitment home with us, that we will demand more of ourselves as we finish our years at Stanford, and that the school will reflect our attitude.

I also saw what it is like actually to live with our professors. We saw what kind of people they are in normal life, away from the podium. We met their wives and children, and this, too, is something valuable that we shall seek out in Palo Alto. Many professors have said that it is the students who are too busy to formulate the beneficial relationships with the faculty. The "overseas students" will not be too busy again.

So I remember my months in Italy as a time when I was exposed to exciting new ideas and facts about another country and exposed as well to important realizations about myself and our campus life at home.

# Stanford–in–France

VERNE REAVES, A.B. '63

*Verne Reaves is majoring in English. He attended the
second session of Stanford-in-France. He hopes to become a
writer, and is currently at work on a critique of the Stanford
Overseas Program, as well as a book of poetry which he ex-
pects to publish privately in the near future.*

STANFORD-IN-FRANCE is situated in Tours, in the heart of the cha-
teaux country, and some two and one-half hours from Paris by
train. The center itself is on the Place Anatole France, at the north
end of the main street of Tours, Rue Nationale; it looks out on the
Loire River, and in front of it is a large statue of Rabelais.

There is nothing singular about the appearance of the Center:
it, like the majority of buildings in Tours, is built of scrubbed white
stone, five stories high, with a gray slate roof and a red brick chimney. The students' living quarters are on the first four floors; on the
rez-de-chaussée is a large, comfortable recreation room; and in the
basement are the kitchen, the dining room, and the library (which
is also used as the main lecture room). One floor of the living quarters is all women; on the remaining floors the sexes are separated on
either side of the central staircase.

The burden of the teaching at the Center is divided among two
American professors and a staff of French teachers. During the first
week the students are given an examination in French, testing both
their oral and written proficiency in the language; on the basis of this
examination, they are divided into five levels and assigned to teachers correspondingly. Students ordinarily attend two hours of French
classes each day, two days a week from a professor who speaks English as well as French, and two days from an entirely French-speaking
teacher. Teaching time in the French classes is divided between

244

translations, vocabulary, literature, and the actual speaking of the language. The American teachers and the courses offered change with each session; an effort is made to orient these courses toward providing the students with a greater familiarity with the customs, politics, music, fine arts, and history of France.

The average work load is fifteen units each quarter. This minimal load, plus a four-day school week, and a three-week vacation between quarters, leaves adequate time for studying as well as traveling. There are usually two week-long field trips during the session, the expense of which is shared by the students and the University.

## II

A broad, stone staircase leads down from Place Anatole France to the Loire, a green-black river whose whirlpools and rapids are often challenged by young Frenchmen in flimsy kayaks. There is a well-kept park by the Loire with white benches that attract lovers on many sultry summer evenings. In the quiet afternoons the old men of the town bowl in the shade of the trees, or initiate their grandsons into the ancient tradition of fishing in a river where no one has ever caught a fish.

On the evening of Bastille Day this park is filled to capacity with families who come to see the fireworks set off from the small sand bar island in the center of the Loire. The local band is there, always delightfully out-of-tune, the men handsome in their stiff blue uniforms they remove from storage once each year for the holiday. As it grows dark the crowd becomes very quiet, until the first blue-green-red rocket lights up the sky overhead and brings forth an "Ah, c'est jolie! C'est jolie!" from people who have become one in the wondrousness of light in darkness. There are somber-faced children in their blue school smocks who are seeing their first fireworks and whose eyes, in the reflected light of the bursting rockets, grow wide with astonishment. It is always a long time after the last rocket has reduced itself to yellow-red ashes falling lazily toward the river that the French make their reluctant ways homeward.

## III

Students take their lunches at the Restaurante Universitaire, some two miles from the Center. To reach it one walks nearly the entire length of Rue Nationale, passing many neat, well-kept shops. The department store and the supermarket are relatively new innovations in Tours as well as in France, and most of the shopping is still done in these small stores specializing in a limited gamut of products: the bakery, the delicatessen, the pharmacy, the yardage dealer, the butcher. Shopping, to the French housewife, is not an indifferent activity; as she may very likely shop for each meal separately, her acquaintance with the merchants is personal, even intimate, and may be carried on from generation to generation. The local shop, then, is a center of social activity, like the park or the café, where friends meet each day to share the latest gossip and discuss the most recent news from Algeria.

But shops are not the only attractions on the streets of Tours. Two days each week the flower markets appear, lining the way with red, yellow, green, and lilac colors, and the smells of exotic plants. And on one corner of the Rue Nationale there is always a small, gray-haired old woman with a pushcart, who sells fruits and vegetables and candy. She is shrewd but kind; she always has a little something for the children, and when you buy a big bag of peanuts, the added dividend is as many peanuts as your hand or your pocket can hold.

The Restaurante Universitaire is a modern, glass-and-brick building, typical of the new ideas in architecture becoming widespread in metropolitan France. The students eat on the second floor: French, Americans, Africans, German, English, and many others. The common languages spoken there are French and English.

If one makes the effort, these lunches can be the source of much pleasure and fascinating conversations. There are Africans who still bear the tribal scars inflicted on their faces at birth, but who, in fluent English or French, will discuss philosophy, contemporary literature, or the delicate subject of American-African relations. These Negroes are perhaps the most approachable of any students abroad, and are eager and capable of dispelling the notion of a "black Africa" weighted down under superstition and bloodshed.

I should say that the youth of nearly all Western nations are represented in that restaurant: the French, voluable yet strongly xenophobic; the Germans, alert and eager for the challenges that face their country; the Swiss, the Italians, the Spanish, and the somehow out-of-place English. Each one with something to offer, each one with some unique viewpoint of world affairs as seen from their part of the globe. Yet in spite of superficial differences, all these young people seemed to be in accord on at least two things: that upon themselves would soon lie the great burden of leading the world in years to come, and that they must make this world, some day and in some way, better. I can but feel that the hope for understanding and peace in our world lies in just such exchanges of ideas and hopes among the young people of all nations.

## IV

Now that I am returned to the States and try to look back on the experience in France and evaluate it, I find myself the bearer of mixed emotions.

Certainly, the Stanford-in-France program could be improved; indeed, it must be if it is to fulfill its stated objectives. The courses given by the American professors should be more directly applicable to the European experience; it is frustrating to be studying psychology or American government while a vast number of buildings, paintings, people, and ideas unique to France go unexplained. There should be, before or during the session, a greater emphasis on spoken French; many students, even after six months, could not speak enough French to carry on a rewarding conversation with a native; and I have seen, too many times, this language barrier force otherwise enthusiastic students into a frustrated resentment against the French due to a lack of communication. And lastly, there must somehow be more contacts with the French at all levels of social activities and at all levels of social classes; the peasant-farmer is far more intriguing, but unfortunately far less accessible to students, than the all-too-similar-to-us upper bourgeoisie.

On the other hand, none of us who studied in France returned to America unchanged. If the Stanford-in-France program was designed to broaden our view of the world, its people, and its cultures, our outlook on the diverse opinions of diverse peoples, and heighten our response to America itself, then in this it achieved a high degree of success. We have returned at once more critical and understanding of the course of world events and of the role that France and the United States play in these events.

But I think most of us agree that the greatest value of the European experience was one that no one really told us about before leaving: that of learning to live with our fellow Americans. The pettiness, the banality, and the tired cynicism that are all too common on the college campus cannot long endure when you live and eat and travel with the same eighty students for six months; friendships, lasting friendships, form when people of our age surmount the social barriers that youth erects against itself and dig deep into the real fiber of other people. Our girls learned what boys look like unshaven; and our boys what girls look like with their hair in curlers. And that unicorn of modern life, the platonic friendship between the sexes, was seen to spring up everywhere, and revealed to us the true nature of affection.

And lastly, suspended as we were in the limbo between French and American customs and mores, to neither of which did we feel really obligated, we, I believe, had the opportunity to find out just *who we were*. We saw ourselves, for perhaps the first time, as each of us really was, and not as we appeared to others. New determination, new perspectives on our places in life and our possible courses of action in life took form in our minds; enjoying a freedom completely new to us, we formed our own personal moral standards, based on unselfishness, sharing, contributing, and tender frankness.

In Europe, at Stanford-in-France, we had the chance to form the philosophies by which, hopefully, we shall lead our lives. And for this and many other things, we are all grateful.